Bounded Divinities

Other books by the author

Lives of the Psychics: The Shared Worlds of Science and Mysticism
(University of Chicago Press, June 2000)

Public Reason: Mediated Authority in the Liberal State (Cornell University
Press, Fall 1999)

Healing Powers: Alternative Medicine, Spiritual Communities, and the State
Morality and Society Series (University of Chicago Press, Fall 1992)

Rational Association (Syracuse University Press, Spring 1987)

Special Care: Medical Decisions at the Beginning of Life (University of
Chicago Press, Fall 1986)

Abortion: A Case Study in Law and Morals (Greenwood-Praeger Press,
1983)

Public Policy: Scope and Logic (Prentice-Hall, 1979)

Normative Political Theory (Prentice-Hall Foundation Series, 1974)

The Nature of Political Inquiry (Dorsey, 1967)

Bounded Divinities

Sacred Discourses in Pluralist Democracies

Fred M. Frohock

BOUNDED DIVINITIES
© Fred M. Frohock, 2006.

First published in 2006 by
PALGRAVE MACMILLAN™
175 Fifth Avenue, New York, N.Y. 10010 and
Houndmills, Basingstoke, Hampshire, England RG21 6XS
Companies and representatives throughout the world.

PALGRAVE MACMILLAN is the global academic imprint of the Palgrave Macmillan division of St. Martin's Press, LLC and of Palgrave Macmillan Ltd. Macmillan® is a registered trademark in the United States, United Kingdom and other countries. Palgrave is a registered trademark in the European Union and other countries.

ISBN-13: 978–1–4039–7538–6
ISBN-10: 1–4039–7538–8

Library of Congress Cataloging-in-Publication Data

Frohock, Fred M.
    Bounded divinities : sacred discourses in pluralist democracies / Fred M. Frohock.
        p. cm.
    Includes bibliographical references and index.
    Contents: Divine ordinances—Words and things : religious and political domains—Sacred texts—True colors : public and deliberative reasoning—Recursions, infinite regresses, and public reason—Modeling public reason : political liberalism and realpolitik—Political and religious practices : a case study continued.
        ISBN 1–4039–7538–8
        1. Religion and politics. 2. Democracy—Religious aspects. 3. Religious pluralism—Political aspects. I. Title.

BL65.P7F76 2006
322′.1—dc22   2006041587

A catalogue record for this book is available from the British Library.

Design by Newgen Imaging Systems (P) Ltd., Chennai, India.

First edition: September 2006

10 9 8 7 6 5 4 3 2 1

Printed in the United States of America.

For all the ophthalmologists and retina specialists who have so far helped me maintain at least a working version of my eyesight, in particular (in Syracuse, NY) Drs. John Hoepner, William Griffith, Theodore Smith, and Paul Torrisi, and, especially (in Miami, FL, at the Bascom Palmer Eye Institute), Dr. Philip Rosenfeld

"Maybe that's how it always has to be with philosophers. We who think we understand truth, wisdom, utility, freedom, liberty, happiness and the cosmos really know nothing at all about life as it is. Those of us who think we really understand power—state, monarchs, tyrannies, despotisms—have seen those things only as we enjoy wine by looking down the neck of a bottle. For what a difference there is when we see a painting of a tiger painted by Oudry at the summer exhibition, and when we meet a real tiger in the forest. Well, I have seen the real tiger in the forest."

—Diderot in a letter to his lover,
Sophie Volland, and her sisters
("My Dear ladies"), in Paris as quoted,
inferred, or imagined by Malcolm Bradbury
in his novel, *To the Hermitage*, page 452.

Contents

Acknowledgments ix

Preface xiii

1. Divine Ordinances 1

2. Words and Things: Religious and
   Political Domains 23

3. Sacred Texts 49

4. True Colors: Public and Deliberative Reasoning 83

5. Infinite Regresses, Recursions, and Public Reason 113

6. Modeling Public Reason: Political Liberalism
   and *Realpolitik* 145

7. Political and Religious Practices: A Case
   Study Continued 175

Notes 199

Bibliography 231

Index 249

Acknowledgments

The Santería study which organizes this work was published as "The Free Exercise of Religion: Lukumí and Animal Sacrifice" in the Institute for Cuban and Cuban-American Studies Occasional Paper Series, University of Miami (November 2001). An early version of the second chapter was published as "Words and Things: Religious and Political Domains" in *The Journal of Religion* © 2002 by the University of Chicago Press. All rights reserved and parts of chapter three as "Sacred Texts" in the journal *Religion* (January 2003). A kind of amalgam of pieces from chapters 4 and 6 was published as "An Alternative Model of Political Reasoning" in *Ethical Theory and Moral Practice,* © Springer (February 2006). I am grateful to the editors/policies of these journals for permission to reprint revised versions of the papers here and the anonymous readers used by the editors for their critical comments on the work.

Also, I do not know how even to begin thanking my spring 2003 graduate seminar for the wonderful discussions that allowed me to refine my thinking on this project. Absent this seminar and I would not have finished a full draft of the manuscript perhaps in my lifetime. In different ways the following individual members of the seminar were helpful: Amanda Dipaolo, Dimitria Gatzia, Michael McFall, Michael McKeon, Roald Nashi, Paul Prescott, Joshua Vermette, Amy Widestrom, and the two regular auditors, Cyril Ghosh and Darrell Driver. I have also profited from numerous discussions with other graduate students, including, early in this project, Steven Benko and, more constantly, Ali Shomali, who is pursuing his own project in religion and politics, one quite different from my approach, and has been an excellent and welcome critic of my work. Faculty colleagues who have commented on the work and suggested literatures for me to read and references to track include James Bennett, Hans Schmidt, Peg Hermann, Elizabeth Cohen, Jim Watts, Jim Wiggins, especially David Miller (for comments on an early draft of the paper on sacred texts) and, for years of discussions on so many topics, Thomas Green. I am particularly grateful to Everita Silina, a graduate student who has been a constant friend and invaluable research assistant for the past five years. A special thanks also to Mr. Ghosh and Ms. Silina for putting together the Bibliography, and to Mr. Ghosh for checking the accuracy of the quotations and their citations. Mr. Ghosh also prepared the Index. (Please contact him to complain about any remaining errors or omissions.)

The Miami Theory group has provided a double benefit. In early 2001, when this project was so inchoate it was more dream than reality, I presented a paper to the Group that mutated into the first two journal articles (above) and mainly the second and third chapters of this book (the meeting was on January 26, 2001). Seeking again a critical venue to try out portions of the later text, I gave a lecture to what was then called the Miami International Relations Theory group (both sessions held on the University of Miami campus), April 23, 2004, on alternative models of political reasoning (chapter 6). I later presented another version of the paper to a Philosophy Department colloquium at the University of Miami on April 22, 2005. The comments made by those who attended one or both of the sessions were very helpful, including those by Nick Onuf, Vendulka Kubalkova, Susan Haack (who graciously provided a separate reading of the earlier paper that eventually became the second chapter), George Gonzalez, Elise Guliano, Ben Bishin, Harvey Siegel, and so many others. These comments were helpful in making the work more accurate and modest than its initial version. I regard the deficiencies now in the book as not so much a result of egregious outreach but more nearly attributable to failed arguments. I am trying to believe that this is an improvement. I am also grateful to Ken Baynes and Ned McClennen for allowing me to be an unlisted third instructor in their seminar on "law, economics and public reason" in the fall semester 2004 at Syracuse University, and for the opportunity to present some of this work at one of the seminar meetings. If anything demonstrates the importance of a good collective setting on intellectual work this seminar was one such occasion.

Then there are the random conversations over the years, too many to count, with friends and colleagues. For example, the passage I cite in footnote 43 in chapter 6 from Rawls on defining evil (p. 439 of *A Theory of Justice*) was cited and read at the May 2, 2003, meeting of the Upstate New York Chapter of the Conference for the Study of Political Thought. This moment, the reading of the passage, and the rancorous discussion of reasoning and deliberation in politics that filled the evening (centered on Rawls and my upstart introduction of *modus vivendi* and reason-of-state to public reasoning) was revelatory and so very useful to me. My thanks to the participants. Another memorable exchange occurred in Da Andrea (one of my favorite Village restaurants in New York City) during the Thanksgiving break of 2002 with Everita Silina and my wife, Val. These two complex and thoughtful women started talking (strangely enough) about incommensurability (I had been writing on the concept that morning in my younger daughter's apartment in the Village) and I just interrogated them and absorbed the ideas going back and forth. Thanks, guys.

Preface

Eighteen years before Galileo abjured his opinion on the Copernican system, a Carmelite friar, Paolo Antonio Foscarini, attempted to reconcile the heliocentric view with Holy Scripture by distinguishing the truth of a text from its interpretation. He affirmed that all of Scripture is true, but we still have to determine what the text teaches or intends, what the text means. Galileo himself, in staged debates, dinner party conversations, and various published works, consistently subscribed to the truth of Scripture in the years before his trial. It is God's word, he said, and true everywhere. But, relying on Foscarini's distinction, he proposed that we can be mistaken about what it means, in this case on the issue of the geocentric or heliocentric view. Cardinal Bellarmine, accepting the contested view that Scripture makes claims about the workings of the natural world, acknowledged the interpretive powers of natural science with a concession: if Galileo could demonstrate his theory, provide a conclusive scientific proof of the Copernican system, then the Church would accept a non-literal interpretation of the passages in the Bible that bear on the issue.[1]

Galileo played a very high card in acknowledging the divinity elaborated in Christianity as an external resource given that he regarded mathematics as the text of the natural world. But his endgame strategy provided a distinction between truth and our understanding or knowledge of truth (the concept of truth). This difference is vital in elaborating levels of religious dispute and accord on sacred texts. Put in Foscarini's terms, we may disagree on the meaning of Scripture and the proper way to find meaning even as we acknowledge the divine truth of Scripture. There is little doubt on the historical record that this distinction would have been beneficial to Galileo if religious authorities had accepted it. It permitted him to argue that physics may not be antagonistic to religion but instead an instrument to reveal the true meaning of God's words. The robust scope of

Galileo's realism, which he extended to both religious and scientific inquiries, also allowed him to claim that the truth of Scripture must be consistent with Nature since both are expressions in different ways of the divine word. In the case of Scripture the text is revealed to the assiduous reader while (on Galileo's program) Nature must yield to the inquiries of natural science. This proposed congruence led to Galileo's suggestion that trained physicists can provide insights into God's revelations, not just clerics specializing in pure textual exegesis.

This argument could not carry the day at a time when the Church claimed ultimate authority on the meaning of sacred texts. It suggested, however, a demarcation between disputes over whether a text is the word of God and those concerned with the meaning of a text that all disputants concede is divine. Reflect on Foscarini's distinction yet one more time. A dispute can still occur, and be prolonged indefinitely, over the true meaning of a sacred text and how to find this meaning without extending the dispute to whether the text is true. The distinctions between truth and the concept of truth, and between exercises of discovery or revelation and those exercises that aim at constructing texts and crafting agreements, suggest a theoretical pluralism that can map differences between religious and secular domains, and perhaps even identify a venue for a freestanding language independent of either domain.

This book is an exploration of the freestanding languages of politics, meaning those public languages of political or state reasoning that in some way are detached from private or nonpublic languages. For those inclined toward metaphor, the work at hand is a kind of map, a handbook that trades on secondary languages of interpretation to guide the reader through the thickets of religion and politics. The one vivid case study of an unconventional religion (Lukumí, which originates in Africa instead of Europe or the Americas) and its contacts with law in the United States organize the book's theoretical excursions. Like, maybe, recent work on justice or scientific practices—and without comparisons of quality—the book sets up possibilities for rigorous empirical work on any number of topics while only touching the practices at issue on its own journey to what I think are significant clarifications and reconstructions. Mainly I offer revisions of the prominent frameworks that track and present connections between religion and politics in the modern Western world with the aim of turning our discussions in a different and more productive direction. This work will not directly address such fashionable (and important) topics as fundamentalism, evangelical Christianity, and the U.S.

Government, though if it succeeds we can reach new understandings of the political techniques appropriate for presenting and governing all versions of strong religious communities in all forms of liberal democracy.

*   *   *

But, at the end of the day (a British phrase I have always found irresistible), and even with these illuminating words and sentences, I am prepared to concede that this book is hard to categorize. On that concession I maintain a studied indifference. One of the better books on sports is Michael Lewis's *Moneyball*. (Lewis also wrote the best book on the bond market I have read—*Liar's Poker*—but then I am partial to narratives as support for even the best theory.) *Moneyball* is an account of a conceptual revolution in evaluating baseball players, a sea change occasioned by the efforts of a few statisticians and one general manager (Billy Beane, with the Oakland Athletics) to see the actual grammar of baseball—what makes for success and failure on the field of play—in terms of revisionist market evaluations rather than the received wisdom of traditional baseball (which was and is ignorant to the core). Some of the funniest parts of the book are descriptions of the traditional scouts, who mainly don't rely on whether an individual is a good, well, *baseball* player, but on other matters, like dismissing a candidate for the annual baseball draft because he doesn't look like a baseball player, supporting another on the grounds that "He has the best body in the draft." Well, all of the works I cite and the summaries I offer may not look like political philosophy, the arguments invoked and developed here certainly don't have the best body around, but I think this book breaks new ground in theory exactly as it defines and radicalizes other works, and synthesizes literatures in strange and sometimes outrageous fashion. A plea to the reader: see this work, whether it succeeds or fails, as an effort to get out of the box with an introduction of a grammar of *politics* to political philosophy.

Here is a concession now on another front. This book, as an exploration in political theory, comes with all of the destructive possibilities of abstract thought. I have always felt that one of the risks in doing theory is located in its duality. Theory sometimes seems to be a kind of setup for field work (endorsing or critiquing existing research, proposing different agendas, getting the language straight, offering definitions of experience, etc.) and yet also oddly complete on its own terms as theory. Maintaining harmony between these functions carries a well known and very steep slope for failure if the relevant concepts do not coalesce successfully. A physician once told me that he knew if he practiced medicine long enough that he would accidentally kill someone. He just hoped that no one would notice. I can only hope that no one notices if I have inadvertently crippled, maybe killed, some areas of political philosophy and religious studies with a type of theory that includes over-the-top scans and unchecked uses of so many different literatures, especially since the unintended casualties can easily include the work at hand. Or worse, that I have missed all targets completely. Then there are failures of style. Ethan Hawke, one of our better actors and street philosophers, has lamented the demise of the manual typewriter. "The computer has destroyed fiction. Paragraphs get so perfectly sculpted they lose all their juice." Later Hawke advances his theory of filmmaking. "You don't make a movie like this (*Before Sunrise* in this instance) without putting some blood, spit, and piss in it."[2]

I don't know about the blood, spit, and piss in my book, but here's a cranky allusion. I think all writing, at least occasionally, is more like prizefighting than we like to admit, with the work itself as one of the combatants along with all the sad deceptions of that strange sport. Hemingway, remember, would ask of other, usually younger writers whether they could go the distance, finish all the rounds in a pugilistic/ literary career. Norman Mailer famously squared off against his top literary rivals once in an *Esquire* article replete with Mailer in gloves and boxing trunks in an unforgettable photo opportunity.[3] The real world of that "sweet science" is filled with bravado.[4] Joe Louis said that when he was young he knew if he kept fighting long enough that on some night some guy would beat him. But before every fight he thought, not this night, and not this guy. Given these high and finally unrealistic expectations maybe it's a good thing that the author-as-pugilist is spared making the requisite public judgment, the decision on whether a work succeeds. The reader is now the decisive figure, a kind of combined referee, judge, possibly even a boxing commissioner, maybe the wily manager. My efforts are done. I extend the traditional and solemn invitation to feast on the text that follows. Me? I'm going to find a dressing room and slide into a willing and welcome state of amnesia. What night? What book?

Divine Ordinances

It is easy to forget, within the comfortable landscape of social religions, that the metaphysical and the practical are fused in a way of life throughout many cultures, and this way of life is governed not by the social but by a transcendent reality, often configured as God. Look, for example, at a religion—a term indicating a distinct practice only, it seems, in recent Western history—that is not part of the mainstream in Western life. The religion (or way of life) is Santería, and a santero, Ernesto Pichardo, began transforming it in 1974 from an underground practice held in private homes to the church of the Lukumí Babalu Aye in Hialeah, Florida. Pichardo incorporated his church that year as a prelude to making it the first public institution in Osha (the African term for the religion). He was guided by intuitions or what he calls "supernatural indications" that this public manifestation of Osha was part of the family mission predicted before his birth by a Yoruba priest in Cuba. Pichardo wanted to provide a venue that could express the consciousness of Osha in a public manner.[1]

In the spring of 1987 Pichardo and his associates located a piece of property in Hialeah that they thought might serve as the initial stage for a church. Pichardo and his group liked the setting, even though it was in a depressed economic area and the store was in bad repair. But they had no history of the land. All they knew was that an auto dealership had occupied the premises until about three months previously. More accurately, the site had been a used car lot. So they decided to protect themselves a bit. They signed a lease for the property with an option to buy at the agreed price. The understanding they thought they had with the owner was that they would first use the site to recruit members and raise funds. Then, if these campaigns went well, they would exercise the purchase option and build a church on the property. They signed a contract and put down a substantial deposit in April 1987. This commitment, they believed, was the beginning of a movement to give public expression to a religion that had remained secretive throughout its history.

The Pichardo group became aware of the community's resistance to their efforts almost immediately after their plans became public with the purchase of the property in Hialeah. Pamphlets began circulating through the neighborhood warning that a satanic church was going to open. Various churches in the area, including Baptist, evangelical, Jehovah's Witnesses, began opposing the installation of the church. (The Catholic Church remained silent throughout the entire episode.) The Humane Society was especially virulent in its opposition. It charged that Osha members drank both animal and human blood during ceremonies, tortured and sacrificed cats, dogs, snakes, other exotic and protected animals, and occasionally humans, and ritualistically abused children as well. The Society also blamed Osha for spreading AIDS (because of blood drinking) and for every animal carcass found on the city streets. Animal Rights groups joined the opposition. By the time of the first city council meeting on the issues, held June 9, 1987, the Osha group faced one of the oddest coalitions in American politics: a heterogeneous collection of organized Christian churches, the Humane Society and Animal Rights League, various economic interests, the majority of the area politicians and their natural constituencies, and the Hialeah police chaplain.

2

The destiny that guided Pichardo in organizing a public setting for Santería originated in the manner of his birth. He was born in Havana to a middle-class family. His mother had been introduced to Osha (a religion known also as Lukumí or Santería) as a child through a first generation olorisha (priest) who was the family cook.[2] The father's side of Ernesto's family, socially prominent with an economic history that included ownership of some sugar plantations, was active in both Catholic and Espiritismo groups. Pichardo recalls no conflict in these religious activities, except that the Espiritismo activities were kept private for social reasons. The gradual shift in the family to a complete reliance on Osha began for health reasons. His mother had toxicity problems during her second pregnancy that caused a miscarriage. The doctors could not control toxic reactions then and so they warned her that a third pregnancy would kill her.

The olorisha had moved out of the Pichardo home by the time of this warning and was marketing his skills to a number of families. He had also become a priest of Shangó, an Osha divinity believed to have been the fourth king of Yoruba, and commanded considerable respect on medical issues and problems. The young Pichardo woman who was to become Ernesto's mother began visiting this priest and complying with the rituals he recommended. He became an authoritative force in her religious life. He predicted well in advance of Ernesto's birth that she was going to have another child, a male child, and that in spite of what the doctors had said nobody was going to die and in fact everything was going to go well. He also predicted this child would become a priest in Osha and described a number of events and accomplishments that would occur in the child's life.

Ernesto was born without any complications and was raised in one of the affluent barrios in Havana. The family moved to the United States in the early 1960s and settled in the "Little Havana" area of Miami, a zone on and near Calle Ocho (S.W. 8th Street). They were extremely poor at first. Their home was a garage that they slowly converted to an efficiency apartment. By this time Ernesto's parents had divorced and his mother had remarried. His stepfather was a professional with five college degrees who could not find work because of his green card status. He would get up at 4:00 a.m. every day and start walking, looking for any kind of work. Finally he landed a job parking cars in the Eden Roc Hotel in Miami Beach. His mother went through a scary time in the hospital after accidentally poisoning herself while fumigating rats in their garage apartment. But she eventually recovered her health and found employment at one of the local garment manufacturers. Ernesto and his older brother Fernando were basically on their own during the day. They would get up in the morning, scratch up something for breakfast, and then leave for school. Resources were exceedingly scarce. The government assistance program for Cuban refugees would not be passed for years.

The economic status of the Pichardo family soon improved, however. In the late 1960s they located a relative in New York who had arrived earlier and been somewhat successful economically. The Pichardos convinced him to invest as a partner in a garment factory to be managed by Mrs. Pichardo. The factory did very well, at one point operating two shifts, one at night and the other during the day. The Pichardos became caught up in the American dream of economic independence and comfort. They bought their first automobile. They purchased a comfortable house in Hialeah, a municipality adjoining Miami. Ernesto and his big brother went to public schools in the city of Hialeah. He became an altar boy in the Catholic Church during his years in elementary school.

At about that time Ernesto began to feel that it was time to "pay up" on what the Yoruba priest had outlined as his destiny. The Osha religion was growing very rapidly in Miami during these years, in part because of the increased immigration from Cuba but also because of the intrinsic practical appeal of the religion to the Cuban-American community. Ernesto explored its beliefs and rituals and felt that his tendencies, his instincts, were more inclined toward Osha than Catholicism. His mother was initiated into the religion in 1970. Ernesto's conversion to Osha followed three days later. His ordination was into the priesthood order of Shangó. Three years later his brother and grandmother became Osha priests, and then his grandfather followed him and his mother into the religion in recognition of what they had been told by the Yoruba priest in Cuba many years before.

The ordination destroyed Ernesto's chances for a degree from Hialeah high school. He was sixteen years old and in the middle of his junior year. He had to be out of school during the seven-day confinement period of the ordination ceremony, and for certain events during the first months after that week. The school required a doctor's letter attesting to an illness in order for a student absent for that length of time to be reinstated. Ernesto had no such letter. Moreover, he reported back to school after the confinement period with the signs of an Osha initiation still prominent on his person: his hair was completely shaved off, he was dressed entirely in white, and religious paraphernalia adorned his body. The principal went berserk on seeing him. He expelled Ernesto from school and even threatened to have him arrested if he was seen on the streets.

Pichardo recalls the experience as a complete transformation in his life. He had been very popular in the neighborhood and school. Suddenly he was this weird thing to be avoided at all costs. From best friends all the way down the line to social acquaintances, except for his girlfriend, he was shut out entirely. The displacement included both the everyday routine of school attendance and his social life. This abrupt isolation from friends and schoolmates was devastating. At the same time he had the extended family of a new religion. Suddenly he had new grandfathers, grandmothers, aunts, uncles, all absorbing him into the religion. His life changed from that of a typical American teenager to an ordained priest completely immersed in the social framework of Osha.

Pichardo's first priority was finding a job. It was difficult. He was young and he still looked bizarre from the perspective of secular employers. He convinced his elders in Osha to give him an exemption from religious attire for work purposes. He could go about with his head uncovered (and by this time his hair had grown in a bit, though it was still very short) and wear pastel colors instead of white. But this exemption applied only to work hours. As soon as he returned from his job he had to change back into religious attire. This dress code was in effect until the completion of the ordination (one year). He managed to get a job in a retail shoe store during the Christmas rush. They kept him on past the holiday season. He later became a manager in the shoe company and then a district troubleshooter for the whole Florida region. During this time he enrolled in an adult education program at the University of Miami and in two years had earned his high school degree. He also opened a botánica (an Osha shop for the sale of religious items) and operated that as well. In 1977 he left the shoe business and became a bill collector. The pay was much better but he found the work just as stressful. His life by then had become completely defined by his job and his business, and the Osha religion that dominated his leisure time.

Eventually Pichardo was accepted for training in the higher priesthood of Osha. In 1977 he completed a period of study and was acknowledged as an italero in the religion, though he says that the study regimen never ends. He likens his efforts to going to college forever. His curriculum included extensive work in cultural anthropology, which he believes he used (without knowing at the time what it was called) in his investigative work as a bill collector. In the courses he took at local colleges he began engaging scholars who had extensive knowledge of Nigeria and Osha traditions. He became a kind of apprentice to some of those scholars, helping them with insights into the practicing world of Osha while learning the historical and anthropological bases of the religion. Soon Pichardo began organizing workshops with a foundation grant that brought academics and priests (both Catholic and Osha) together to discuss issues in the Osha movement. Public forums were held that included university professors, olorishas, and representatives of the Catholic Church. Pichardo continued to expand his economic interests in corporate America, accepting positions on the executive boards of a number of area businesses.[3]

3

Regla de Osha, in some ways a syncretic religion, originated in an odd and painful historical accommodation between Yoruba and Catholicism in the slave culture of Cuba. Yoruba is a culture that can be traced back at least 5,000 years in Africa.[4] The Yoruba people lived in what is now the southwestern part of Nigeria and eastern Benin. It was one of the regions in Africa from which blacks were enslaved and transported to Spanish colonies in the New World during the sixteenth, seventeenth and (primarily) the late eighteenth and nineteenth centuries. The Africans taken to Cuba were sent to the sugar and tobacco plantations. The conditions of life there were as bad as one might expect in the practice of slavery. In this coercive and hostile setting the Africans encountered the Catholic Church and its message of eternal salvation through Christ and the sacraments. All of the slaves were routinely "converted" to Catholicism through mandatory baptism upon arrival in the colony. The result was a tense and radically incomplete surface fusion of Yoruba and Catholicism.

The encounter story, whatever its form, must be seen as coercive in all respects. The slaves arriving in Cuba had no knowledge of Christianity. The baptisms were administered to recipients who did not understand any part of the ceremony. Some priests did visit the plantations later to give informal instructions in Catholicism. But the obvious asymmetry in power between instructor and student invested these lessons with compulsion. Even those slaves who were freed entered a society dominated by Catholicism, and understandings of Catholic practices and symbolism were crucial to survival. This frame of reference helps explain why the coercive introduction of Catholicism to Yoruba culture never produced the contradictions of principle one might have expected in the forced joining of two discourses or practices. Slaves have always found it useful (in the deep sense of survival) to align in some way with the institutions, if not the beliefs, of their owners, and the incentive among slaves in Cuba for a pragmatic acceptance of Catholicism was predictably strong. Lydia Cabrera, a folklorist who did important early field work on Osha culture, saw the new religion as an instrument fashioned by slaves to avoid retaliation for pursuing heathen practices. Leavening this survival strategy was the fact that the two religions had much in common—beliefs in a single overriding God, an external reality, interventionist spirits, the sacredness of nature, blessed objects, miracles and the power of prayer, the importance of ritual, and the possibility of spiritual healing and divine protection from harm.

But the absence of strong contradictions may also be explained by the fact that no complete fusion or even an equitable balance of Yoruba and Catholicism has ever emerged from the acceptance. The incentives in Yoruba to maintain the beliefs and practices of the homeland during the diaspora must have been compelling. A collective memory of Africa, which most of the slaves never saw again, was embedded in the Yoruba religion. We know that the Ifá priests memorized and retained the Odu Corpus, the core content of Yoruba, and kept it secret from the slave owners. (One word for priest in Yoruba is babalawo, which also can be translated as Father of Secrets.) Any fusion between the two religions was accordingly layered in crucial ways along the dimensions of surface accord and underground convictions. The result is an alignment that is little more than a surface wrapping of parallel structures from distinct cultures, or at best a re-expression of Yoruba with a Catholic veneer. Some members of Osha, and several scholars of the religion, maintain that the syncretism assigned to Yoruba is found only in the pragmatic responses of members to a dominant culture, not in the religion itself. Also, the coercive origins of Osha led to a hostility between the two religious groups, and cultures, that has kept the religious structures independent to some degree, a hostility which exists in various forms even today.

There is a case, and an impressive argument, for syncretism in Osha. In the work developed by Mercedes Sandoval, for example, we must understand Osha, and all religions, as a chamber, a generous and open vault containing many cultures. Sandoval reminds us that the Hispanic culture during the slave trade was itself heterogeneous, consisting of a patchwork quilt of contributions by the Jews, Muslims and Catholics residing in Spain, as well as markings from the cultural regions of Catalonia, the Basque country, Galicia and other areas. The Catholicism taken to Cuba was definitely pluralistic and distinctly Mediterranean, and included the worship of saints and a fascination with mystical languages. Cuba itself was dense with beliefs in miracle healings and supernatural events in general, and was influenced by an Espiritismo movement that traded in magic and even witchcraft. The country presented a culture of ambiguity reinforced by the multiple and conflicting subcultures that stretched across the island. Catholic culture was a dominant force in Cuba, but never commanded a numerical majority of the population. It was commonplace for individuals to cross over from one religion to another with little difficulty, and certainly without reprisals. In telling this story Sandoval argues that it was impossible in a setting as heterogeneous as Cuba even to identify a pure African religion. Whatever came over in the slave trade was immediately thrown into a cultural mix so deep and compelling that a syncretic religion was an inevitable outcome.

The problem for all syncretic claims, however, is that any glance at the structure of Osha reveals Africa, not Spain or Cuba, or Catholicism. The dominance of African religious culture can be easily tracked in the parallels between Osha and Catholicism. Olodumare, the distant and absolute God of Osha, is incarnated in a life force known as ashé. This force roughly parallels the Catholic understanding of grace, but only roughly. Grace is a divine state of love that, when granted by God, transforms and sanctifies individuals. Ashé is a more active sacred current, a power that infuses the universe. Ashé is personified by orishas, who represent aspects of God and intervene actively in human affairs. They are worshipped by followers of the religion and occasionally possess individuals in order to communicate with humans. Catholicism has saints and angels. Orishas, saints and angels are superficially similar. For example, Oshun is generally regarded as a correlate of the Catholic saint, Our Lady of Charity (the patron saint of Cuba), and Saint Barbara at one time was offered as a correlate for Shangó. But the first is weak, the second absurd when the features of saint and orisha are inspected and compared. The distinction is also one of sense in addition to signification. By definition, saints are deified humans. Orishas are holy beings, natural phenomena sometimes represented in human form but also as natural phenomena simpliciter. Also, on sheer numbers, orishas are both more numerous than saints (scholars count more than 50 in Cuba, and some students of the religion accept over a thousand orishas in various regions worldwide) and seem always to represent particular things and functions. Catholics have many patron saints, but they also pray to saints and other divine beings who have diffuse and general powers transferred to them by God. Also, most Catholics today do not worship saints (though Catholics did so in medieval, and sometimes early modern times), nor in the contemporary world are Catholics ever possessed by saints.[5]

Osha is filled with divinations, spells, curses, and protections, not as powers of any individuals but as forms of divine intervention. Ifá, the path of divination, is mastered by those who would know the will of God. Three types of priests are recognized in the religion. They are, in ascending order of rank or importance, the awolorishas, italeros and babalawos. The most respected of the priests in Osha are the babalawos, for they are masters and interpreters of Ifá. This means that they have partial access to and can interpret the destiny of all beings (which is known in its entirety only by God). Those who petition these priests for oracular advice can gain entry into the divine order in sufficient scope to address practical problems. No comparable access to the divine plan is found in Catholicism, which (on Aquinas's hierarchy of laws) allows only rare and incomplete glimpses of divine law. Osha also uses divination to solve (by defining and interpreting) the personal problems of those who seek counsel from babalorisha or iyalorisha (Osha priests). Catholic priests, by contrast, administer the sacrament of penance and reconciliation (also known as confession) and distribute communion, which are offered as God's instruments for human redemption. But no Catholic priest of any rank would claim privileged knowledge of the cosmic order to introduce to life's ordinary difficulties.

It is precisely in the relentless joining of the eternal with the practical that Osha exhibits its distinctive character. A practical union with higher beings is part of Catholicism, but the methods found in Osha mark in yet another way the differences between Christian and African influences in the Yoruba religion. The individual member of Osha tries to establish a close, binding relationship with the orishas, who are the spiritual figures instantiating the divine power of God. The believer does this through divination (where the orisha speaks to the human), sacrifice (involving offerings of food shared between human and orisha, sometimes including animals offered as sacrifice), possession (in which a human experiences a rapid trance followed by a physical state of possession by an orisha or ancestral spirit), and ordination into the priesthood of Osha. The last method commits the individual to full eventual union with the orishas or Ifá, and is regarded as the fusion of spirit and human in one person. Traces, and sometimes heavy marks, of each of these methods of contact with higher beings are part of Christianity's long history, but the Catholicism that evolved in the New World has little remaining of these rites. The religious forms and rituals of Osha are primarily expressions of African culture.

We must remember, however, that any comparisons among cultures, any exploration of syncretism, of fusion, dominance and independence, are filled with the intractable problems of identity and causal paths found in all cultural encounters. The easiest and certainly simplest way to proceed is to assume an original African model, identified mainly with the Yoruba culture, which is carried in the slave trade to countries in the New World, primarily Brazil, Haiti (with the Dahomian people) and Cuba, but also (in less significant ways) to the United States and other countries. Then its instantiations in each of the three major countries yield the variations we know as Candomblé, Vodoun, and Osha, variations produced by the indigenous cultures of the host countries acting on the African model in different (and disputable) ways. But this simple account is painfully inadequate. It is not clear at the outset that there is, or ever was, a structure in Yoruba (in the sense of a formal expression generalizable to all Yoruba practices) that could be transported to the New World from Africa. All non-Western societies tend toward a holistic sense of culture which absorbs religion, so that the term Yoruba refers more accurately to a way of life, not a distinct religion of the sort demarcated in the West from other practices. Without a distinctive practice or a written theology Yoruba may be just what individuals did in Africa when they worshiped orishas. It is indicative of the dominance of practice over belief that the sign of membership in Osha has never been an expression of faith but participation in the rituals of the religion. Also, one of the acknowledged features of Yoruba is its pragmatic openness to different beliefs and practices, suggesting variable rather than fixed structures. Among the expressions of this spiritual pragmatism are the sectarian variations that occur even within different cultural manifestations of Yoruba in the New World. (In this sense Yoruba is like Christianity and all other religions.)

The problems of identity are compounded when we realize that traditional ways of life are closely linked to a sense of place. What were the effects of a loss of African terrain and the introduction of a new geography to the Yoruba culture? Even if some type of structure was somehow taken to the West with the African slave trade it is still difficult to distinguish the Yoruba structure from the structures that are a product of Yoruba's encounter with Catholicism. An undefined and practical way of life, taken as background or as a seamless component within a culture, may become precise and visible and different when challenged by another way of life. Even the simple request for a description of a religion may elicit an answer that is an artifact of the question, the tacit made explicit and changed as a result of the interrogation. Or, the dependence of position on observation at the level of particle physics is alive and well in the macro world of human communities whenever a structure is the product of one culture encountering the gaze of another. It is probably safer (and better) to say that there is an expressible structure in Osha that is African, but whether it was carried intact in this form from an original African model cannot be known. Also, even if we concede that the central model is African, without important syncretic influences at the systemic level, the syncretism of Osha practices (not rituals), beliefs and progenitor (within families) is legion and impossible to deny.

We do know that Osha, originally a religion of slaves, was adopted eventually by portions of the white population in Cuba. Membership rolls were kept only in memory, however, since Osha continued to be a loosely organized religion practiced in private homes rather than in churches or public institutions of any kind. Even today the religion has no final written code or theology in the sense of a Koran or New Testament, though Ifá exists in a written text that is still evolving. Its origins and traditions, including its core ideas and practices, have passed from generation to generation mainly as oral history. Osha was brought to the United States mainly in the late 1950s and 1960s by Cubans fleeing the Castro regime. The first wave of Cuban immigration was in the years immediately after 1959, an influx to South Florida of mainly the professional classes in Cuba. In 1980, approximately 125,000 Cubans came to South Florida in the Mariel boatlift. This second wave of immigrants brought Cubans from all classes, and included substantial numbers of Osha practitioners (and, to the faithful, the orishas who followed the priests).

Reliable demographic data on the religion do not exist. The best estimates on membership in the United States vary widely. The regional figures mentioned most frequently today are that 300,000 members of Osha reside in New York, many from Puerto Rico and the Dominican Republic as well as Cuba, and at least 100,000 are in South Florida, mainly from Cuba, though many of these practitioners may also call themselves Catholics. (Census figures for the year 2000 put the number of Hispanics in Dade County as 1,284,416 in a population of 2,253,362 million residents.) The lowest estimate on the larger picture from scholars and members, partly drawn from an informal survey in 1985–86 of the written records of elders in Osha and from sales of animals and other paraphernalia in stores, is that the core of just Osha members in the United States is roughly one million. Some scholars, for example Migene Gonzalez-Whippler, set the figure of practitioners (not just members) as large as five million (a figure regarded as too high by most other scholars).

4

Animal sacrifice, the explosive issue for much of the opposition to Osha in the United States, is a ritual deeply embedded in many religious practices throughout history. The Book of Leviticus provides detailed instructions for the Israelites on the slaughter of animals, including the statement that "The priests shall dash the blood against the altars of the Lord at the entrance of the tent of meeting, and turn the fat into smoke as a pleasing under the Lord" (17–6). Not all writers of the Bible endorsed sacrifices but "burnt offerings" were very much a part of Hebrew traditions. Christianity did not conduct animal sacrifices but the influence of Dionysian rites is evident in the communion ritual, which is described as the eating of Christ's body and the drinking of his blood. In Christianity Jesus assumes all sacrifices by offering himself as the ultimate sacrifice, the "lamb of God" in the Catholic Eucharistic Liturgy. Pre-Western cultures in the Americas, including especially the Aztec and Mayan, practiced sacrifices that included both animal and human victims. In all of these rituals blood is regarded as sacred, and the spilling of blood from a live animal an offering that placates the gods. More precisely, sacrifice is a conciliatory gesture that intends reciprocity between human and deity. The ritual offers the sacrificed animal as propitiation to spare the life of the human disciple.

Seen in this historical context, the reliance on animal sacrifice as a central and even defining ritual in Osha is continuous with virtually all religious practices in the past. Put in crude metaphorical terms, sacrificial rituals are to religion as apple pie is to American popular culture. But there are two important breaks with religious traditions in the Osha ritual. First, modern religions have largely substituted virtual sacrifice for actual sacrifice, relying on tokens and symbols instead of the real thing.[6] Osha continues to do the real thing. Second, Osha is a religion that appears to be entering the contemporary world (the Lukumí Church has its own web site) while yet maintaining its core primitive rite of animal sacrifice. The conditions of this new world are shaped in part by influential and unprecedented animal rights movements unalterably opposed to any abuse of animals. Here are found the contours of a struggle.

One signature statement of the contemporary West is the extension of rights vocabularies to forms of life traditionally regarded as chattel, embryonic, or fair game: children, fetuses, non-human animals. Animal rights groups protect non-human animals from harm primarily with rights driven tactics, meaning that they assign rights to life and freedom from harm to non-human animals. But these groups also sometimes develop utilitarian themes, for example that a brutal attitude toward all forms of life will be an inevitable consequence for human communities if the torture and killing of animals continues.

Animal rights groups currently restrict experimentation on animals, join ecologists to block developments of land that threaten endangered or rare species, demand and receive assurances from American film companies that no animals are harmed in films, and present no fewer than 25 Web sites for different organizations intent on preventing a robust inventory of harms to animals. The Lukumí Church, by default, enlists the virulent opposition of all animal rights organizations with its practice of animal sacrifice. An Amicus Curiae brief supporting the city of Hialeah was presented to the U.S. Supreme Court in the Lukumí case by a group consisting of People for the Ethical Treatment of Animals, New Jersey Animal Rights Alliance, and the Foundation for Animal Rights Advocacy.

The opposition between Santería and animal rights groups was more than a standard political confrontation. It was (and is) a textbook type of intractable dispute. (Yet note: like all seemingly intractable disputes, it yielded a solution when political or legal measures were assigned to it.) The dispute was visceral, and framed in terms of foundational principles. The differences extended even to descriptions of the sacrifice ritual, creating a Rashomon effect of vivid dimensions. Here is a presentation of the ritual by Gary Francione, one of the lawyers representing the American Society for the Prevention of Cruelty to Animals (published in *The Houston Chronicle*, July 24, 1993, immediately after the U.S. Supreme Court decision):

> Presentations by the faithful surround and even bury these descriptions with elaborate religious procedures. Listen to the words of Julio Garcia Cortez on animal sacrifice:
> "A young goat is the first offering, a piece of coconut is put inside his mouth, and tied with a rope. Two assistants will hold him while the Oriate (a senior olorisha) peels a bit of hair from the goat's neck and starts chanting. (Here Cortez lists the chants in Yoruba between the Oriate and a Choir). While chanting these phrases (the Oriate) will introduce the knife through the side of the goat's neck. (More chants.) . . . . With the knife still inside the animal's neck, the Oriate will continue to do the next chant. (More chants.) These chants will be repeated until the goat is left without blood . . ." (from The Osha, pp. 317–18)

Cortez goes on to describe the sacrifice of fowl and other animals. These accounts differ from the horrific descriptions provided by opponents primarily in the setting. It is clear from the texts of the faithful that the sacrifice ritual occurs as part of an established practice with

fairly precise rules and criteria for correct performance. These ceremonial trappings are not to be underestimated. The Catholic Church
is known for its lush pageantry (exactly what occasioned Luther's
scorn and Reformation sparseness in Protestant churches). The pro-
cessions, statuary, colorful garments, stained glass, religious medals
and rosary beads, holy water and holy pictures, clusters of brightly lit
votive candles, the smells of incense, and the layered ceremonies at
Mass are forms of religious art, expressions of an interior spirituality
in terms of transcendent symbols. These sources transform human
meanings by suffusing them with an eternal perspective. The controlling thought is that an event in human terms can be quite another in
God's terms. To the Osha believer it is exactly the thick religious
dimension represented in ceremony that leavens and justifies the sacrificial ritual. The ritual, as an offering to God, must be evaluated from
God's point of view.

5

The political opposition coalesced that year (1987) in the June 9 city
council meeting. From Pichardo's point of view it was an exercise in
oblique power. Since the city could not deny a religion its church without violating First Amendment rights, the council charged that Osha
was not really a religion but a cult, and that it violated hygiene laws
and laws preventing cruelty to animals. The meeting concluded with a
passage of the first of Hialeah's resolutions opposing animal sacrifice.
It was an emergency stipulation that declared it city policy to oppose
ritual sacrifice and prosecute violators of state and local law. The resolution adopted the language of the state's anti-cruelty statute and
applied the statute's provisions to the city of Hialeah. The Florida law
specifies the terms and conditions for the humane slaughter of animals, primarily in the slaughter of livestock for food, as set forth in the
Federal Humane Slaughter Act of 1958. These terms and conditions
prohibit unnecessary and cruel killing of animals, though the Florida
law does exempt "ritual slaughter."

The debate and public condemnation continued through the summer. Occasionally Pichardo and his colleagues found themselves dodg-
ing cars trying to run them over. Cassettes containing Christian
sermons were tossed onto the property. Once a wooden plaque with a
crucifix was thrown in like a Frisbee. Crank calls, death threats, letters
addressed to Dr. Satan were common. The city council enacted additional ordinances in September that specifically targeted and prohibited

the Church rituals of animal sacrifice. On September 24 the Lukumí church filed a suit in U.S. District Court against the mayor, the city council, and the city of Hialeah alleging that their constitutional rights to religious freedom had been violated. Pichardo labels this period as the start of the chicken wars. The city, in his view, had arranged to reduce all of the complex issues of religious belief and church–state relations to the morality of animal sacrifices.

The legal core of the dispute was whether the municipality of Hialeah, Florida, could constitutionally pass and enforce ordinances that prohibited animal sacrifice when the practice was and is a core ritual in Osha. The narrative of the dispute exhibits some of the political and legal patterns of reasoning that follow the introduction of external references, the commands of God, to secular contexts, and displays the antagonisms toward those pragmatic moments that seem to fulfill so much of conventional American religious practice. The illustrative quote is from Pichardo. At one point in the District Court proceedings Judge Spellman asked Pichardo this question: If the law forbids animal sacrifice, what was he going to do about the practice of his religion? Pichardo responded, "Obviously then we have a contradiction. The ultimate judgment displayed in history is that man does not have the right to tell God that he cannot be offered an animal."

Pichardo is a man whose movements are graceful and deliberate. He seems very relaxed, with a kind of controlled energy. But it is clear that he is driven by what he considers destiny, and like all who believe that their life's path is received from God, not chosen, he is solemn and unbending on his understanding of his religion. On this point, the supremacy of God's work, he is adamant. "It is an integral part of our philosophy that we cannot tell God how we're going to worship. God has already established that. If we can tell God what He can do, then He is not a God to begin with."

On June 11, 1993, after the expected long legal process, the U.S. Supreme Court ruled the city ordinances unconstitutional. All nine justices agreed that the ordinances violated the free exercise clause of the First Amendment. In the majority opinion written by Justice Kennedy, the Court found that the ordinances intended to suppress the Osha religion even though they did not state such a goal. The use of the words "sacrifice" and "ritual" was not decisive for the Court since Kennedy admitted in his opinion that current usage of these terms also admits secular interpretations. But the Court did rule that the ordinances, by intending to prohibit animal sacrifice conducted by the Lukumí Church, failed both the neutrality and general applicability tests of *Employment Division v. Smith* (1990). The problem was that the clear objective of the regulation was the suppression of the main ritual of the Osha religion, which effectively targeted religious beliefs for regulation. This "is never permissible," according to Judge Kennedy.

Lukumí v. Hialeah was a dispute extending to a variety of compatible and contradictory interests, including that most influential of incentives, the possibility of economic gain or loss for some of the disputants. But the dispute was not just a conflict of interests defined in secular terms. Animal sacrifice for Pichardo is mandated by God, thus outside the mediating forces of political adjustment and compromise. The church cannot concede anything on this point. The methods of reasoning in Osha, and the conclusions drawn from them, are controlled by background beliefs in God and the commands He has given to the faithful. This seamless external reality, which provides a form of guidance for human decisions that must be honored without dissent, cannot be introduced to the nominal partitions of a secular liberal state without compromising and ultimately contravening the authority of God. The social side of the religion, in other words, gives way to the principle-driven side when the core rituals and beliefs are at issue. It is precisely this pattern of reasonable intransigence, yielded by those defining features of religion, which marks it off from other social practices.

The complexity of the relationship between principled religion and the democratic state suggested in Pichardo's acceptance of God's authority is familiar but still hard to exaggerate. Pichardo believes that secular law cannot prohibit offering an animal to God without contravening God's command, which would be unintelligible from his point of view. Even though the final legal ruling by the U.S. Supreme Court was in the Church's favor, Pichardo's reasons for supporting animal sacrifice, and his explanation of the dispute and its outcome, are outside secular frameworks. He accepts a higher order of being that is not entirely accessible to the human mind or soul, and believes that this higher level of existence must dominate human experience. Acceptance of the divine, of sacred texts, draws Pichardo's thinking away from secular modes of thought, and suggests radical breaks between the religious and the secular.

6

The familiar distinctions raised by the Lukumí narrative between the sacred and the secular take us into areas that underwrite the special standing of religion, a standing recognized by Locke (among others), and then into a critique of the dominant strands of public and deliberative reasoning developed in current versions of liberal political theory. This type of discussion, which opens the theoretical excursions of this book, offers a first cut into religion and politics that identifies what does not work, a kind of precursor for a theory of political governance that succeeds in addressing religion on its own terms, not those versions of religion that accommodate liberal political theory. Or, put more directly, the Lukumí case suggests a critique of public reason and deliberative democracy (as deployed in the literatures selected here) that pays special attention to religious discourses and church–state in liberal democracies and leads us to a sketch of an alternative concept of public reason that is wider and more political than found in current works in political theory.

Can we define the working vocabulary introduced by these discussions? The traditional literature presents religious communities in terms of ontology, morals, and ritual. To this standard collection of terms I will add a belief in insensate realities (by which I mean those realities not defined by human sentiments), an acceptance of the unknown as a condition of experience, and (to use the quaint demarcation of post-axial religions) views of the self as dualistic rather than unitary. My main energies early in the work are marshaled to distinguish sacred texts in terms of their acknowledged connection in religious communities to a supernatural realm, meaning that the interpretation of such texts must be negotiated on the acceptance of a domain not contained by human experience but external to it. I define politics, the second entry in the binary set of concepts, as an authoritative practice that secures a range of prudential goods in a geographical territory. The defining exercise tries to represent these differences through the identification of core terms in the practices at issue. I mean by core terms those that are reasonably generalizable across many, perhaps most, versions of the practices. Their introduction here is in large part a management strategy shaped and limited by the specific assumptions and purposes of this inquiry. The key methodological assumption on this matter is that the absence of definitions with some generalizing powers restricts us to a kind of conceptual botany, cataloguing differences instead of developing theory or even arguments. This can hardly be useful, and core terms are helpful in avoiding these limitations.

The critical entry on this lexical menu is divinity (an orientation to a realm beyond human understandings of nature) as a core term in religion. One clear indication of the nominally essential standing of divinity in religion is in the type of inquiry characterizing a religious sensibility. Any strong religion is framed by a set of questions (not answers) that secular orientations typically do not and perhaps cannot address. These include (1) why is there something instead of nothing, (2) is there life after death, (3) is the universe a product of a higher design, (4) what is the purpose of pain and suffering in human life, (5) do we have contact with higher beings, and (6) is there a God? The methods of inquiry generated by these questions sometimes overlap with secular inquiries and at other times do not. The near-death experience, for example, presents a kind of evidence for life after death that invites both secular rules of evidence and inference, and also metaphysical conjectures. The defining logic of ritual, by contrast, is more completely within religious domains, a distinction seen whenever we consider the purposes and rationale of religious rituals. Ritual is understood as a way of ensuring a continuity of form and meaning, an expression of faith, a physical representation of spirit, the presentation of something that cannot be interpreted in natural terms (or an enactment of the mystical as a reminder that at least some parts of the world must be seen as exceeding the natural), a token of universality (when performed in the same way all over the world), a method of purifying the self, the celebration of symbolic over sensory reality, a reproduction of religious belief, evidence of a permission to interpret ceremony, a form of access to religious imagery (especially for those who are not intellectually inclined), a definition of membership in a religion, and a propitiation to God. All of these uses of ritual are confined to the religious, and so help mark off the religious from the secular. These questions, and the attempts to answer them, are primeval in form and origin, and differ from inquiries characteristic of political thought and action in requiring the concept of divinity as an instrument of classification and interpretation.

The concept-formation exercises put into relief the basic theoretical question driving this work: how can politics manage radical disputes that absorb all the rules and principles typically used in managing disputes? I will argue that the acid test for such a question is represented by strong religions in secular democracies. I will also argue that in negotiating strong differences between religion and politics, church and state, one is required to explore the possibility of freestanding political languages (those detached from community vocabularies) that might serve as resources to govern relations among disparate communities. The versions of political reason and deliberation drawn from dominant strands of political liberalism simply do not work in sharply rendered, or what I call divisive or deep, pluralism. I maintain that these conditions sometimes require a version of political reasoning crafted more nearly in terms of the diplomatic languages of reason-of-state in international politics than the consensual expectations of liberal political theory. But these state languages still require a frame to evaluate the conditions favoring liberal or reason-of-state models of political reasoning. I suggest that a kind of collective pragmatism provides that frame. A recursive system of argument guided by collective references takes us to models of reasoning that can match, coordinate, and, in general, accommodate institutions that are dissimilar in the extreme sense in which the religious and secular differ in orientations to human experience. The operations of complex systems, curiously enough, correlate happily with the reflexive logic of conscience in religious thought.

In the midst of these excursions into theories and models it should become apparent that the book is as much about religion as it is about politics. I believe that the successful identification of freestanding political languages capable of attending to religious communities requires more detailed explorations of religious thought and practice than usually found in the prevailing literatures in political philosophy. These explorations are provided here. I confess to redefining some of the material in religious studies and political theory. My arguments for a restoration of the supernatural in religious practices, for example, oppose much of the constructivism of postmodern thought. But this opposition is not inspired from a believer's point of view. It arrives from a sharper delineation of language games. It doesn't matter for the arguments here on divinity whether a supernatural realm exists. It is just that the interpretation of sacred texts can require something like the ground rules of internal realism, which instruct us to treat certain terms (or texts) as if real objects exist whether they exist or not. In this sense divinity is a token for a religious grammar. This is the strategy that opens a critical space between religious and secular political discourses, and suggests that sacred texts cannot be read from a skeptical or dispassionate perspective.

The end game of the book, the introduction of a managing device for transformative liberalism and reason-of-state models, should be irresistible in presenting the kind of tiered arrangement so intriguing to (at least) traditional social theorists: a sketch that extends a meta language across disparate communities, in this case a background grammar of politics across the pluralism of a secular democratic state. This small enchantment, summoned from within the logic of recursive systems, provides a freestanding political reasoning to manage the parallel universes of religion and politics. The background mechanism just *is* the generic form of political reasoning in discerning the conditions favoring the liberal model or *realpolitik*, or some amalgam of the two and perhaps even other models of practical reason, and as part of this effort adjudicates the appropriateness of each of these orientations as conditions differ. It is also the mechanism that can lead to a justification of force when political extremes defeat the uses of any model of reasoning.

Yet even as we state the practices of religion and politics in systemic terms we cannot systematize the real-world complexities that relate the two. The arrangements for state and church (meaning religion here) are so various across the world that they defy even classification.[7] We can list the current arrangements, cataloging them as entries in a book or manual. The list would include establishment religions (sanctioned by the state as the official religion), represented by England and Sweden; a dominant religion in a secular state (Israel); quasi official religions, such as Hinduism in India; pluralist democracies with a favored religion factored into multiple denominations and numerous other religions (Christianity in the United States); pluralist democracies like Japan with no favored religion and multiple religions and sects; and more. The one stipulation of this work in the face of such diversity is that divinity be recognized as the mark of a strong religion on the grounds that this concept yields the more interesting differences between religion and the secular state even as religions differ on the role and importance of divinity in their organization.

The narratives of the liberal state are typically rendered in terms sufficiently vague or ambivalent that diverse groups can appropriate them to some degree as their own. The regulatory powers of liberalism can be shaped and interpreted by different communities, and these communities may have different reasons for compliance with their demands. Put in more extreme fashion, liberal democracies can represent the secular ecumenism that accompanies a toleration stretched to foundational levels. Ambivalence is also a part of religious practices in the negotiation of meanings that connect human and divine experience. But the invitation of the religion narrative is framed by a summons, a set of commands issued from a reality not completely enclosed by human experience. These distinctions help explain why the persuasive powers of church and state are so different. It is also precisely these more radical differences, illustrated by the gulf between divinity and the bounded forms of reason used to negotiate differences in liberal democracies, that chart a need for different forms of public and deliberative reasoning.

Words and Things: Religious and Political Domains*

One of the more compelling starting points in social theory is defining the experience that one is studying. This Aristotelian exercise is irresistible when comparing two or more experiences that are demarcated for reasons independent of any research or linguistic project, and seem deficient accordingly. Church and state, for example, are separated in the United States on constitutional grounds, and almost never defined within constitutional law as organizations, institutions, or practices. Yet the reasons for separating church and state must rely to some degree on what we make of religion and politics. If the two (in this case) practices are identical or essentially similar, then arguments for separating church and state would be different than if the practices are radically unlike one another. My effort in these opening chapters will be to engage in what might be called concept-formation (or discovery). I will offer definitions of religion and politics, and explore the defining strategies that yield various productive concepts of church and state with the thought of providing a first cut into the distinctions, overlaps and mutual effects of the two institutions in democratic political systems.

The importance of definitions is evident when we recognize that every theory has break points that require specification from some interpretive sources. Break points are the terms, the words or arguments that allow access to the interior of a theory where strengths and vulnerabilities are on display for the observant critic. Illustrations? Look at Mill's *On Liberty*. This work, published in the same year

(1859) as Darwin's *Origin of Species*, provides the framework for relations between individual and state in liberal political theory. The framework is both simple and effective. We are to imagine individuals as competent and autonomous creatures possessing natural liberty. The only justification for government regulation of these creatures is when they harm one another, when, in short, the model of discrete and free individuals breaks down. Harm as the occasion and only justification for state regulation follows in some sense from the initial celebration of individuals. The premium value ascribed to individual life is exactly what justifies state intervention when liberty of action produces harm to creatures who are so highly esteemed.[1]

Liberty, Harm, Competence.—These are break points. They are the controlling terms that sketch the signature propositions of Mill's theory. They also disclose the parameters of the theory and the openings that transform Mill's arguments into malleable parts. By now it is indisputable that the terms are open to rival and reasonable interpretations even within the confines of the theory. Liberty is famously divisible into negative and positive. Harm yields the equally well-known senses of direct (and usually physical), offensive, and structural (e.g., market deprivations). Competence is clearly jurisdictional, variable with differences in rules of inference, evidence and argument found across cultural groups. Now, the important thing is that the position one stakes out on the sense of these terms helps define the scope and meaning of a theory. That, for example, Mill settled on negative liberty, direct harm and the type of competence drawn from scientific forms of reasoning marks his theory as libertarian within the secular traditions of the modern state.

Occasionally terms outside break points will introduce competing extensions of a theory. Where, for example, one sets the beginning of life for individuals will have strong effects on the assignment of legal protection to embryonic life on Mill's considerations of harm. There are typically also internal competitions among terms as conditions for implementation are recognized. For example, and still inside Mill's theory of the state, competence depends on having information. But on occasion information can coercively restrict liberty (as acknowledged in the majority opinion in *Thornburgh*, 1983). Or heresies may gain the high ground. The suggestion by Rousseau, for example, that coercion and liberty are complements may invert the main claims of Mill's theory. Also, there is the strong possibility that the moral pluralism anticipated in a free society may make it impossible to secure the consensus on governing vocabularies that permits a reasoned state regulation on Mill's conditions. But even on the recognition of these (and other) delicious possibilities, there are break points in every theory, and the terms that represent break points in Mill's *On Liberty* are the frame for the modern liberal state.

The truly intriguing question is how different communities use break points, and what these different uses tell us about the communities. Will a religious sensibility interpret such terms differently than a secular community, for example? And do religious beliefs present a different type of reasoning than the dominant forms representing a secular community? It does seem intuitively true that, with respect to Mill's terms, at least harm and competence will vary between religious and secular communities (if not liberty). To have this kind of discussion, however, requires the exploration of definitions that help sketch religious and secular domains as resources to specify content for break points.

2

The first entry in the binary set is religion, and in identifying or defining this term we might ask if there is a model of religious experience that is reasonably generalizable to a variety of religions. Again, we will work with a definition in terms of ontology, morals and ritual, with the three additions of insensate realities, an acceptance of the unknown as a condition of experience, and a binary view of the self.[2] To get to these terms in the most productive way we should begin with the broad demarcations historians recognize among pre-axial, axial, and post-axial religions. These demarcations are cut roughly along the years of antiquity to BC 800 for the pre-axial age, from BC 800 to 200 for the axial period, and of course the post-axial period from the end of the axial age to the present. John Hick, in *An Interpretation of Religion*, describes the pre-axial period as representing a fusion of the natural order and social stability, and driven by an understanding of the natural so utterly pervasive that no distinction can occur between the secular and the sacred. All of experience is religious, and reality is a seamless and stable cosmic order in which human individuals are regarded as inextricable parts of nature and subject to the same deterministic laws governing all items in the natural world. In the axial period a radically different understanding of experience is developed, largely through the insights of extraordinary human individuals (the list that Hick provides includes Confucius and Lao Tzu in China, the

Buddha in India, Zoroaster in Persia, the great Hebrew prophets in Israel, the Greek philosophers Socrates, Plato, and Aristotle, and, a bit later, Jesus Christ). These insights led to a stipulation that individuals are distinct from the cosmos, and an awareness that the acknowledged deprivations of human existence could be alleviated by a human consciousness open to transcendence. The prospect of salvation, redemption, or at least liberation promised an open set of possibilities for individuals. The individual who found and was absorbed by a higher reality could escape ordinary human life and its limitations. Individual transformation became part of what Hick labels a "cosmic optimism" in post-axial religion. The failures of human life, including its temporality, now could be overcome through acceptance of the eternal order. These propositions led to the formation of the great world religions that are found in post-axial cultures.[3]

Marcel Gauchet tracks some of these historical shifts in ways that signal a possible end state for religion. For Gauchet antiquity is dominated by the familiar absorption of individuals in a unitary cosmos controlled by destiny. The initial historical transition in religious practices is an organizational expression of this cosmic authority. Gauchet labels this expression the logic of superiority, where hierarchy, rigid organizational forms, and objectivity dominate, and even extinguish the concept of, individuals. The important shift is the Christian resolution of the Judaic contradiction that tries to couple a universal God with a sectarian (chosen) people. In placing divinity and authority within each and every individual Christ resolved the Judaic paradox by introducing and extending to all individuals the sense of otherness that separates all of us from God. Individuals were now marked by an interior consciousness, which opens a space between the external empirical world and dynastic authority. The resulting dualisms of God–human and soul–body arrived at an extended organizational point with the Reformation and the development of liberal democracies. But, Gauchet argues, while this movement from organization to individual resolved the issue of God's universalism it also disseminated the toxin of religion's demise by undermining the importance of all structures with the introduction of a subjective religious sensibility. One might also say that it produced a chasm in religious thought between cosmic and individual orientations that no general model of religion can bridge.[4]

So we start with a concession: any model of religious experience is bound to be abrasive to the differences between pre- and post-axial, cosmic and individual religions. Yet there are also certain features of religious experience that might capture some of the attributes of both orientations, though post-axial religions are probably more nearly the norm in any contemporary model of religious experience. The influence of historical conditions on models of religious experience is probably most evident in the use of current versions of science to present secular contrasts with religion. Modern science to the postmodern critic is an eminently historical creature, a local occupant of a restricted time and place. A set of contrasts between contemporary science and religion on local venues must accordingly be limited to historical conditions. The standard exit route away from crippling historical restrictions is content neutrality. All models that extend across difference in practices and cultures are to avoid particular claims and distinctions. For example, the sacred for Aristotle is likely to be defined or adjudicated successfully today with secular methods even when the formal properties of a model remain constant. On these terms, so long as a model fits both pre- and post-axial definitions it succeeds as a general expression of religion. But the particulars of rough edges and bad fits, even with the aspiration to content neutrality firmly in place, will become uncomfortably clear as we proceed.

The main sources of discomfort are found in the partisan traps, which seem to capture and break the many efforts throughout recent history to define religion. Neither the Old nor the New Testaments in the Bible mentions the term religion with any frequency. Roughly in the sixteenth century the literatures in anthropology begin the modern efforts to define the term for primarily research purposes. The early colonial excursions use the term from the outside of the cultures studied and dominated, usually as a device to conclude that no religion is present in the indigenous culture, or that if present is primitive (translation: non-Christian). From current historical perspectives these impositions are predictable, since it would be difficult to understand from within Western cultures a religious sensibility that recognized no distinctions between human and nature (a term that is also an artifact of Western cultures), or religious and secular practices. But colonial impositions do put into relief the potential for bias in any use of the term religion. Jonathan Z. Smith has organized various definitions of the terms religion, religions, and religious. The definitions he targets are elaborations on ceremony, virtue, faith, naturalness (in two senses: rational demonstration and commonality), spontaneous versus instituted, local versus universal (usually reducible to theirs versus ours), and an orientation to (what one supposes the West would call) the supernatural. Smith concludes with the proposition that the term religion is not a native term but "a second-order generic concept that plays the same role in establishing a disciplinary horizon a concept such as 'language' plays in linguistics or 'culture' plays in anthropology."[5]

Any number of alternative strategies is available to negotiate these issues, but some combination of humility and restricted ambition is always welcome. First, there are alternative ways to conduct and complete the exercise of concept-formation, and rival concepts do seem to find a family identification in proposed definitions, meaning that the exercise here is an entry in a crowded and respectable field.[6] Second, since many cultures past and present do not express a distinction between religious and other experiences, any definition of religion must be incomplete and in some way culturally limited even as it presents generalizing powers. The conceptual sketch offered here is primarily an inventory of items that allows us to demarcate political and religious venues in particular and contemporary Western settings where church and state are not fused in a single seamless cultural fabric. It is this second caveat that allows the present exercise to avoid the numbing critiques that all attempts to define religion produce terms that are too inclusive or restrictive, and exhibits a cultural bias.[7]

Variations on the term religion require us to be attentive to yet another issue in any effort to identify a general model of religion. Western literatures on and from religious experience seem consistently to divide according to whether the account provided is framed from the outside or the inside of the experience. Sociological/ anthropological definitions and explanations are outsider accounts. They describe and explain, and indeed mark off and sometimes create, religions from the perspectives of the observer. Consider, for example, Geertz's famous definition of religion: "a system of symbols which acts to establish powerful, pervasive, and long-lasting moods and motivations in men by formulating conceptions of a general order of existence and clothing these conceptions with such an aura of factuality that the moods and motivations seem uniquely realistic" (Geertz: 90–1).[8] This is a description that articulates the function of religions in cultures. It leads easily into what Hick labels non-realist versions of religions, which are informed by the view that religions are collections of beliefs intertwined with skills and needs in social practices, and that religious ideas are human projections, expressing human thoughts and ideals. This view represents the way that religion is understood in liberal democracies. It also complements the secular practice of teaching about religion without addressing the internal center of religious experiences. The insider account, by contrast, may not define religion at all. But if it articulates religion it would have to be as a set of texts (not books necessarily) referring to a reality that exceeds human understanding. These texts are not regarded as human artifacts on the terms of the insider view, but as issues from an insensate reality. Such texts are not adequately accounted for on the terms of functional or dysfunctional. Religious teaching on an insider account would be instruction in the requisite skills, ceremonies and knowledge indigenous to religious practice.[9]

Religion does not easily fit into the research frameworks of contemporary social inquiry for many reasons, not least because of the truth it claims to present. This truth, realist from a contemporary point of view, seems to argue against the standard program of reducing the practitioner's beliefs to more-or-less purely functional explanations. Such reductions beg the question by ignoring the resistance of realist truth to epistemological understandings of truth. But let me bracket the issue of truth at this point with a promissory note to return to it later in this work in the context of the outsider–insider distinction, especially since both go to the center of church–state distinctions. I want to try now to provide an insider account of religion that avoids the strong endorsement package of the believer by accepting the stipulative powers unavoidable in any definition of religion. The task is familiar. Concepts in social theory are drawn to some degree from the indigenous beliefs of the subjects under study, but these concepts have to meet the rudimentary condition of all explanations, which is that the account have a generalizing power outside the belief system under study.

Note also, however, that morality is not included in the account that follows. The take here is that all religions have moral implications in specifying or implying attitudes toward experience, and perhaps guidance for actions. But morality is neither necessary to, nor an exclusive property of, religion. A full account of religious experience can be provided with morality as little more than an adjunct and perhaps not even that. For example, if we take as the start of morality a sympathetic understanding of the other, and perhaps formalize this in Golden Rule morality, then some religions are even hostile to morality. It would be hard to insinuate a concern for the other as the self if, as in Buddhism, the dualism between self and other is regarded as an illusion to be overcome. Also, robust accounts of morality can and have been provided (in different ways, for example, by social contract and utilitarian theories) that make little or no reference to religion.

With all the proper reservations and caveats implied by the need for this balancing act of cautions, conditions, inclusions and exclusions, the following are offered as features of religious experience.

1. All religions are concerned with ultimate matters, usually by accepting planes of reality beyond the conventional boundaries of the senses even as amplified with instruments.[10] The contrasts with contemporary science again clarify the proposition. Traditional scientific approaches regard the domain of the scientific as coterminous with the boundaries of actual and potential human experience. Nothing that science must attend to is assumed in principle to be outside human experience. Religious perspectives, by contrast, routinely assume that human experience is a limited area within more comprehensive domains of the real, and that these more robust domains are the locus for religious inquiry and the reference for our deepest understandings of human experience. In William Christian's formulation, "Someone is religious if in his universe there is something to which (in principle) all other things are subordinated. Being religious means having an interest of this kind" (Christian:61).[11] Any inspection of religions will reveal that this ultimate something typically extends beyond the parameters of the conventional realities of the time and place where it is employed. Seen still another way, a religious community provides a wormhole (as in physics, not biology) from a thick inside to some ultimate Archimedean point that defines the community in holistic terms. This observation stays in place even as we acknowledge that the ultimate is put into dramatic relief only with the modern development of a scientific temperament that restricts knowledge claims to human theatres of existence. Contemporary science (perhaps in its cosmological modes) posits alternative realities to which we cannot have direct access, such as, for example, negative or parallel universes. But these universes are scientific matters to be treated as objects of inquiry so long as they are admissible with the techniques and theories of science. If they are regarded as both inaccessible to science and sources of insights on human experience, then one might reasonably conclude that science and religion are indistinguishable in approaches to these matters.

2. Partly as a consequence of (1), there is a sense of the unknown in religions that is a token for human limitations and a reference for understanding experience. Scientific temperaments typically regard the unknown as a problem to be solved. It is to be retrieved and brought into the domain of the known with the explanatory powers of science. Of course religions also attempt to explain what we do not know or understand, and in ways not always consistent with science. But a religious sense of the unknown is a position marker for human limitations, and humility, in the full range of experience. At least some senses of the unknown in religious perspectives are testaments to human imperfections and indicators of a larger theatre of reality.

To science the residue that stands for the unknown is a needed premise or an area yet to be explained. It cannot be a token for a domain of reality inaccessible to human understanding.

3. Given the limited access to higher planes of reality we might expect a religious sensibility to rely on what might be called oblique or indirect forms of knowing. These include a strong narrative orientation that folds easily into myths, parables, allegories, and generally into intuitive forms of knowing. This use of narrative powers is not just the introduction of a surrogate for some otherwise inaccessible state of affairs, a representation of higher realities that cannot be described explicitly. It is also the formation of instruments to gain at least partial access to complete or transcendent realities, often by deciphering the codes that are thought to issue from the insensate. These oblique forms of thinking complement the importance of faith in religious experience as a form of homage to the limitations of the human intellect and the scope of reality.[12]

4. Again as extension of (1)–(3) religious sensibilities assume that at least some of the concepts used in human reasoning, presumably those attending to comprehensive or transcendent realities, originate in areas that exceed the conventional limits of human experience. The terms of our thinking are not amalgams of intention and context but are rather the received frames of insensate domains. One cohort of this assumption is that knowledge is not completely an artifact of decisions but at least in part the result of discovery. Religious knowing is thought in some sense to impose itself on the subject from the outside. One important side effect of this approach is that sacred documents present what today we would label as realist, not epistemic, truths. All religious figures throughout history have taken for granted that their religion cannot be satisfied with the consensual accords that define epistemic truth. Instead, like logicians, scientists, historians, and others, they have sought, and claimed to have discovered, statements that are true independent of anyone's beliefs. The particular type of realism implicated in religion, however, is often believed to be revealed truth, in the sense that a core religious truth is made evident by issuance from an alternative reality. Prophecy, on this frame, is revealed truth spoken through the instrument of a human voice.

5. The one important last addition to this list of features contains the items marking the changes from pre- to post-axial religions. These are the important shifts in concepts of the individual that have influenced Western thought and social organization. From the residual categories of the pre-axial period the individual is assigned a distinct and reasoning consciousness that allows the meta reflections on nature that make moral thinking possible. Conscience occurs as a type of reflection on rightness that implicates the integrity of the self. The binary self that houses (in substance dualism) a soul or (in property dualism) a mind appears and leads to the belief in many religious discourses that persons exist in two venues: the material and spiritual worlds. This thought leads in turn to an understanding that an incorporeal self

survives after the death of the body. The vocabularies of survival, redemption, and transcendence easily follow these shifts in concepts of the self or person. Modern relationships between church and state are also nurtured on an interior consciousness. The mental venue of religion (strikingly put into relief with Christ's admonition that the thought of adultery is as bad as the act) established an individualism that is both the origin of the state and the source of resistance to its authoritative scope.

3

The dominant narratives of political life differ from religious stories. In all historical accounts of political theory one finds epochs in which the terms of politics represent distinct cultural meanings. The classical period of ancient Greece is the iconic source for essential definitions, which (paradoxically) have referential powers primarily in the conditions of their historical origins. In the story, classical philosophy, on its own special conditions of epistemological certainty, offers a normative vision of the state in which justice and authority can be pleasingly fused (as in Plato's *Republic*). The long traditions of natural law following this vision claim that concepts of law and politics are incomplete without some references to moral terms. Just as influential are the practical reminders from the classical age that the political world is a communal world knitted from language, and that concepts of politics must allow for both just and unjust regimes. All extensions of classical inquiries, however, offer introductory lessons on the importance of certain vocabularies that elaborate what we mean by the political: power, authority, legitimacy, obligation, and—later—consent.

Classical theories of the political community stressed the primacy of community (the whole or collective) over the individual. The contract theories of the seventeenth and eighteenth centuries regarded the individual as the starting unit in theories of the state. In a sense contract theory is possessed by early forms of methodological individualism in trying to derive social states from descriptions of individuals who are both primordial units and the constituent elements of the state. This reversal of conceptual direction predictably elevates consent to dominance in the modern world, explaining and justifying political arrangements by tracking them to some formulation (for example, the social contract) which represents an acceptance of political authority by individuals. These two orientations, classical and modern, are obviously influenced by ontological perspectives adjudicating which entity, whole or individual, is the primary or original variable in experience. One implication of selecting one or the other of the entities is that political theory is wedded (at least for a time) to either the political society (whole) or the modern state (individual) as the locus of politics.

Contemporary theories of politics are inclined toward the state and its coercive dimensions as the primary linguistic filler for the concept of politics. In Max Weber's influential definition the state is the "monopoly of legitimate physical force within a given territory." David Easton's definition of the political system as that which authoritatively allocates values in society attempts to combine systems theory (in trying to identify the defining function of politics as a system of actions) with the coercive emphasis of Weber. The same preoccupation with ultimate power and directional or organizational function also informs most of the recent attempts to define politics: politics is "integration and adaptation . . . by means of the employment, or threat of employment, of more or less legitimate physical compulsion" (Almond and Coleman, 1960); politics is "authority patterns" (Eckstein, 1973); and so on. These definitions are largely taxonomic efforts to state the meaning of politics in a single phrase, with the attendant hope (accompanying all taxonomic definitions) that the phrase can capture most or all of what we mean by the term at issue. In this sense contemporary definitions are mirror images of the classical attempts to define politics. The two—classical, contemporary—are alike in the sense that both provide a defining property for politics generalizable to all authentic instances of the concept. But they present reverse images on method. The classical schools seek an essential definition while the contemporary approach offers research utility as an adequacy criterion for definitions.[13]

Taxonomic definitions are notoriously deficient in political inquiry. They succeed even minimally only when the defining term can in fact extend across all instances of what we call politics in ordinary language. (They formalize lexical definitions for philosophical or research purposes.) But the extension of taxonomy (and indeed even with essential definitions) can work only in reasonably homogeneous settings. If the political setting is strongly heterogeneous for almost any reason then the extension is bound to fail. The more embarrassing versions of these failures seem to be part of a cultural diversity within the political system that can control meanings with local languages.

Think of how the term politics varies from the inner city to city hall or from academic settings to practitioners in the occasional hardball of ethnic politics. The fact is that the sense and reference of a term that designates power and its distributive influence on primary goods can be expected to display sensitivity to divisive beliefs and interests in the political society.

Only one strategy seems able to maintain single-property definitions. A workable taxonomic account of politics must select the minimal conditions possible in meeting the requirements of a linguistically reasonable definition. We would expect, for example, that the properties must at least describe important dimensions of politics, and to be completely successful must pick out those features necessary for the descriptive use of the term politics in any cultural setting, while doing no more than this. There are minimalist candidates for this function. A necessary though not sufficient condition for the concept of politics may be the directive functions noted in systems theory joined to the group or aggregate settings of all political contexts. This minimal specification (a) allows a full range of settings for actions that direct, including moral persuasion, rational demonstration, oblique and direct uses of force, and more, (b) permits both the collectivist sense of community found in classical thought and the numerical groups that seem to accommodate the strong individualism of, say, populist democracy, and (c) excludes from the domain of the political system all non-directive communities, which comfortably leaves anarchism outside the boundaries of the political society and the modern state. The minimalist logic of the strategy (restricting the definition only to necessary, not sufficient, conditions) also can avoid the intellectually partisan content provided by cultures and subcultures. Of course aligned against all directive or power oriented concepts of the political are communitarian arguments denying a particular locus for the political (power, for example, distributed throughout the human community) and allowing for non-directive state functions (the political system as, for example, essentially meliorative and cooperative rather than controlling). But theory and experience provide accounts of the modern state in essentially directive terms (writ in heterogeneous form) even to those who would wish otherwise.

The accounts of politics meeting the conditions of directive minimalism are of course spare in content, but they are always crafted in terms of spatial norms that secure certain prudential goods in a group setting.

1. The first and most direct rendition of the state is drawn from the thought that it is a set of authoritative actions concerned with the maintenance of organizational norms within a geographical region. The libertarian state is the sparest expression of this function. This state (described in accessible form, along with justifications, in Mill's *On Liberty*) is designed to guarantee the security of individuals without extending political authority to the issues of producing and distributing goods. Nozick's (1974) night watchman state (and the slightly less pallid Minimal Protection Association), for example, protects its citizens from physical assault and ensures negative liberties, but does almost nothing else. Put another way, the minimal state is a kind of spare criminal justice system that exercises a directive function in ensuring against the breakdowns in order that threaten physical safety and property. Distributive justice is left to other social practices. The bare bones state of libertarian political theory illuminates a condition that all theorists might accept, which is that some directive function, and likely one interpreted in libertarian terms, is the minimal property of any state. A state that does not direct in some way the behaviors of its members is not a state. Anarchy, the absence of political authority, is the condition where direction, and consequently a political system, is absent.[14]

2. The goods typically at issue in political systems are those accepted as material in the culture housing the political society/state. We must be careful here. We have noted that distinctions between material and what we know as metaphysical goods vary with time and place, and are difficult to establish even in the best (meaning the least complicated) conditions. But the long traditions of classical and medieval political theory generally acknowledge that the state is concerned with a certain range of goods illustrated by security of life and property, freedoms of various sorts, group and individual respect/integrity, in general those items that make civilized life possible for human beings and which now are designated (by Rawls, for example) as primary goods.[15] When the state is distinguished from the church in these traditions it is accompanied by a recognition that certain metaphysical goods like the security of the soul are the proper concerns of religion. Granted, in certain cultures these distinctions cannot be made in part because church and state, material and spiritual, are indistinct. But insofar as a political system can be identified as a political system within a particular culture, meaning a set of practices described and marked off by the languages of politics, then certain goods seem to be linked to its organization. Many of the more contentious discussions over the scope of the state are directed toward the active role, if any, that the state should play in the protection, production and distribution of these goods.

3. All political action is group oriented. Robinson Crusoe, or Tom Hanks, or any creature living on a desert island, natural or contrived, cannot be a political creature. Again, the languages of politics are the give-away sign. Any survey of political vocabularies will easily demonstrate that all of the terms within the family of politics are strongly transactional. For example: liberty,

in both its negative and positive incarnations, refers to others (freedom from and freedom to both presuppose a possible resistance or support from other persons); obligation implies others to whom one is committed; power and authority require a figure who is authoritative and others who are the recipients or subjects of influence/coercion; and so on. It may be that a collective or aggregate sense of human action is the one indisputable, so obvious as to be the not-worth-talking-about, property of politics. But note that a religious experience can be isolated in human terms. The sole individual can claim to have a religious experience, a connection to God or the cosmos, that is entirely outside of any group. These experiences may be resisted by some organized religions, but they are within many religions. An isolated experience by contrast, is outside of the political system by definition.

4

Suppose we accept these rudimentary accounts of religious and political experience. How can we cash them out in a comparison of the two practices?

Here is a simple first-cut entry into this exercise. If we set up the accounts side-by-side, like ledgers, we will be able to see surface differences and similarities. The most obvious are the spread sheets that take the participants in each of these practices in different directions. The first differences are in scope. All political systems are confined to spatial regions; a condition of the political that is exceedingly visible in the era of sovereign states but also very much a feature of empires throughout history. Religions, by contrast, are not always restricted by geographical boundaries. The world religions assert universal appeal and authority. It was common, for example, for Popes in medieval Europe to say that they were Princes of the whole earth because the dominion in question was spiritual in nature. By contrast, the Roman emperor typically knew that his authority was limited to the areas of the earth he did in fact control (even if he did claim de jure authority over those he could not de facto govern).

Membership also occasionally varies between the two practices. Political systems are constituted by citizens, who are persons with formal or testable membership in the system. Some religions propose membership for all persons in any area of the earth, and assume authority over persons as such, regardless of their beliefs. Again from the Middle Ages, Pope Innocent IV held that God's laws applied everywhere to all persons, and so infidels, invited to become Christians, could be punished for breaking these laws even if they refused the membership appeal. Political systems may dominate non-citizens on geopolitical considerations, but typically have no parallel to the open and sometimes aggressive enrollment practices found in inclusive religions. Persons acquire citizenship by satisfying sometimes stringent entrance criteria often designed to keep people out of the system. Crusades and universal conversions are the mark of inclusive religions, simple conquest and regional authority the sign of states. The closest parallels between religious membership and political citizenship are found in those exclusive religions that sometimes restrict affiliation by birth, or require initiation rites at least as stringent as those qualifying persons for citizenship. Then there are the natural differences in scope between a secular democratic state and any of its constituent communities. If we survey the communities typically found in a democratic polity—education, market organizations, religious—we will see that they are each limited in scope (in any sense of that term, membership, influence, etc.). But the state is always ubiquitous by comparison, an umbrella that extends benignly or perniciously across its member communities. More specifically, in an empirical reversal of universality of intent, religion is a communal activity of restricted domain within the political system in any secular democratic state.

Second, both epistemology and ontology offer different programs in religion and politics. It is true that the wide sweep of theory from classical to contemporary literatures comfortably extends to a full range of epistemological views. Plato's reliance on the forms, on certainty and complete knowledge, yields a political theory and at least one form of government that accepts an epistemic authority so pristine that it courts realism. Modern models of bounded rationality, with its conditions of risk and uncertainty, seem to produce the critical democracies that are consistent with the indeterminate states described in contemporary physics. These easy compatibilities of types with a wide range of epistemologies are not found in religious practices. The comfortable fit of various certainties with religious beliefs is legendary. The radical uncertainties of the modern world, on the other hand, present problems at least for theism. One signature statement of science (among several) is a willingness to abandon statements that fail critical tests, one mark of religion a proclivity to maintain a range of fundamental truths on the basis of faith. It is more than a bit curious that an acceptance of a larger theater of the real in religious discourse is consistent with radical doubt. The larger reality, after all, may be chaotic on human terms. But the sense of truth as a discovery of issued propositions typically includes a belief that certainty may be a condition somewhere in the universe even if it is inaccessible to humans.

Third, we have mentioned the senses of the individual crafted by various practices. The simplest way to describe a religious person in the West is that s/he occupies two venues, one material and the other spiritual. This ontological dualism represents a domain outside the material by acknowledging dual membership in two worlds: body and soul/spirit. No problems here for liberal democracies, for the political individual requires a demarcation culture, one that partitions experience into spheres, so long as the political is one subset of the culture. It is just that the opportunity costs of membership in demarcated political worlds are different, presenting (as we have seen) a demand for loyalty that is by definition partial, which in turn proposes a distinction between religion and politics, church and state. Of course naturalistic religions admit no distinction between material and spiritual. A holistic rendering of experience would collapse the metaphysical and the material into a seamless version of the natural. Holistic cultures, however, entertain no possibility of a political individual since there is no political dimension providing identity that is separate from other practices. It follows that for both demarcation and holistic cultures the invitation to be religious is contrary to that required to be a member of a political domain in liberal democracies, even as this domain exists in an imaginary world in holistic settings. In either culture the individual is configured in separate fashion for religious purposes, either as a political person in contradistinction to the spiritual or as a totally integrated person in a culture that does not recognize the political as a separate sphere.

Fourth, and a variant on the definition and role of the individual in religious and political practices, a religious orientation to human experience must re-shape the boundaries of that experience and absorb the self in the re-shaping in ways not required in liberal democracies. Though members of purely social religions seem to forget this, the defining feature of religion throughout history (and proposed here) is the acknowledgment that at least some of our understandings of the world come from a domain outside human experience. The high standing granted to revelation, the use of parables and myths, the priority of faith—all are tokens for the belief that we have only partial access to these external domains even as these instruments of metaphor are used to provide a more complete account of experience than the practices of secular thinking (including that most powerful of icons, modern science). Being religious finally means accepting the higher powers of an alternative reality beyond sensory planes, and this acceptance is thought to re-define the self and provide guidance in all aspects of life. In brief, religion is a summons to the whole self, mind and body, while a secular democratic state requires only a commitment of the public self for civic behavior, and does not require individuals also to act from the right thoughts.

But these side-by-side comparisons are little more than police lineups, blunt and even crude recognition exercises that illuminate some broad differences between religion and politics. Conceded, they are part of any genealogical tracing of historical relationships. They also are useful in presenting simple areas of conceptual hostility and compatibility. We can see more clearly that the two practices cannot be merged without significant modifications of one or the other, or both, as they are presented in Western democracies. The palpable effects of domain differences on concepts and principles are a general phenomenon, and can be seen whenever an entry in one domain is introduced to another. Note, for example, the way in which Rawls sculpts the difference principle (inequalities are justified only if they benefit the worst off representative person) differently in different settings.[16] Look even more carefully at how the normative reference for the difference principle is inverted in some practices. The difference principle is a principle attending to the structure of a society, not particular settings. But there may be no society-wide "worst off," only "worst off" persons in particular settings, and the settings may come with different implications. In an intensive care ward, for example, the "worst off" may be set aside by the triage nurse as those not to treat (i.e., assign resources for benefit) precisely because they are worst off. Different interpretations of the principle are common and even sharper in differentiating political and religious settings. Who exactly are the "worst off" in these settings must differ according to whether one believes in the primacy of the soul or not.

These lineup differences between religion and politics exclude reductionism as a strategy of benign reconciliation. No secret identity between the practices will be revealed if one absorbs the other. The side-by-side match up of concepts in each practice tells us that an absorption of religion into politics, or politics into religion, will result in significant losses because the practices are different from one another in important ways. To move deeper into the practices, however, we need explicit instruments of comparison and contrast. We need theoretical devices that monitor more subtle change and maintenance than the recognition of seismic faults provided by conceptual lineups.

One alternative to a lineup of concepts is an inquiry into the functions of each practice, not in the ways in which they carry out moral duties in the larger society and meet cultural needs but in the internal logics that help identify a practice. Consider tripping mechanisms, for example. Any social practice can be cast as a coping or maintenance mechanism, responding to an environment in different ways by adjusting to or resisting stress. Think for a moment of the ways in which religion and politics respond to a challenge aimed at core principles or practices. Again, in the case study organizing this book, a Santería church sued the city of Hialeah when the city council passed a number of ordinances prohibiting animal sacrifice. The Church eventually triumphed in the U.S. Supreme Court ruling but it was clear in all of the legal hearings that animal sacrifice is a core ritual of Santería and because of that the Church cannot under any circumstances trade-off or compromise on the practice. If there is collateral reasoning on the practice it must be crafted to ensure the continuance of animal sacrifice, not its restriction or abandonment for some other good.[17]

Are there comparable responses in democratic political domains? Even the loosest of democratic arrangements contain some core area of principle. The entire history of political theory is concerned to elaborate the governing principles of politics. But these principles are mainly frameworks within which disputes are located and managed. This sense of principles as marking off areas for discussion and adjudication provides the important concept of public space, the metaphor that allows us to see claims being introduced to an impartial domain for discussion and possible resolution. True, there are claims that are excluded as illicit. Attempts to legitimize violence against minorities, for example, are typically excluded today in democracies before discussion begins. They fall outside the parameters of acceptability. This sense of principles as gatekeeping instruments is quite different from the more substantive roles of religious principles. The differences are not that one (the religious) is a more rigid or brittle practice but that the other (political democracies) relies on principles that have different roles to perform. Religious principles define the meanings of religious practices. Political principles in democratic arrangements typically craft the central and sidebar discourses that can manage disputes without defining the practice of politics.[18] It would be surprising if the tripping points, meaning in this case the points where proposals for change are resisted or accepted, were not different in religion and politics given these differences in the logic of principles in each practice.

A second alternative is to track influence patterns. For example, does one practice exclude or dominate the other? In collective choice theory an alternative dominates another when the presence of the alternative excludes the other. Nothing this draconian occurs in standard demo-cratic practices, though there are religious movements that require an end to politics. Usually these movements aim to absorb the political, meaning extinguish it by reducing all practices to religious practice. Orthodox Judaism and Islam, in rejecting secularism, are versions of encapsulating religions in which the political must be an extension of religious practices. A state crafted in this way is a religious institution, and so (by definition) must be hostile to religious pluralism. Suppose, however, that we track corruption effects. One of the commonplace justifications for walls between church and state is that the practices tend to compromise each other. Note that arguments for corruption assume that the practices are different, and that differences in concepts cannot be transferred from one practice to another without change that is harmful. In the examination of religion and politics the conceptual lineup scans the implications of making each practice to some degree like the other. If they were different practices then of course the changes would be real and possibly unwelcome, especially as they affect core beliefs or principles.

Also, yes, these comparisons indicate that at least some of the break points in the governing terms of politics are appropriated differently by religious and secular communities. Consider again Mill's break points. No particular sense of liberty is easily assigned as an exclusive property to either community, but the two other terms yield critical differences on an acceptance of the definitions suggested here. The sense and scope of harm must vary according to whether one stresses a spiritual or a material dimension in experience. The very rendering of individuals in terms of a soul or spirit indicates a range of harms not available to a more strictly material orientation. Similarly, a belief that the meanings of sacred texts issue at least in part from an insensate domain must affect the rules of evidence, inference and argument representing competence in the two communities. The year 1859 is notable for the introduction of two disparate theories that abandon received truth in favor of a truth that emerges from competition. Mill's last standing opinion in open debate is a complement to Darwin's natural selection. In both cases truth is an outcome of a competitive process. It is not discovered in some external domain and imposed on experience. That this version of truth is hostile to communities that rely on a truth issued from an external source of authority is part of Western lore. All of this is simply to say in yet another way that religion presents a way of rendering political experiences intelligible that differs from at least the secular approaches of modern science.

5

The core differences between religion and politics may be located in the models of reasoning distinguishing each practice. To get at these differences requires a leap of faith that is often dismissed on postmodern relativism. The leap is an acceptance of a very general framework of reasoning that extends across practices and perhaps even cultures. One might say that a framework of this sort is required even to begin discussing reasoning on any grounds. But leaps of faith are often intelligible only after they have completed their redemptive tasks. Let me present a framework that might illuminate reasoning patterns across religion and politics with a second promissory note, this one to assess its effectiveness after its mission is accomplished.

The framework consists of three components. The first is the background beliefs (often functioning as unexamined assumptions, tacit or explicit) that influence the rules of inference and evidence used in all reasoning. The second is the depiction or characterization of reason, whether, for example, it is to be seen as a kind of puzzle solving, a search for truth, or a mediated solution—generally, a representation for what it is we are doing when we reason. The third is the set of rules or patterns that identifies forms of reasoning, the inventory of tactics, strategies, licit and illicit moves, types of expression—generally (again), the visible stuff that allows us to say that this is political, scientific, religious, etc. thinking and talking.

As illustration of background: Susan Haack, in *Manifesto of a Passionate Moderate*, distinguishes between the quality of evidence as objective and our judgments of the quality of evidence as framed by our background beliefs. This demarcation allows us to maintain objective standards while accepting perspectival effects on evidential quality:

> whether the way a candidate writes his "F"s is evidence relevant to his trustworthiness is an objective matter, depending on whether graphology is *true*; but whether I judge it to be relevant evidence depends on whether I believe *graphology* is true. (Haack, 1998:144)[19]

It is difficult to conceive of any form or reasoning that is not influenced, at least loosely, by background beliefs of some sort. Look, for example, at the deductive nomological model of explanation so fashionable at one time in philosophies of the natural sciences. This model is an imperfect formalization of a background belief that events can be expressed in a law-like relationship to one another, and that the intelligible world is ordered in such a way that explanation and prediction are symmetrical. Various background beliefs are notoriously important in scientific explanations. Contiguity, for example, is vital in ordering correlations as worthy or useless in explanations, yet the conducive effects of events on one another are usually just a matter of the way we believe that the world works. (Sunspots can be correlated perfectly with business cycles yet regarded as null explanations because Western cultures do not have any mechanism connecting the two phenomena.) Arthur Koestler (1984) has shown us how the ancient Greeks developed and clung to the geocentric system because they held the view that man was at the center of Creation, a background belief that kept them from the heliocentric system that their mathematics and observations could easily have expressed.[20] Or think about the competing and congenial roles of direct explanations and metaphorical presentations of experience. A direct explanation is the product of a background belief that experience is essentially accessible, and will yield its forms to explicit modes of thinking. Metaphorical presentations represent background beliefs that reality is both layered and translucent, a medium to other realities, and requires indirect and primarily symbolic texts as instruments of access.

As illustration of characterization: Haack (1998) suggests that if we understand the model for evidence as a crossword puzzle rather than a mathematical proof, then many of the famous difficulties of relativity will slide away. For example, the great debate over the superiority of Western versus non-Western epistemologies will be exposed as "a kind of conceptual illusion" (p. 145). While all cultures do not employ mathematics (at least in the same way), all are attempting to use evidence in some objective fashion to make experience intelligible by solving certain puzzles. The differential effects on evidence of background knowledge are still in place, but the puzzle depiction reveals "commonality underlying surface divergences" (p. 145).

The characterization of practices can also heighten differences in the uses of evidence, even within cultures. A legal trial, for example, can be depicted as either a contest, in this case an adversarial struggle between the state and a defendant, or as a search for truth. If, in the first depiction, one regards the state (as Justice Brennan did) as having a disproportionate advantage, then the exclusionary rule drawn from the Fourth Amendment to the U.S. Constitution might be interpreted to rule out any evidence from the prosecution secured illegally or connected in any way to an illegal search ("fruit of the tainted tree") even if relevant to determining the guilt of the defendant. But if a trial is seen as a search for truth, then even illegally secured evidence, if sound, might be admitted as helping determine guilt or evidence. Or, the characterization of a legal trial affects the rules of evidence, in this case by establishing differences in including and excluding information.[21]

The third component is an inventory of items. This inventory includes the types of decisions made in reasoning, the explanatory models endorsed, the expressions of effective thinking, and more. In this component we might find the more standard marks of reasoning offered as purposes or aims that craft form. For example, practical reasoning as an attempt to provide deliberative conclusions on what to do here and now has been singled out since Aristotle as a distinctive form of reasoning by virtue of its practical aims. Explanatory and persuasive forms of reasoning similarly are distinguished by their purposes in (respectively) rendering experience intelligible and getting an audience to do something. That all forms of reasoning are influenced by background beliefs and characterizations almost goes without saying. The easiest way to present this third component is to say that it is the surface on which we identify expressions of reasoning, but only with the commonplace understanding that surfaces have depths that are below immediate appearances. If this is not hyperbole, imagine identifying a corpse (in the sense of who exactly has died) without yet defining the cause of death. The third component of reasoning is the collection of marks or signs on which the post-mortem recognition is based.

These three components of reasoning are helpful in distinguishing among reasoning domains (practices, institutions). I propose to use these items to segregate science, religion and politics on the most rudimentary terms, and offer on the basis of these distinctions a truly very quick sketch of some gross (as opposed to net) differences in reasoning that will lead us to some distinctions between religion and politics.

Scientific reasoning has been oriented toward method in all of its incarnations, but it may be represented in blunter terms. Perhaps the bluntest of these terms is the goal of explanation. The point to science is to render experience in explicit and generalizable terms. The characterization of scientific inquiry may be multiple—puzzle-solving, open and contentious debate, falsification—but the purpose of such inquiry is an explanation that can be presented in transparent and replicable terms to any objective (read: neutral) observer. In one popular form, for example, the central explanatory feature of science is the practice of subjecting all statements to critical tests, to the extent that (in Popper's felicitous phrase) even our most cherished principles are no more than hypotheses that have so far resisted disproof.[22] This contemporary effort to avoid the paradoxes of confirmation with falsification has itself been restricted by the acknowledged need to protect core propositions and (one imagines) the methodological commitment to falsification. But the protective belts of science are typically justified as instrumental to good explanations and, in principle, to be dismissed if evidence requires it. The unknown in this form of reasoning is a problem to be solved, not an occasion for faith.

Religious reasoning must differ here in crucial ways. The literature we have reviewed suggests that the point to religious inquiry may also be seen as explanation, but the background beliefs influencing this form of reasoning (for example, a preoccupation with ultimate matters) accept a layered reality that renders explanation incomplete as a matter of necessity. Unlike the expectations in science, religious sensibilities, in anticipating that the whole of reality is only partially accessible to the human intellect, must concede that even our best theories and data sets can only represent a partial look into the real world. This background belief, when joined to a belief in higher powers outside the scope of human communities, is the most likely source for faith (defined by Mark Twain, and accepted by Carl Sagan, as belief without benefit of evidence) as a complement to, and occasional trump of, direct explanations. The natural concomitant of these beliefs is what might be called substance shielding, or protective belts around methods and core propositions that may have robust retentive powers in the face of falsifying events. Put another way, the mechanisms of change and maintenance differ across scientific and religious discourses. A form of reasoning that is self-limiting on a background belief in human limits is not governable simply by its own methodology. It must be eminently open to external insights provided by a partial seeing into dimensions of existence that exceed the human. It follows that the unknown in this form of reasoning is a condition of human experience that is testimony to our intellectual limitations. The best characterization of religious reasoning is probably a cryptogram, with a profound reliance on metaphorical modes of reasoning. Truth must be realistic by default.

Now, with these two sketches in place, consider political reasoning within the framework of any type of government. A generic form of political reasoning is organized around the need to secure a communal order that makes possible the realization of certain prudential goods that help define a human community. This part of the political is unas-sailable. If we flesh out this minimal form within the context of a liberal democracy, we would enrich the goal of order with a recognition of diversity and a negative liberty to pursue different versions of the good life. Various freedoms of expression are the natural correlates of these arrangements. The characterizations are multiple, but the Mill model of uncoerced dialogue seems most apt. The protective belts of reason in this case are wrapped around constitutions and symbols. The background beliefs seem to consist of shifting understandings of the political mission within the broad mandate for order. Within these understandings the unknown is negotiable as both asset and deficit, which means that it can be used to justify incrementalism and undermine synoptic planning, and provide reasons to employ a fusion of rhetorical and more direct languages in political discourses. The unknown in political reasoning scans easily into uncertainty, in this way collapsing ontology to epistemology. Truth is epistemic, meaning in this case consensual within parameters of legitimacy.

6

These are the briefest of renditions of three famous species of reasoning, and they are indeed surface excursions. But the sketches do reveal the effects of background beliefs on each of the forms of reasoning. The belief that reality will yield to explicit modes of explanation, for example, conditions much of what passes for scientific inquiry, including the set of characterizations and forms that make science a visible or public practice. But the effects of background on religion and politics are more impressive. The belief that concepts originate in areas outside human experience is decisive in crafting religious practices. It leads to realist truth in the sense of discovery, the unknown as an intractable condition of human experience, and the role of faith in inquiry and understanding. Note that even if we accept the proposition that working scientists are seeking truth, meaning that they are trying to provide an account of how the world is rather than how it seems, the distinctions still hold. Here is a redemption of the first promissory note. The decisive internal background belief in religious temperaments requires a deferential approach to the world, leading to methods (the central uses of metaphor) and shields (faith) that make inevitable a different account of how the world is than that sought and produced by scientists.

Also note carefully how the absence of this decisive background belief influences political discourses. The vocabularies of politics, including the most revered of political principles, are notoriously open to rival and reasonable interpretations. This indeterminate standing for the governing terms of politics is the sign of politics, from antiquity to the present. The identifying feature of authoritarian states is the attempt to force closure on open texts, the sign of democracies the public recognition and tolerance of the open and elastic qualities of political languages. Democratic politics just is the seemingly endless definition and redefinition of political terms in disputation and action. But these welcome contraries would indicate something quite different if one believed in a realistic truth emerging from domains not coterminous with human experience. In this case, with this background belief in place, the appealing disputes that characterize liberal democracies could be regarded as cacophony in need of an imposed order. The defining constraint of a democratic state—that it not adjudicate the truth of political claims but mediate their differences with negotiable criteria like those drawn from Mill's harm thesis—might be unintelligible as a permanent solution to differences. The appeal of a democratic polis is that it accepts no stable background belief as reference for truth, with the implication that a political world is constructed through and through. The appeal of a religious order is that the disorder of an empirical world is a surface feature that invites order on the basis of a truth that is untouched by the disputes of a human community, with the accompanying thought that a religious world is given rather than constructed. The second promissory note underwriting the effectiveness of segregating religion and politics with a model of reasoning depends on the presence of realist versions of truth in religious thought and practice.

The easy rejoinder to this argument is that texts in all discourses are finally products of interpretation. Religion on this view is in substantial part the history and practice of interpreting sacred and other texts, an exercise that is needed even to say what those terms mean that issue from another domain of existence. One might also say that the common feature of both religion and politics is their constructivist power over experience. But this rejoinder, which extends Mill's critical program into religious discourses, not only misses the historical divide over the role of authoritative interpretation of texts versus the dominance of the text as such (the Reformation, in other words), but also glosses very real differences found in interpretive practices. If all social practices are viewed as no more than various constructions of experience (text), then we still must be attentive to different mechanisms of change and maintenance for terms. I have argued here that the decisive feature of religion is the background belief that meaning issues from another reality. Of course this belief must be put into practice by the practitioners of religion to say what it means. But the point to the present reflection is that this belief constrains discussion in important ways, and these constraints are not found in discourses that do not accept the belief. One could see secular and religious discourses as language games and the point still goes through. The acceptance of an external source for meaning provides a different grammar for religious terms. It doesn't matter whether the claims for an external source are valid. Like internal realism's acceptance that some terms must be treated as if they referred to real objects even on the view that language is constructed (or risk distorting their logic), so too must some religious terms be understood as originating in an external reality if they are to be used correctly whether the origin is valid or not.

One might maintain that there are still no redeeming distinctions that demarcate practices. But think for a moment of what this stipulation does to language. It is a type of reductionism familiar at one time in moral philosophy, the efforts to collapse altruism to egoism. One effective response to these efforts is a reminder that the two terms point to different experiences described in ordinary language. Imagine, for example, the difference between a woman giving her life for her daughter and a man maximizing returns for himself on the stock market. If one wants to view both actions as forms of egoism then language needs a subscript to represent the ordinary differences between the two cases: the first instance is egoism 1 and the second is egoism 2. Then egoism 1 means altruism and egoism 2 means egoism. At this point the dispute is just over words, what to call actions that are clearly different in ways that must find their way into language.[23] If the background belief that meaning issues from an area outside human experience is decisive, then the constructivism found in religion requires a subscript to represent its differences from constructivism without this belief. In this civilized sense all practices may be viewed from the lens of constructivism, but the differences in types of constructions are more telling than the ascription of constructivism to all practices. Or, perhaps better even if less fashionable, religion is engaged in some way in discovery rather than just construction, and this makes all the difference in demarcating religious and political texts, and eventually in identifying relations between church and state.

Sacred Texts

I

Osha, like many religions, appeals to those who have problems that need to be addressed by a third party, and also to those whose lives are unusually hazardous and want protection of some sort. For eminently pragmatic reasons the religion is the choice of those in high-risk professions: deep-sea divers, boxers, certain gamblers, smugglers, artists, drug dealers in particular. Entertainers, curiously enough, are also found in these ranks. Practitioners fondly remember Desi Arnaz and at least his surface homage to Osha by opening his act with the chant of "Babalu" culminating with the full name "Babalúaiyé" (the orisha of disease and health). The practical reliance on Osha may be a celebration of use, as in the maxim, whatever works in any world: the prayer, the amulet, the incantation, the money bribe for border patrols, favors for the agent to get a movie role. But the ordinary, risk-averse person also turns to the religion for help. An individual might have a health problem, for example. He goes to an olorisha for assistance. Suddenly his problem is not his alone. It now also belongs to the olorisha. The olorisha will usually begin by trying to determine the cause of the problem, whether the client has a natural illness, for example, or if the origin of the health problem is supernatural, say the result of someone working magic on him. Or maybe the olorisha will conclude that a deity wants something from the client. Then he may take the person to a babalawo. The method of divination, Ifá, is conducted by the babalawo. In one method, the babalawo speaks to the oracle, ikin, by ritualistically tossing and interpreting the patterns of sixteen consecrated kola palm nuts to find the odu, or particular sign of the client. In all versions of divination the babalawo is trying to ascend in order to get the orisha to descend and reveal the cause of the problem and a possible remedy.[1]

Solutions vary according to problems. The illness may be part of the man's fate, and must be allowed to run its course. Or it may be an item in his destiny for which a remedy is available, something that can be modified by human interventions. If the illness is a spell conjured up by others, then the olorisha will identify a ritual to cancel the spell. Perhaps the illness can be passed on to an animal. One of the oldest African rites is an exchange ritual that transfers illness from one body to another, usually from humans to some power animal like a ram or goat. Then the animal has the illness, or evil spirit causing the illness, and so of course must be sacrificed rather than left sick and perhaps dying. Or it may be that the client must offer food and gifts to an orisha, perhaps Babalúaiyé. On many occasions the olorisha will send an ill client to a regular physician for treatment after the Osha rituals are complete. It is the established view of Osha that illness must be treated holistically, as both a physical and spiritual manifestation. No hostility to modern clinical medicine is found in Osha, though in fact psychological conflicts in individuals do occur as they try to avail themselves of both spiritual and conventional healing techniques.

The practical effects of consulting with an olorisha are some combination of distraction and renewed confidence in oneself. One measure of these effects is the widely acknowledged success that olorishas have in solving problems of love, where the heart is broken figuratively rather than literally. A woman comes to an olorisha with a common story. Her husband is leaving her for another woman. The olorisha immediately sympathizes. He bonds with the woman emotionally. He may tell her that the other woman has cast a spell on her husband, that the loss is not her fault but rather the result of black magic. He may even say that she will get her husband back if she follows his directions. In the meantime he keeps her very busy with instructions to light candles, put honey on some of the orisha's favorite food (maybe squash), take a bath with consecrated herbal water, get someone working on her hair, take this specially blessed perfume, buy a new dress, and so on, all leavened with the decisive promise that the olorisha will solve the problem. The woman may return home with a different, more positive attitude. This result alone is a kind of magic performed by the olorisha. It is a hybrid between the Homeric ontology that assigns responsibility for problems to the gods and the Christian reassignment of blame to the individual sinner. The individual in Osha accepts responsibility for modifying her behavior while understanding that the remedy has a higher or supernatural origin with dynamics that she can only partially comprehend. At the end of the day the intervention may bring the husband back, or—more likely—reconcile the woman to the loss and lead her to see that she can succeed in life without her husband.

This holistic strategy is obviously a form of practical therapy. It is also used to heal a variety of illnesses that respond to changes in attitude, including drug habits. The more intractable problems of daily life may yield only if an individual is initiated into Osha, either as a priest or through some other rite of passage. One does not choose ordination into the priesthood. It is offered to worthy individuals, those destined to be priests, and costs from 8,000 to 12,000 dollars and sometimes more. (Olorisha counseling fees are much more affordable, usually in the ten to hundred dollar range.) The impact of ordination on the iyawó (novice) is thorough, and typically described as a rebirth. The entire ordination takes 12 months to complete, and is broken into a preliminary period followed by different activities in intervals lasting several months. The first stage of the ordination takes place over a seven-day period of confinement, in the house of the initiate's godparent, and is open to friends and family. The initiate's hair is sometimes completely shaven and certain ritual symbols, understood primarily by the clerical community, are painted on his head. During the confinement the iyawó (novice) bathes with consecrated omiero (a liquid extract made from herbs). A divination ritual known as ifá occurs on the third day. At this time the iyawó will be given the pre-scriptions and prohibitions s/he is to follow for a lifetime in order to secure the material and spiritual benefits that render existence mean-ingful. As the week progresses the initiate will go through complicated rituals that extend and strengthen the mental and spiritual faculties needed to fulfill the requirements of a spiritual life. The entire process requires considerable physical stamina and psychological strength.

The result of ordination is a kind of abandonment and commitment. The individual gives up a range of freedoms to accept the guidance provided in Osha. The italero priest tells the newly ordained priest what is allowed and forbidden for the rest of his life, a program that comes directly from the divination ceremony. In return the priest joins an extended family consisting of all those individuals who are members of Osha. This support network helps the individual in making a range of decisions, primarily through interpretation and instruction, while providing a spiritual and practical framework of love and assistance. The success in redeeming individuals from destructive practices like alcohol and drug abuse is reported to be very high, for members are part of a spiritual community that—like Alcoholics Anonymous—redefines the self. But Osha is a religion, not simply a secular support group. It offers a detailed ontology that explains reality and human experience. No promise of salvation in an afterlife is held out to members, though Osha does contain beliefs in reincarnation. The problems of this life are resolved in Osha by transforming understandings of the ordinary world through the introduction of a transcendent world.[2]

Empirical experiences are regarded as derivative in Osha, drawn from ashé. Orisha consciousness is true consciousness, conventional truth only a reflection of a higher timeless reality. Like Plato's allegory of the cave, humans in Osha must be shown another reality, one set forth by ashé as the design of an ultimate God. In divining that higher reality one can come to see where one's own life and its problems fit into the pattern of fate. Stories that illustrate the higher reality communicate both timeless truths and practical lessons to the member or priest. These stories (apataki) form the order (or destiny) of a particular individual and are provided as answers to practical problems. But they are not simply pragmatic solutions. They introduce spiritual dimensions to ordinary concerns.

Percussion, singing, dancing, and chanting are very important expressions in Osha. One of the more dramatic devices used in the religion to gain access to orisha reality are the batá drums, played in drum celebrations known as wemilere (the orthodox Lukumí term for a drum celebration), a toqué, or just a tambor honoring one or more orishas. These celebrations are usually held in a private home (remember that there are virtually no churches or public facilities in Osha, though sometimes Osha people rent banquet halls). The ceremony typically begins with the oru igbodu, a phase where the drummers play before the orisha's trono (altar) without chanting. This event is followed by a ritual meal for the drummers. Then, and finally, there is the oru iyará nlá, the public ceremony where the apuón (singer) will chant traditional verses in Yoruba to traditional rhythms played by a team of drummers (omó añá) on three sacred drums with dancers responding. The sounds produced from the trio of double-headed hourglass shaped drums, the batá, and the movements of the dancers easily fuse to conjure a mood that affects both participants and spectators. One function of the batá is to present the recently ordained iyawó (technically the spouse of the orisha, but in practice a term that refers to the novice being inducted into the priesthood) before Añá (the deity of music and drumming) and the batá drums in a ritual of movement and chanting, after which the individual olosha is authorized to dance in future ceremonies in front of the batá. During this phase of the bembé many iyawós may be presented in sequence. Once this phase is concluded the celebration continues with general dancing that is still performed according to learned movements representative of the individual deities (spontaneity is in low regard in these ceremonies).

The bembé, a term which refers to a specific drum ensemble, is typically a celebration where the ensemble (agbé) of one or two conga-type drums, two or three shekeres-gourdrattles, and a gong is contracted to play in a dance that is less structured than the wemilere, and more social than ceremonial. Oloshas gather (again in a private home) and dance both planned and spontaneous movements to the drums (both sets of movements deriving from Africa). The ceremonial forms and styles vary within an acceptable range. The event can include yesá ensembles, various styles of bembé, and unconsecrated batá known as aberikolá and cajones. The range is set by African and Spanish traditions, and the quality one expects of any artistic expression ("as long as the ensemble is good," one participant told me). The initial goal of the bembé is to call forth Eleggua, the orisha who is the guardian of the path, the one who can open doors to higher planes of existence. He occupies a very high standing in Yoruba and is usually propitiated first in ceremonies. In the bembé he is the first orisha summoned, and the one who closes the evening. In this context he is viewed as a spirit of the random and unpredictable, the trickster who introduces spontaneity and creativity to an orderly universe.

As bembé progresses different individuals come forward to dance, with different orishas represented in various dances. Oshun, the river patron (cool power), may be represented. Another dance may represent Oshosi, the hunter, or Ogun, the patron of smiths (who stands for hot power). But the patron saint of the batá, and owner of Aña, the deity of dance, is Shangó. As the evening progresses more and more people dance to the drums with a frantic energy that seems to sweep across the room. At random moments in the dance various individuals may be possessed by one or more of the orishas. The orishas are said to "mount" the human, using him or her as an instrument to harangue, predict, warn, and in general utter truths to the human assemblage. Possessions occur in both the batá and the bembé, though oloshas say that they are more frequent in bembé in part because it is less controlled by ritual. Those who are truly possessed remember nothing of the experience, though they feel the physical effects of whatever they do during the possession. In bembé several people may experience flash trances, and are thought to be radiated momentarily with the energy of the orishas. Only a few of the trance experiences continue to possession.[3]

Some of the moments in the bembé are terrifying if, for example, an enraged orisha verbally castigates some individual. Other events are amusing. Purists believe that the darker or wilder ceremonies sometimes described in the bembé are not genuine expressions of Osha, and are more accurately classified with the types of ceremonies conducted in palo mayombe, the black magic rituals brought over from the Congo, and more particularly with Vodoun in Haiti. In these ceremonies lower level spirits or deceased ancestors possess the individuals. At one irregular session a deaf mute from ara orun (dead ancestors, or "people of heaven") mounted an individual and began communicating with sign language. The crowd, in frustration, finally shouted "mata este perro otra vez!" (kill that dog again). On another occasion a possessed man began eating candles. After the second candle the group took pity on him (realizing how sick he was going to feel afterwards) and brought him down from the trance. In general the group will not allow individuals to do anything dangerous or harmful during the spells, though embarrassing moments are usually allowed to occur on the grounds that it is really the spirit who is responsible, not the human.

In one memorable palo mayombe session a Marxist economist was possessed by a dead ancestor who did seem (really) to have the power of clairvoyance. The spirit (via the individual) was able to describe exactly the interior of a woman's house and the light blue car that had recently been brought to her yard by her nephew. (The "mount" had never met the woman or her family.) The woman's husband remained skeptical (and even lied about the house's contents when asked to confirm the accuracy of the description). So the spirit turned to the husband and said "I will be in the blue car with you the next time you drive it." To which the husband responded, "Then be careful, because I carry a large gun with me whenever I drive." The woman was overcome at the spontaneous absurdity of the response. She fell on the sofa laughing at the prospect of her husband "killing" the spirit of a dead ancestor.

The trances and possessions in the Osha bembé, by contrast, seem to be genuine mystical experiences that unite the human and spiritual worlds. They are brought on by music, primarily drum rhythms, without drugs of any sort. Individuals get so intensely into the movements and sounds that they are "occupied" by an external entity. The orisha is accepted in Osha as the incarnate power of the higher reality. Its presence in a human body is proof to participants in the ceremony of the possible union of human sensibilities with a reality beyond sensory experiences.

2

The supernatural dimensions of so many religions, and the consequent inclination to regard religion as distinct from political practices because of its reliance on divinity, can be tracked to differences between sacred and secular texts. It does not take much acumen to concede that reading any text is deceptively complex. Analysis and interpretation are sometimes regarded as methods that, once explained or justified, are generalizable to all texts. Strong pragmatists like Richard Rorty, for example, see *use* as the dominant criterion for all textual interpretation. But it must be true that the way we define and classify texts influences the way we read texts, which suggests that there is no criterion, and certainly no interpretive grammar, that extends to all texts. I want to identify some methods for reading and understanding texts that are influenced by distinctions between the secular and the sacred, and then draw out some preliminary implications of these methods and distinctions for relationships between church and state in liberal democracies.

The obvious and least complicated way to start this exercise is to arrange methods of textual analysis in terms of their relationships to a text. Of course all textual analysis is related to the text under scrutiny in the sense of method-to-subject (even when the text is regarded as a function of method). But some methods stay primarily within the text while others move outside it. If we tried to use predicate logic in ascertaining the meaning of a text, where words are assigned symbols and a single or restricted set of meanings is tracked for each word throughout the text to determine consistency as a confirmation of meaning, the analytic methods would have to be confined to the text itself. If, on the other hand, the historical context of a text is regarded as decisive in settling on its meaning, then the reader must do some outside work in determining what the text says.

The most aggressive use of external conditions is probably a political or utilitarian reading of a text. An example is a constitutional interpretation guided by aggregate or collective considerations, for example what the document implies for the larger political society. Mark Graber (1999) argues that we should read the U.S. Constitution as a kind of institutional design that privileges some interests and groups over others. He urges that our primary understanding of the document should be in terms of its political consequences. In this form of interpretation internal textual analysis gives way to empirical consequences and perhaps thoughts of the greater good. These species of interpretation are noble on the face but (and Graber allows this) textual meaning must still count. First, the consequences of the Constitution cannot be understood independent of what the document says about institutional design since the effects of a text cannot be tracked without some description of the text as antecedent. Second, one of the important ways to monitor and evaluate consequences is with the Constitution. These two simple points tell us that a text read in terms of its consequences must still be understood as a text in order to track its consequences.

Perhaps the important hybrid method in this arrangement of textual analysis, one that also combines in-text analysis with external conditions, is author intent. Here the text means what the author intends it to mean. Some empirical work is required in accurately determining the intentions of an author, but since the author is so intimately connected to a text s/he wrote one might fairly say that this method of analysis uses an extended text whose boundaries are set not exclusively by the palpable document we see and read but also by the document framed within the thoughts of the author. We look for a text that represents more-or-less exactly what the author sees, or, more loosely, a text crafted as the author sees the work. One form of author intent, original intent, is especially important in the interpretation of written constitutions. Its importance derives from the acknowledgment that a political/legal constitution is to provide some form of stable guidance in governance over time. Retrieving and adhering to the original intent of a constitution establishes the consistency that such a document sets out to achieve. One might say the interpretation of a written constitution without at least some reference to original meaning drawn from the intent of the constitution's authors misses the main reason for crafting a constitution (one wants to add, "in the first place"). Original intent is an influential method in determining the meanings of the U.S. Constitution. If we were to use original intent in settling on the meaning of any part of this document we would be bound to retrieve as completely as we could the intentions of the document's framers, and use these intentions as the primary linguistic references in interpreting the clauses.

Textual analysis guided by author intent, perhaps because it is such a simple and natural way to proceed, has always been singled out for criticism and defense in the literatures on interpretation. In the oft-told story, summarized by Stefan Collini (1992) in his Introduction to Eco's *Interpretation and overinterpretation*, the New Critics developed arguments separating the text (the aesthetic object or verbal icon) from its author, maintaining the text as a freestanding item independent of author intentions. These separation arguments played the children's game of labeling, in this case tacking the sticker, "the intentionalist fallacy," on the proposal that the intentions of the author are in any way relevant to textual meaning. The arguments led with remarkable speed to the rich discussions that now occupy us on what exactly does produce meaning in a text if not the author. The main current takes in this discussion can be stated easily enough. First, there is little reason to think that the author has privileged standing in assigning meaning to a text, especially a meaning that is at variance with conventional understandings. Words, phrases, sentences change meaning over time. Or, definitions of words are a matter of shifting grammars and practices, neither of which is controlled by the author. The practical use of language is represented in all theories of speech acts, which demarcate the syntax and semantics of a text from the conditions of language use. Language use is best seen as a linguistic token, which is that the meaning of an utterance is a function of the speaker's intentions, yes, but also a range of immediate and distal conditions, including the language of the text itself and, in the broadest sense, the assemblage of rules, traditions, beliefs, in general, culture, that thicken the context in which a text occurs. The author's intentions are just one entry in this thicket (Searle, 1969, 1995).

Second, even when intention dominates meaning, it is not easy to say what intentions are. We know that intentions are states of mind. We also know that states of mind are unstable and not directly accessible. Anyone doing field work can testify to the ways in which a subject can see and assign fresh meanings to texts with each new reading and interview. But, more importantly, retrieving states of mind is impossible without palpable evidence for mental states, and the best evidence for intentions may be a text. Put another way, the meaning of a text is good evidence for intentions, but intentions are not always reliable, or even available as independent evidence for the meaning of a text. Intent analysis seems to reverse the providential direction of this evidentiary chain, a reversal that is often set back in the right direction with the use of additional texts as public evidence of intent for the text at issue. Also, the passage of time makes it difficult to identify evidence that scholars may concede goes to establishing intent. Original intent, the most important type of intent for constitutional interpretation, may be among the more difficult of intentions to establish on a time line in any complex and decently mature political society, even when disputes over relevant evidence are settled, because such intent occurs at the very origins of a political society when cultural orientations may still be inchoate.

For these and other reasons textual analysis based on the intention of the author is usually fleshed out with a consideration of historical conditions and the internal logic of a text. It is interesting that the critical lines on the use of intentions also apply to one of the more radical alternatives in the interpretation of texts in legal discourses. I refer here to legal realism. In strong versions of legal realism the law is thought to be primarily what the judge says it is. More reasonable versions simply grant judicial discretion a dominant position. But this movement of interpretive powers is no better than original intent since it simply transfers privileged standing on the text from author to particular types of readers. If linguistic theory in general and speech act theory in particular tell us anything it is that no user of language, author or reader, can utterly determine what words and sentences, and a text, mean. Interpretation must be a practice with shared rules that in some complex way provide constraints on individual interpretations. The judge may have considerable discretion in interpreting law, but only within a linguistic and cultural framework supplied to her stipulated jurisdiction. As Ronald Dworkin (1986) and others have noted, discretion seems always to occur within an area of discourse governed by standards, and these standards permit and help identify discretion as a measured departure from established norms. A judge who starts making up the meanings of words and statements in the law in some idiosyncratic or random sense, who ignores relevant principles and accepted rules, and is creative on the side of license, will soon be revealed as deranged in uninteresting ways.

Umberto Eco (1992) has argued recently that the text itself can have intentions, in the sense that it presents limits on interpretation by virtue of its contained sense and reference, and coherence. Also limiting interpretations in Eco's framework are the range of textual readings deemed acceptable by a relevant community. Eco's approach to a text is a rich mix of maxims and techniques that employs standard methods of interpretation in fresh ways. For example, he invites us to think about distinctions between empirical and model readers, and perhaps even authors. The distinction in types of readers is tantalizing and imaginative in allowing us to regard a text as designed to find and perhaps even to craft certain ideal types of readers. Then there is his almost subliminal proposal for a bifurcation in types of authors, the real live breathing author who writes and may even try to comment on his art, and the idealized author that the text creates. In constructing a model author by mapping back from the artifact to the writer we may become impatient with the breathing author who sometimes seems to get his own creation all wrong. Dialectical movement among these constructs seems a requirement in Eco's approaches.[4]

3

A range of different but overlapping interpretive methods is infamous in interpreting written constitutions. Akhil Reed Amar (1999) casually lists the main approaches in opening his own arguments for the dominance of the text itself in interpretive exercises, in this case the U.S. Constitution: "parsing the text of a given clause," securing information on the history of the Constitution, recognizing what the document entails as a text, measuring the practical effects on the law and society of different interpretations, "appealing to judicial cases decided under it," and "invoking the American ideals it embraces." Note in passing here that ideals have always been at least a tacit part of Constitutional interpretation and their usefulness has been illuminated in fresh ways recently by Dworkin. If we grant a reasonable indeterminacy in primary languages, at least to the degree that judges cannot deduce imperatives from the languages of the law, then one constraint on judicial interpretation will be the collateral restrictions provided by moral discourses. Hercules, the well-known metaphorical figure standing for conditions of certainty (Dworkin, 1978), can provide moral ideals as one rational device to decide hard cases and presumably interpret the Constitution.[5]

Amar's arguments for an internal form of textual analysis takes as the guiding frame for interpretation the document itself. In his article, "Intratextualism," he offers an intriguing case for using the Constitution as a kind of unconventional dictionary in which the meanings of words can be determined primarily by revealing consistencies among phrases in the document, specifically by "establishing the meaning of a word in one constitutional clause by analyzing its use in another constitutional clause"(p. 757). Amar illustrates the method with a set of terms, for example interpreting the phrase "the people" by "reading the first words of the Preamble alongside the last words of the Tenth Amendment, and harmonizing their invocations of 'the people' " (p. 759). Intratextualism is not an algorithm. Amar allows that the method can be used by different individuals to reach contrary interpretations. But a more important difficulty for his program is that linguistic rules and conventions come into play at every turn. For example, Amar accepts Marshall's suggestion in *McCulloch* that "necessary" be read differently from "absolutely necessary," but he resists reading "due process" differently from "due process plus equal protection." Why? Because "Where a particular clause is best read as declaratory, glossing earlier words and making explicit what these words only implied, the presence or absence of this gloss should generally make no difference" (Or, "Do it—I mean it" = "Do it.") But this explanation relies on a convention of language use that must be imported into the Constitution.

The text of the Constitution as a document is sometimes remark-ably broad in intratextual analysis, in the sense that its meaning and even the effectiveness of intratextual analysis depend on external con-siderations. The coordination of precedents is often vital. Amar reminds us that *Brown* cannot be understood without *Bolling*, and in fact the former would not have had the same meaning had the latter been decided in favor of segregation. Amar scores some of his best points in recording Blackmun's initial use of the Constitution as a dictionary in searching the term "person," and then chronicling the collapse of the lexical search engine when Blackmun turns it to the wide canvas of history for the meaning of "person." The intratextual search is indeed far more impressive. But then Amar allows that the fail-ures of the external searches can be explained in part by the absence at that time in history of a general (external to the Constitution) "theory emphasizing gender and the particular ways in which abortion laws burden the liberty and equality of women" (p. 778). Intratextualism wins by default, meaning that its superior effectiveness in this instance is an artifact of exogenous conditions.

The tendency in intratextualism to move to more robust considera-tions may be a defining constant it shares with all other interpretive approaches to a text. For example, the method slides on occasion into a broader view of the Constitution itself as a document ". . . intratex-tualism always focuses on at least two clauses and highlights the link between them" (p. 788). But a holistic textualism (where the docu-ment is more than its constituent parts) may be different and better, as per Douglas's heroic efforts to infer privacy from a survey of the entire Constitution (p. 797). This tendency may indicate that a partial viewing of anything, whether term, clause, sentence, even document, is difficult to maintain, and the issues of accommodating the whole that appear when we analyze parts are non-trivial. In the old example used in discussions of methodological individualism, the individual notes in a melody cannot be understood as notes without invoking the holistic term "melody." Sometimes a subset of the notes offers partial melodies, and in constitutional interpretation we might say that subsets and partial melodies arrive as constructions outside the document to extend it into areas of case law. The abortion cases since *Bellotti v. Baird* have been guided by whether state laws regulating abortion practices pay allegiance to *Roe v. Wade* and do or do not place "undue burdens" on the woman seeking an abortion. Ian Shapiro, in *Abortion: The Supreme Court Decisions*, tracks the use of the "burden" phrase through *Planned Parenthood of Pennsylvania v. Casey* and beyond in describing a Court that measures an acceptance of abortion regulations with an "undue burdens" test. Yet the reference to appropriate and inappropriate burdens is brought to bear on the Constitution from theories of equity in the larger worlds of practical thinking. The "burden" phrase is a complicated reference, a kind of partial or conceptual whole that is needed to assign practical meaning to the document.

If wholes are always the eminence grise of textual analysis, including intratextualism, then rules or criteria are needed to order, select and use the appropriate whole as reference for interpretation. Wittgenstein suggests that rules should tell us how to go on in our thinking. In textual analysis we may also need resources that tell us when to stop searching for the right textual reference, even in intratextualism. If, as Amar acknowledges, "the same words sometimes sensibly mean different things in different contexts" (p. 799) and "sometimes different words should mean the same thing" (p. 801, n) we need and in fact always use external considerations to define and judge the meanings of words even within a text. We might even say that intratextualism goes wrong in presupposing that a palpable text is the text, when every indication (even using this form of interpretation) is that the text cannot stop at the printed or spoken word.

4

If we parse speech acts for a basic set of variables that represent what we do when we use language, four areas invite more detailed initial analysis: the speaker, the text, the audience, and (there seems never to be a good term here) the cultural setting. Each of these areas is enriched, we might say dense, with possibilities and shifting nuances of references. In the most basic terms, we might start by saying that the (empirical/ideal) speaker issues the text with at least some set of intentions. The text is a document with unclear parameters even when it is written. The audience (readers, listeners) assigns meanings and understandings to the issued text. This too-simple arrangement still limns the even more simple notion that a kind of social contract between author and reader, and among members of the audience, establishes textual meaning, and the way to get at a text is to explore the consensus and arrangements that yield a text. (Note how constitutional interpretations rely on evolving agreements in the body politic on key terms: citizen, the people, person, etc.). The fact is that any text occupies a location in culture, and its parameters, durability, and the methods appropriate for interpreting it will in part be a function of culture.

For example, a political society in flux and in conditions of divisive pluralism will stand differently to a text than one which is stable and represented by high consensus. John Rawls (1996) distinguishes between societies that are and are not "well-ordered," and allows different entries into public space in each of these conditions. He maintains, as a demonstration, that the abolitionists could use comprehensive doctrines because their society was not well ordered, while the pro-life people on abortion today are denied such doctrines because current society is well ordered. In effect, political doctrines have different effects, and perhaps meaning, in different conditions. Then there are the numerous interpretations of the U.S. Constitution in times of crisis that seem exceedingly oppressive when the document is read in times of stability. Read, for example, civil libertarian Justice Hugo Black's concurring opinion in *Korematsu v. United States* (1944).

Are there conceptual devices that can impose stable orderings on interpretive methods that are reasonably immune from the complexities of speech acts? It is instructive that virtually all textual interpretation today in the West is guided by coherence tests at minimum, epistemic truth at the most demanding levels. Amar, in his article, says that "the ultimate proof of any given tool must be whether it in fact ever works: does the tool in real and hard cases even help us to reach satisfying and sound legal results?" The results on this kind of test must be framed by terms like intelligibility, consistency, elegance, utility—the usual panoply of effective responses in science and other practices that go toward conceptual map making, meaning the construction of working "tools" that help put things together in a satisfactory way, move from point A to B, and in general lead us to a coherent account of a text (including experience) that will enlighten a domain of inquiry filled with other texts. This approach to interpretation represents the best of secular thinking even as the interpretations that the methods yield are not and can never be conclusive (though they can reasonably have retentive power or dominance for extended periods of time), meaning that, like Popper's ubiquitous hypotheses, we must accept the caveat that even the best interpretive results will be supplanted at some time and in some place by something different.

Provisional interpretations may not suit sacred texts, however. The U.S. Constitution, for the record, is what I am calling secular, in the sense that it is primarily a framework to manage and resolve disputes in a political/legal system. This is a way of saying that the Constitution, whatever else it also may be, is first and mainly a political document. First, the text structures the government. The Preamble opens by expressing the people's desire "to form a more Perfect Union." The first order of business in the body of the text is to distribute governmental authority: "All legislative Powers herein granted shall be vested in a Congress"; "The executive Power shall be vested in a President"; "The judicial Power of the United States, shall be vested in one Supreme Court, and in such inferior Courts as the Congress may from time to time ordain and establish." Second, the Constitution fashions relations between the government and the people, primarily by circumscribing the power of the government. The Bill of Rights provides a list of prohibited acts, for example: "Congress shall make no law . . . abridging the freedom of speech"; "the right of the people to keep and bear Arms, shall not be infringed"; ". . . nor cruel and unusual punishments inflicted." Third, the Constitution distributes burdens and benefits among individuals and groups. For example, certain rights are granted to citizens of a certain status, as in the provision that only persons of eighteen years of age may vote, while other rights are assigned to all citizens regardless of status, as with the Fourteenth Amendment's "equal protection of the laws" clause. As a political text the Constitution has normative powers. The rights vocabularies found in the document are clearly normative, largely in the form of constraints that prohibit impediments on the bearer of rights. (If I have a right to speak others may not stop me from speaking.) These normative powers sometimes represent connections between moral laws/principles and politics, connections that are themselves sources for the document's high political standing. The Constitution, for example, will occasionally be used to implement a political morality, which is arguably the case in *Brown v. Board of Education* (in stipulating racial equality via integration in public schools).[6]

Some might view the Constitution's high standing in the political community as a reason to regard it as a sacred document. But it does not meet the tests of a sacred text in the strong or religious sense of that term. The meaning of "sacred" is drawn initially from a family of terms under the umbrella of special or separated use. If I say a text is sacred I am saying that it is set apart for use by a particular group or community. Dworkin links the term "sacred" to "inviolable," and suggests that "Something is sacred or inviolable when its deliberate destruction would dishonor what ought to be honored" (Dworkin 1993, pp. 71–81, sentence quote on p. 74). A distinction between the profane and the sacred is regarded by Durkheim (1912) as the distinctive trait of religious thought. The sacred entry in this binary ranges across a conceptual terrain where the term is unpacked with the numinous (Otto, 1917), the transcendent and irreducible (Eliade, 1968), intriguingly designated as manifestation (instead of proclamation) coupled with an antihistorical standing (Ricoeur, 1995), and, in the other direction, shaped by reductionist exercises, including both benign (Segal, 1983) and judicious variations (Edwards, 1999). Rappaport (1999) argues that the sacred is (in part) an invariant form of expression, and functions to ensure the integrity of language in protecting against the chronic tendencies toward erosion, subversion and degradation that accompany usage.

I want to rely on some of the earlier traditions, for example, Otto and Eliade, and map these concepts into Rappaport's invariance condition with the stipulation of properties additional to special or separated use. One is primary standing. The sacred is valuable in itself rather than just an instrument to secure other goods. The other is independence. A sacred text is not just an expression of human wants, needs, or goods. It is a freestanding resource that functions to recognize, interpret and order the values of such expressions. To the second stipulation add the proposition that the independent standing of a sacred text in religion issues from an insensate reality. This means that the source of sacredness is a place not completely accessible to human efforts, nor entirely intelligible to human understandings. An insensate reality is one that is fully describable in terms that have no reference to human sentience. Such a reality is either discovered by appropriate methods of inquiry or (in some religions) issued to believers, and sometimes spectators, as a revealed truth. We would also expect a sacred text in religion to be able to summon the whole person to a total commitment by providing full instructions on the moral life. These extensions of the term capture the sense in which the "sacred" is that which is worthy of respect, venerable, and, in religious discourse, made or declared holy.

It is worth noting that discussions of insensate realities are found in both religious and scientific discourses. John Mackie (1977) tells us that a something can be objective only if it can be fully described in terms of properties intelligible without reference to sentient beings. He concludes that values are not objective because they cannot pass this test. James McAllister (1996), in discussing Mackie's view, and others, within a treatment of aesthetic evaluations in that icon of objectivity, scientific inquiry, provides arguments for a supply-side view of values, meaning in this case that aesthetic values are projected into theories by scientists. It is exactly the arguments in subjectivist accounts like these that put into relief (by opposing them) the view of the sacred delineated here, since they attempt to reduce all normative texts, including sacred matters, to human constructs.

5

There is a sense in which the U.S. Constitution satisfies some of the defining terms of a sacred text. The Constitution has intrinsic value, is in some important ways an independent measure, auditor and legislator of human values, and is inviolable in the minds of many. But its summons to the moral life can only be partial. The moral dimension in the political life of a liberal democracy is at a meta level, meaning that citizens are invited to participate in a collective undertaking that requires placing some of one's deepest moral beliefs in abeyance when this is needed to tolerate those with opposing moral beliefs. This exercise is profoundly moral, producing as it has a negotiable public space that can ensure the great human goods of peace and stability (among others). The commitment required is dualistic, however, occasioning a public loyalty to the state while reserving the private self for other moral undertakings. The Constitution also is a document that represents in complicated ways the preferences of persons, at its origins especially but also throughout its history in a dialectical play with its own authority as a Constitution, and the procedures for amending the text are explicitly in the text itself. Though it may have originated in beliefs that certain truths are self-evident, its meaning is not settled with references to an external, or certainly insensate, reality but by its fidelity to those criteria and rules crafted by (most broadly) the people in the political system that the Constitution serves and regulates.

A sacred text in religion, by contrast, typically invites the whole person to the community of believers, and attends to a full inventory of rules and principles for the moral life (including the integrity of the person). The self can be unified in the religious community, not divided according to public and private dimensions. To say this is not also to say that all religious communities attend to the complete moral life. A religion would still count as religion even when moral instructions are incomplete or missing, and some divided identity is afforded the believer. But completeness in instruction and sense of self is an easy sell in religions, in no way contradictory of the religious mission. A complete package of moral terms would be contradictory for the liberal democratic state, however, since public space must be emptied of comprehensive views in order to allow a variety of moral and religious beliefs into the political system (Rawls, 1995, 1996). Finally, though even core religious beliefs can be modified and dismissed by various institutions and groups, like churches, it is unusual for a sacred text to contain its own prescriptions for textual change. The reason may be that a sacred text is thought to issue from a reality that is to some degree insensate. This kind of text cannot be just what its people say it is, since its content and form are matters settled at least in part by reference to domains that are not solely artifacts of human preference or belief.

These stipulations do not exclude diversity within religions. The fourth-century Nicene Creed is a brilliant text that states the Christian faith in such a way that a wide variety of beliefs can still fall under the Church rubric. One might see parallels between the Creed and the U.S. Constitution in the measured toleration of diversity. But the parameters are different, and drawn up on different criteria. The boundaries of the permissible are typically narrower in religions than in the guiding frameworks of a liberal democracy. One cannot imagine some of the obnoxious (and welcome) extremes of free speech, which can properly denigrate the democratic frame itself if safely located within no-harm limitations, as escaping the judgment of heresy in religions. The reason again is that religions have different expectations of commitment. Membership in a religious community goes deeper than the requirements of democratic citizenship. Beliefs, whether in the pre-Reformation sense of following actions or the post-Reformation frame of establishing prior legitimacy for actions, are crucial to religious commitments, at least in the West. The atheist going through the motions of taking communion while denying that the bread is the host is denigrating the sacrament, and one might argue is not engaging in the religious ceremony. Beliefs are not similarly located in liberal democracies. Citizens affected by the civil rights movement, for example, could have sought and achieved moral standing if they believed in racial equality, but the law required only that they behave as if they did. The history of liberal democracies is testimony to the importance of shielding beliefs from the regulatory and judgmental powers of the state. The fragility of consent requires that stability in conditions of strong pluralism be founded on compliance in behavior, not beliefs. Citizens must subscribe to the democratic framework through their behavior while tolerating the beliefs and behavior of those they oppose. Wide diversity in belief and behavior, if within acceptable parameters of the reasonable, is celebrated in democratic arrangements, but properly regarded as a problem in many religious communities.

None of these distinctions implies that church and state always in fact follow these stipulations. Every liberal democracy is occasionally engulfed by religious movements. The free speech provisions of the First Amendment to the Constitution seem perennial targets of churches aimed at delineating proper conduct in a political community. But it is a category mistake to conclude that the empirical failures of these distinctions between the secular and the sacred constitute evidence for the failures of the distinctions themselves. The opposite is the case. We use this conceptual design in those political systems that separate church and state to evaluate and remedy the wrongful incursions of religious zeal into the political sphere. Absent the design we have no understandings that can reject efforts to absorb politics into religious domains where church and state are separate as a matter of constitutional structure.

6

Not all religious texts are sacred in the strong sense. Even foundational texts in a religion may be little more than pragmatic instructions bearing no marks of an insensate reality. The main texts in Confucianism seem to be an amalgam of religion and philosophy, and generally are regarded as lessons for proper worship, work, family relations, in general for living well by cultivating moral character and correctly organizing public life. Nor are all texts regarded as entries in the secular world unmarked by at least some of the signs of the sacred. The sacred is often regarded as a power that moves through much of human experience. In this broad sense the Constitution, like many other texts (including some in art and fiction), may be regarded as sacred because it can occasion a sublime or awesome experience as we absorb and use it. Yet the document can do this without being regarded as a religious text. Examples of a fusion between the sacred and the secular abound. It is understandable that the viewer of Velasquez's Las Meninas might have a kind of mystical and even trans-forming experience without believing that the painting is a communi-cation from God. Or when Newton explored alchemy it is conceivable that he encountered some versions of sacred texts that in his mind extended the boundaries of human experience. But he could have con-ducted these explorations without also thinking that the texts were religious, at least as he defined the principles and practices of the Puritan church (to which he belonged). There is also a strong sense of the sacred that is one of the marks of the religious. This version of the sacred, informed by its connection to other realities, indicates distinc-tions between religious and secular experiences in Western cultures, and differences in reading religious and political texts.

Let's review, and track implications. First, a sacred text in religion must be concerned with ultimate matters. Though primarily a Christian term , some non-denominational sense of eschatology seems to be central to religions everywhere. The meanings and significance of life itself, death, the origins and fate of the universe—these are the usual subjects of the sacred in religion even when the content is organized by particular religious ontologies and/or mundane con-cerns. Second, a sacred/religious text is an invitation to think further about ultimate matters after the reading is complete, offering both insights into these things and depicting them as concerns that require the thoughtful attention of the reader. The distant and impartial reader is not in a congruent state with a sacred/religious text since he will have to resist the summons that is part of the text. Third, the strong sense of the sacred introduces insensate realities (at least in part) to human experience. The sacred text in this way becomes a resource to clarify connections between the human and the divine. It is not an arti-fact of either human author or reader, nor an instrument that occa-sions free interpretations. It is more like a manageable cryptogram given by another with a truth to be deciphered by the reader (with the implication that a text can be realized as sacred as the deciphering goes forward successfully). In an odd way, sacred texts in theistic religions require a restoration of author intent with God as the author, restoring the older literary method of a privileged author into its original form as a theological exercise. Fourth, a sacred/religious text offers an arrangement that combines the unknowable with the knowable. This arrangement inevitably requires a complex negotiation between text and reader on relating these two dimensions to each other and to additional considerations. Finally, the state of mind of the reader must be dominated by humility rather than hubris given that a sacred text in religion is assumed to represent an insensate dimension. In Christianity one might think of such a text as given by another from the position of another world. This special sense of the sacred is a defining feature of many religions.

Let's return to reading a text. If we abandon the dominance of the author and reader in textual interpretation then the text itself must yield its meaning according to some set of methods. We might reasonably expect these methods to be sensitive to the distinction between outside and inside points of view. Paul Ricoeur (1974) has delineated a line of interpretation that moves between outer and inner domains. Ricoeur suggests binaries of event–meaning, writing–reading, and explaining–understanding. The left entry in the pairs represents the natural sciences, the right entry the human sciences. A reader approaching a text must guess at the whole meaning of a text in part because the exercise of reading is focused on sentences. This guess is an attempt to explain the text as a written event in the world, essentially as the author responding to something. But evidence for explanations is limited, and in any case the text is existential in the sense that it changes through time and responds differently to different readers. Readers must move to an understanding of the text as it refers to itself, meaning that each reader must find meaning in the writing by appropriating the text for herself. This appropriation then shapes the world as the reader begins seeing experience through the frame of the owned text.

Reading on this account requires an intelligible shifting back and forth between explanation and understanding, and in each of the binaries appealing to relevant communities for validation (in explanation) and meaning (in understanding). We might say that a textual interpretation that weaves Eco and Ricoeur together composes the objective (outside) and subjective (inside) in a single complex arrangement that identifies the relevant communities to which one appeals in reading a text. Mediating this arrangement is the standing or categorization of a text. For example a political text, especially a constitution, must include an analysis measured in terms of political consequences. To exclude consequences in reading a political text would be to miss its main design and purpose as a document, even conceding that consequences cannot exhaust textual interpretation.

Suppose now that the text we read is sacred. What are the appropriate methods of analysis?

This question is best answered by identifying the relevant communities of appeal given the standing of a sacred text. The easy first cut at making this identification is—those acknowledging the sacredness of a text, and thus capable of being drawn into its logic, constitute a community for reading such texts. This entrance test is not a litmus for salvation, or a kind of moral ordering. It just marks off the common ground for the shared reading of any text, which is that we first recognize its genre. Imagine a reader of the U.S. Constitution who does not acknowledge it as a political/legal constitution, who, say, sees the document as a formal notational system, a pure thought experiment. Or the reader of Newton's *Principia* who believes it is an entry in the literatures on science fiction. The interpretive rules for formal tracts and science fiction are likely to wreak havoc (read: produce implausible interpretations) for, respectively, political/legal constitutions and scientific texts. A proper categorization would, in the first instance, allow consequences in interpreting the text and, in the second instance, require the interpretive use of scientific rules and principles. Note that categorization does not amount to an endorsement of the logic of politics or science. It just means that different types of analysis are appropriate in each of the examples.

A sacred/religious text, as an indication of an insensate reality, must be mysterious. It is a text that is at least on occasion obscure, at times secret, almost never transparent but rather layered with conceptual levels that must be opened, sometimes with deciphering codes. To say that the meaning of such a text is its use (as Rorty does for every text) misses the point of the text in every way that the assignment of fictional status to the *Principia* misses its point. One might think that the collapse of meaning to use distorts all texts, but I think not, at least not in the same way. Every text whose truth is epistemic may include use as one of the tokens of consensus. Consensus, after all, is the source of this type of truth (though use seems unlikely as a dominant component of meaning). But the reliance of sacred/religious texts on insensate realities excludes use as a source of meaning from the very start of interpretation. Readers who have categorized a text as sacred must look for other interpretive methods for producing meaning than use. This must be so because the sacredness of a text determines its special uses in a community. Its sacredness is not a function of its use.

There is one complication in the exclusion of use in understanding sacred texts. Religions are practices that rely on rituals. A ritual in religions is a set of repetitive actions performed with the aim of expressing a supernatural attachment between the human and the divine. All rituals exhibit structures, usually in the form of a passage with preliminary, transformative (or liminal), and postliminal stages (Smith, 1995, pp. 930–1). The initiation of individuals into regla osha (or Santería), for example, is a well-defined passage from secular to holy standing. On a surface examination we might think that use can create or become meaning in a ritual through the repetition of the actions. But consider Rappoport's (1999) more generic take on ritual as a term denoting "the performance of more or less invariant sequences of formal acts and utterances not entirely encoded by the performers" (p. 24). Taken generically we can say that external coding governs the meaning of a ritual, so that meaning is assigned to the performance from a point outside the ceremony. It is not created by the ceremony. I have argued that the external encoding in religious rituals has a final source outside human experience, in the sense that the distinctive mark of a religious ritual is its attachment to the supernatural. This attachment distinguishes religious rituals from routines or habits. A supernatural attachment reverses even more dramatically the pragmatic ordering of use and meaning. Rituals have meaning in religions in terms of their supernatural connections, not through ceremonial repetition. This chain of influence accords with the thought that, while ritual may be the primary venue for the sacred and the manner in which its elements are integrated, the sacred is a type of invariant expression that finally controls usage in ordinary language.

Look now at a sacred text in religious literatures, the parable of the wedding feast (a variant on the generic Parable of the Great Supper, discussed by Funk, 1966, in chapters 6 and 7). The narrative, and I am using the one found in Matthew, 22, begins in a familiar way with a kind of simile, or likeness: "The kingdom of heaven is likened to a king, who made a marriage for his son." The king sends his servants out with invitations to the wedding. The invitations are refused, the servants mistreated and some killed. The king angrily sends his armies to destroy the murderers and burn their cities. Then, since the wedding is at hand, the king instructs his servants to go out into the streets and find guests for the wedding. This they do. Later the king visits the wedding feast and moves among the guests. There he sees a man who does not have on a wedding garment. The king asks the man why. The man is silent. The king then says to his servants: "Bind his hands and feet, and cast him into the exterior darkness where there shall be weeping and gnashing of teeth. For many are called but few are chosen."

What methods are appropriate for reading this text? Clearly not any method that employs consequences as a source of meaning, nor one that relies entirely on scientific practices to unpack a text. An interpretation of this text must start with what it says in religious terms. One should be careful here. A religious text can be analyzed in terms of its consequences, and scientific methods may help in locating the causal antecedents of a religious text and perhaps even fix its standing as an historical document. But these types of explanation leave an unusually important residue when brought to bear on sacred texts, which in this case amounts to the religious standing of the text. Taking a text on religious terms means taking seriously its claims to express insensate domains of a special sort. This "taking a text on its own terms" exercise is not an explanation but an understanding of the text, and an understanding gained by entering the text and seeing it in some fashion from the point of view of a subscriber (in this instance, a believer). The exercise may require the appropriation of the text by and for the reader as it is being read and understood.

The one sure thing in reading this text is its classification. As a parable it cannot be a direct text, by which I mean one crafted within the practices of predication. Predication aims at being literal, at an increasing focus on items framed explicitly. In its expression as predicate logic the ideal text is expressed in notational terms manipulated by formal rules. The goal is a precision and an order that allows the reader to see directly what the text is saying. A parable, by contrast, is never literal. It talks about B in order to talk about A. Typically a parable is quite concrete, providing a story grounded squarely in ordinary reality. A wedding feast, for example, is a commonplace event. But very quickly the ordinary reality described in the parable is rearranged, altered in sometimes dramatic ways, so that it becomes strange, its rules, motives and actions mysterious. The parable takes the reader or hearer away from what is concretely described to a reality that cannot be presented literally but which is revealed by the metaphorical powers of the text. A religious parable indicates the spiritual order by presenting the natural order as translucent (Funk, 1966).

Look again at the parable of the wedding feast. The first sentence presents an analogy, which amounts to a linguistic invitation to be open to a truth or lesson for domain A (the kingdom of God) drawn from a description of domain B (a king arranging a marriage for his son). Implied in all analogies are bridge rules to connect two domains. Then the description of the analogous domain (the wedding) is presented as a story, meaning that loose methods must be assigned that decipher the tale and connect it to the kingdom of God. Now we must move into the text, or, better, let the text move inside us, the readers. We read the words, listen to them, and follow the narrative as it is told in the parable. It is a strange world that unfolds. A king without subjects or notables who will respond to his invitations for his son's wedding, the sweep of the area for guests, the terrible judgment of the king descending on a guest inappropriately attired, the silent man summarily brought into the feast from the streets yet thrown out of the gathering into the violence and anguish of "the exterior darkness," and the hard final judgment about calling and choosing. To see this story as a sacred text will still allow multiple methods of interpretation: the crafting of filler narratives or glosses (as in the Midrash of Hebrew traditions, or the theological tradition in Catholicism) that extend the stories in the text and help the reader understand them, a search for consistency in defining terms (as in intratextualism), a detailed reading of the placement of letters or signs, even computer checks of hidden texts deep within the document. But in all methods the text must be seen as a partial seeing into an insensate reality where the strangeness of the story is dissipated with laws, principles, certainly meanings and interpretations that are radically different from those found in human communities.

The most important effect on textual analysis is what is implied by truth in a sacred text. It is impossible to accept sacred truth on a provisional basis. This restricted prospect is not as odd as it may appear. Many human experiences in secular cultures cannot be provisional. Imagine trying to relive the prison experience by visiting a prison as a mock prisoner for a weekend. Mock prisoners on weekend visits miss the defining feature of a prison, which is the coercive nature of the incarceration. Or think of a trial marriage. Or temporary parenthood. The fact is that certain experiences cannot occur without the compelling or absorbing force that defines them. Sacred truth seems to be this type of experience. To say, I will tentatively adopt a truth categorized as sacred, is to enter a contradiction known by all who measure secular and sacred practices side by side: a sacred text cannot be read successfully from a skeptical perspective. To see a text as sacred requires that we read it on an acceptance of the truth that it expresses. In a way, a sacred text is like fly paper. Explaining it maintains distance, but misses the connecting powers of the text. Understanding it in the sense of appropriating it on its own terms takes the reader into at least some parts of the reality it represents. A casual reading of a sacred text is impossible once its sacredness is accepted. Its meaning produces and governs its use, and its readers. No secular text has this connecting power as we read and interpret it.

These differences between secular and sacred texts help mark off the space between a democratic state and a religious community. The former, charged to depict religions within the frame of explanations and at least putatively bound to epistemic truth, allows individuals the freedom of interpretation that follows a separation between reader and text. The latter, summoning individuals to a textual understanding controlled by the sacred, binds individuals to an authority that fuses individual and text. No skeptical gaze at sacred texts can be permitted once the classification and definition of the text is in place.

7

Proposals settling the relations between church and state in liberal democracies cannot be completed, much less justified and evaluated, without an account of the two institutions and the term "walls." Consider again separation arguments. If the state contains many or all of the features of the church then a wall between the two would be like segregating identical universes. Arguments for a wall, and the features of the wall itself, would be attuned to likeness rather than difference. If, however, church and state are radically different as institutions then separation arguments must look for barriers that shield unlike entities from one another. Think, as an instance, of arguments for insulating market commodities and moral goods. If we believe that these items are different, then the corruption of one by the other is a proper consideration in separation arguments. But if we believe that moral and economic items are similar at some foundational level then separation arguments might be irrelevant, and when made are typically framed in terms of the utilitarian implications of adding or fusing the same things. The arguments for relationships among items, in short, are influenced by what we make of those items. The reductionism developed by Richard Posner, for example, diminishes the importance of many of the traditional liberal shields between economic and legal systems because it places economic perspectives in a dominant position within the law, primarily as translation devices that render legal reasoning in terms of cost–benefit calculations (Posner, 1983, 1998, 1999). Put in simple and general terms, if any one of two systems is reducible to the other it is hard to say that either can corrupt the other.

Defining any social practice or institution is (conceded) a difficult and messy exercise. Complicating matters is the paucity of stable references that can control ambiguity with a rank ordering of stipulated definitions. Even the natural in experience (a reference traditionally granted baseline stability) seems to be an artifact of culture and its various devices for seeing nature. E.H. Gombrich (1969) persuasively argues that artists who appeal to natural surroundings in their paintings still see nature in terms of other paintings.[7] Or, like the natural science described by philosophers of science, we seem to approach all experiences, including nature, in terms of devices (concepts, theories, images) that make these experiences intelligible. These devices are influenced by numerous conditions, including culture, and may vary with time and place. It seems that if concept-formation exercises are to find success in defining social practices in generalizable terms they must be pitched inside subtle arrangements with modest goals. But any success at these efforts in the practices of religion and politics can provide us with a more useful statement on church–state relations than, say, the simple proposal of Jeffersonian walls (per Justice Black) between the two institutions.

The temptation to organize material inductively with taxonomic definitions, or simply list the concepts in a kind of police lineup to identify surface consistencies and incompatibilities, will not avoid these difficulties. Concepts bearing on social matters are divisible and sub-divisible on many levels, and influenced by the internal dimensions of social practices or institutions. Any theory, no matter how abstract, will yield models (from analogical theories) and visual interpretations. These more-or-less formal representations are influenced by conventional trends in theories (thermodynamic models, for example, dominating the social sciences in the nineteenth century) and in different ways by the immediate contexts under study (for a discussion of theory, models, and visualizations, see McAllister, 1996). Political languages are filled with metaphors driven by theoretical trends and historical conditions (permanent structures and the city-states of ancient Greece and later feudalism, Newtonian mechanics and the modern industrial state, quantum indeterminacy and contemporary pluralism). They are also related to context in especially complicated and unstable ways as both the targets of power (in the sense that people disagree about political rules and principles) and its primary instruments of influence and domination. Any inspection of political terms must be attuned to the reality that they typically are at the center of the more acrimonious disputes in a society, with all that this implies for manipulation of meanings. Religious languages add to the complication stakes. The concern in religions with ultimate matters leads easily to the thought that religious sensibilities rely on concepts shaped by forces that are not confined to human experience. This external feature of religion disallows a purely constructivist account of experience and undermines conventional approaches to concept-formation. Religion is profoundly different from postmodern theory exactly on the acceptance of this type of objective source for concept-formation.

It is worth noting that incomplete concepts of religion and state have not prevented the assignment of partitions between the two practices, and their representative institutions, at almost every point in Western history. Distinctions have often turned on a separation of functions. (Remember Christ's political admonition to "Render unto Caesar the things that are Caesar's, to God the things that are God's.") In the church–state discussions of the late Middle Ages, the more profound philosophers tried to demarcate the church and the state by recognizing authoritative venues. Aquinas, a moderate Papalist, saw the state as attending to the provision of those common goods needed for communal life in the here and now, the church concerned with the soul and its passage to eternal life after death. The superiority of the church derives from the greater importance of the soul when compared with the body. Marsilio drew even sharper distinctions between the proper domains of church and state on the basis of powers demarcated according to concerns with the temporal or the eternal world. Thus secular punishment is the exclusive province of the state, temporary or eternal damnation in the next life the business of the church. Post-Reformation separations between church and state are eventually developed on a different set of conditions, in particular the presence of multiple churches and a state committed to a measured tolerance of different religious beliefs. Modern walls between church and state are often assigned to shield churches from the secular logic of political systems, to protect religious freedom from the coercive powers of the state, and to uphold the secular autonomy of the political system.

But more complex demarcations are possible when we start getting clearer about concepts of religion and state. One is the natural insulation of post-axial religions from external scrutiny (for the distinction between pre- and post-axial religions, see Hick, 1989). Much of the lore of the contemporary state stresses its surveillance powers. Foucault (1975) notes a major shift in the visible axes of power. The traditional sovereign was on display, the people on whom sovereign power was exercised were in the background. Now, with the architecture of modern society, it is power that is invisible, the objects of power brought forward into the visible realm for detailed inspection. Surveillance is certainly one of the powers of the modern state, leading as it does to control over its citizens, and this power can be tracked to the species of objectivity peculiar to Western thought. The logic of the other presents an observer who is separate from that which is observed. The observer is to reason with transparent methods, meaning they must be accessible to all others equally detached. This model of reasoning is the centerpiece of modern science, and the intellectual resource that tries to see into and through all parts of reality. The interesting and important items in the transparent society are the points of resistance to observation and control. One is the interior consciousness of post-axial religions. A religious sensibility that seeks and finds meaning in a domain invisible to the surveillance powers of the state is bound to resist secular power. It is arguable that this resistance historically created the individualism that yielded the liberal state. Recognizing an interior consciousness also provides a deep first cut into understanding the need for contemporary walls between church and state, dramatically expressed, for example, in the autonomy of religious conscience.

A second cut is made on issues of textual interpretation. I have argued that certain distinctions between sacred and secular texts in Western thought influence how we read texts. These influences can be initially tracked from the much-discussed issue of whether understanding a religion depends on religious belief or understanding (posed by Alasdair MacIntyre as "Is Understanding a Religion Compatible with Believing?" and refined by Donald Wiebe as "Does Understanding Religion Require Religious Understanding?" in McCutcheon, 1999). We start with the thought that a religion can be understood in some senses by the observer standing outside the text, since the visible expressions of traditions, including rituals and procedures, are accessible to the impartial spectator (Geertz, 1973, for the classic "outsider" definition). So may a sacred text be read as a palpable artifact of religious conventions. Conceded also is the typical presence of multiple intermediate positions between observer and subject, outsider and insider, that have occupied virtually all scholars of culture from time to time. But it is also true that there is something about some experiences that is inaccessible to the outsider. An indigenous dimension has been widely recognized in social theory, from Max Weber (1949) through Peter Winch (1958), and more. Two contemporary and disparate takes on this claim are made by Leo Strauss, in a normative vein:

> The historian who takes it for granted that objective value judgments are impossible cannot take very seriously that thought of the past which was based on the assumption that objective value judgments are possible. (1953, pp. 61–2)

and Karen McCarthy Brown, as a methodological comment:

> If I persisted in studying Vodou objectively, the heart of the system, its ability to heal, would remain closed to me. The only way I could hope to understand the psychodrama of Vodou was to open my life to the ministrations of Alourdes. (1991, p. 10)

The higher or alternative sources claimed for sacred texts fit and sometimes fill an internal category of experience, seeming to require for a full textual reading an interior commitment even when these sources have been provided by the scholar as concepts to render religious beliefs intelligible. It also seems that once a text has been categorized as sacred there are few if any intermediate stops between skeptical observation and internal belief. The resolutely non-religious reader who adopts an "as if" attitude toward sacred texts, even when moved by the rhetorical effects of these texts, may have no settled or comfortable space in which the text can be reliably encountered. Sacred texts, with the binding powers of realist truths, have the power to compromise the usual halfway houses found on the path between skepticism and religious belief.

8

Differences between the secular and the sacred refine our understandings of ambiguity and precision. Terms may be ambiguous in the sense that their meanings are unclear or mixed (having several definitions). But sentences typically have a precise meaning in one context or another. Now, the point to locating precision in contexts is that ambiguity is then elevated to meta levels. If a situation presents multiple contexts each of which provides a precise but different meaning for sentences, and there is nothing available to rank order the contexts, then the ambiguity of language, typically leading to uncertainty in the use or meaning of sentences, is a product of the speaker's power to select contexts. Something like this happens in the abortion dispute in completing the sentence, "Life begins at . . . ." Stoic culture, late Catholicism, the common law traditions, and *Roe v. Wade* each present a different context to complete the sentence. There is no "open texture" to the language of life's beginnings, in saying exactly when life begins. Each context provides a reasonably precise answer to the question. The ambiguity occurs as one surveys these contexts and realizes that there is no reason to favor one over the other, with the consequent that the text is arbitrary. The arbitrariness of the choice of contexts sets the ambiguity.[8]

An arbitrary choice, one for which no reasons favor any of the alternatives considered, can be the result of isolated practices which cannot be compared. Are religion and politics *mainly* commensurable, or incommensurable? Do these practices represent or contain isolated contexts that cannot be compared? If we view religion as a system of thought and practice that relies on a type of realist truth located outside human conventions, and politics as a set of organizations concerned to secure certain prudential goods in a human community, then certainly the two practices cannot be measured or evaluated in their entirety by terms that mean the same thing in each practice. Even as a sacred truth is interpreted with methods that overlap with, or are identical to, secular approaches the measures of comparison will be different because the truth conditions of the two practices differ. But there is this one feature of the politics of pluralist democracies that redefines the commensurability exercise: incommensurability among communities does not deny the possibility of a political settlement between the communities. In a very important sense there is no incommensurability in politics. The defining need of liberal democracies is to find or craft that third language which provides an accommodation meeting the general needs of rival communities without requiring the more stringent condition of full accord. The guiding light in politics is found in the structural or holistic requirements of the political community, not the common measures that permit comparability among communities in the political system. Put in the direct language of politics, it is not vital that adversaries agree on the merits, or even on what the merits are, so long as a settlement is reached. Rival communities may agree on an accommodation for different (and incommensurable) reasons, and even define a settlement in different ways. It doesn't matter for the *modus vivendi* arrangements that are the heart and soul of democratic politics. Divided communities can find in these arrangements a common ground that is common only because it is the accepted condition of a political accord.

But the types of distinctions offered here between the sacred and the secular are sharp enough to control even fundamental terms. In a common example, both Aristotle and Aquinas work within the same political framework in subscribing to the good as the natural end of human life. But Aristotle, confining experience to the temporal, conceives of a good satisfied by prudential accounts of happiness satisfied within natural human communities. Aquinas, extending the natural to the transcendence of a Christian God, is required to see all prudential goods as incomplete, with happiness dependent on aligning human experience with eternal law. Distinctions at this level suggest that political and religious discourses are, and perhaps must be, radically different in interpreting the break points of power and authority, in conflict when religion (as it is alleged to do) speaks truth to power, and the arrangements between church and state may be intelligible only in terms of a freestanding language independent of the assumptions of either practice. In negotiating differences like these one is invited, indeed required to present a third domain of language that abandons even minimalist taxonomic models. This third domain might be developed on a looser and more open version of religious and political discourse, developed on family resemblance concepts rather than single-property or analogical models. Evans (1997), for example, uses a family resemblance strategy in delineating the term "religion" and then suggests that legal cases under the free exercise clause of the First Amendment may be oriented toward different entries in this inventory of family properties.

The promised returns in using family resemblance concepts in the framework of a metaphor of cultural encounters are almost irresistible. All cluster concepts are artifacts of cultural diversity, they can be assigned in creative ways to all aspects of language (from theory to models and visualizations), and, partly as a consequence, can more easily elaborate and explain the competing demands of religion and state in contemporary liberal democracies. When we scan the vast differences among secular and religious communities the spectacle of radical translations across distinct language games appears at the center of one's vision. The user-friendly scope of family resemblance coupled with the vocabularies of system-like interactions is especially helpful when we accept the implications of the arguments here on these differences: that discussions of church and state may have to entertain the glum possibility that political and religious discourses are at least partially incommensurable when they negotiate synoptic ways of organizing human communities, and their intersections governable only by third domains, languages that are free of the main assumptions of either practice. At the end of the day we may find that these implications are the conditions on which church and state can forge political compatibilities with each other in modern democratic states, and these conditions are unlikely to be found in the dominant liberal models in contemporary political theory.

True Colors: Public and Deliberative Reasoning

I

In part because of the distinct standing of sacred texts religious communities are probably the acid test for the regulatory powers of the liberal state. One might even argue that it is in addressing religious doctrines that the deficiencies of the liberal model are most pronounced. Liberal theorists are often so troubled by religion that they require revisions in religious beliefs as a condition for their access to the conceptual domains of public reason. The unease clouds both interpretive sides of religion. On one side there is a tendency in the harsher liberal views to underestimate the possibilities of styles of reasoning (not values) common to both religion and the secular democratic state. Ronald Thiemann has presented a list of ingredients in the critical reasoning of public discourse that can be shared with religion, including publicity, the intersection of the religious norms of fairness and concern for the vulnerable with secular norms of equality and mutual respect, and the accommodation strategies that can house secular values of tolerance and mutual respect, a conceptual package that conflicts with more sectarian approaches in religion but still count as religious indicators.[1] Religion has always had (though not universally) its own critical discourses, represented, for example, in the argumentative styles of Jesuit traditions (which include Aquinas's proofs of God from observation and argument), and the recent public efforts of religious figures to influence political policies with arguments and evidence, as, for example, in opposition to war, support of social programs for the poor, and so on. A distinction between a sacred text and its interpretation is ample resource for secondary discourses in religion that seem unavoidably to employ and complement secular rules of interpretation, and the contents of modern practices like science. The gaps between the intellectual styles of religious and secular reasoning are easy to exaggerate in pragmatic contexts.

Then there is the other dimension in religion. On this other side, the history of religions provides ample evidence for the insularity and intolerance despised by liberal champions. Of course impediments to open cooperation are found in both secular and religious camps. But on this side of things the starker differences between core religious and liberal political cultures are real and damage the common ground shared by religion and politics. This is a version of religion with rules of evidence, inference and argument that can never be in a position of influence in secular politics. Liberal theorists do shift in their tolerance for this side of religion. Rawls had moved to a more generous perspective on religion with a wider view of public reason. In his later work he recognized the possibilities of support for democratic regimes within the interpretive strategies of religious discourses. He allowed that a religious community might endorse a constitutional democracy from internal (religious) reasoning, citing (curiously enough) the earlier Mecca interpretation in Islam of Shari'a as supporting an equality of men and women that is consistent with "the constitutional principle of equality before the law."[2] But, generally, the religious perspective is acceptable in Rawls's political philosophy (and this is a view typical of liberal political theory) as it subscribes to liberal democratic values, stated in Rawls's proviso, for example, that religious languages can be useful if stated (in due course) in terms of political languages. In a sense Rawls always recognized the starker differences between religious and political types of reasoning. The opposition to religion in liberal theory does key on those differences that are antagonistic to the liberal model of reason in managing religious disputes. These antagonisms, in turn, lead to the general resistance in liberal thought to the use of religious principles in organizing and governing a secular democratic state.

One helpful way to see these differences and what is required in addressing religion with an adequate model of public reason, *and* also avoid the rhetoric of hostility toward religion in much of liberal political theory, is to understand more about religion than is usually evident in liberal tracts, and how religion differs from the practices of a secular democracy. John Searle has demarcated terms according to distinctions in a kind of ontological rendering. Some features of the world exist independent of human attitudes, like sunlight, mass, gravitational attraction and photosynthesis, and other features depend on human attitudes, like money, property, marriage, and government. It is a given that social facts are not just the products of individual attitudes. There is also an abundant literature that locates natural or physical facts in the dense thicket of social conventions, as relative to the observer as any social fact. But, also, a kind of continuum from the created or contrived fact to the discovered fact is very much in evidence. Other features of the world seem more resistant to mere human needs or interests, possessing a kind of retentive power that shapes human pursuits, while other features accommodate human efforts to shape the worlds we occupy. In the simplest sense, we can change the rules of practices like baseball (and do) to suit our needs, but the rules of biological reproduction and the laws describing planetary motion are impervious to this kind of convenient alteration.[3]

I want to work here with a grammar of religious thinking that places at least some religious facts not just on the far edge of the retentive side of the continuum, but also outside its parameters. Unlike facts established through ordinary experience, or the designed observations and explanatory theories of the natural sciences, a religious fact can be a natural fact which has the property of being visible only in part. We might say that visibility in at least some religious experiences is ineluctably partial, so that unlike the experience in science of incomplete access later transformed into full access, a number of religious experiences are complete when the facts are presented as partial. The assumption driving this thought is the religious belief that reality exceeds the boundaries of human experience, and human access to these external dimensions is only partial. Partial access *is* the entire experience in religious terms and is insurmountable when religious facts are remote from human viewing even in principle. The resistance of such experiences to social construction is obviously incorrigible, since the laws defining a complete religious experience might not be known or even knowable to the human intellect. Discovery is taken to a different and more external level on the continuum of social to natural, with a more distant extension to the supernatural.

2

Both public and deliberative reasoning, the main contemporary candidates for the freestanding and recursive languages of state that are to manage disputes in all viable democratic systems, have recently been identified, tagged, and assigned several notable features by political theorists. These proposals are mindful of both logic and scope, and the demanding opportunity of managing religious disputes as a decisive test of success. But whether these contributions succeed in adjudicating or mediating the hard disputes represented by religious differences is an open question (and the subject of this chapter). In terms of its conceptual or logical form, the contours of democratic political reasoning present a familiar arrangement of overlapping consensus, abundant visibility, and reciprocities of various sorts.[4] As a form of justification, political reasoning has been effectively developed (Nagel, 1987) on common standards of rational justification, a process which relies on two conditions of publicity:

> preparedness to submit one's reasons to the criticism of others. . . . This means that it must be possible to present to others the basis of your own beliefs, so that once you have done so, *they have what you have*, and can arrive at a judgment on the same basis . . . second, an expectation that if others who do not share your beliefs are wrong, there is probably an explanation of their error which is not circular. . . . These two points may be combined in the idea that a disagreement that falls on objective common ground must be open-ended in the possibility of its investigation and pursuit, and not come down finally to a bare confrontation between incompatible personal points of view. I suggest that conflicts of religious faith fail this test, and most empirical and many moral disagreements do not.[5]

John Rawls stressed reciprocity in political reasoning, by which he means a relation between citizens on the fair terms of cooperation "in which everyone benefits judged with respect to an appropriate benchmark of equality defined with respect to that world." Rawls located reciprocity between impartiality, which he regards as altruistic, and mutual advantage.[6] In keeping with long democratic requirements that power must be justified to the one being coerced in terms s/he can understand, reciprocity stipulates that reasons for the exercise of political power have to be reasons that others can accept as a justification for this power.[7] The same spirit is accepted by Gutmann and Thompson in extended form: reciprocity is "the capacity to seek fair terms of social cooperation for their own sake." And ". . . citizens should aspire to a kind of political reasoning that is mutually justifiable."[8] A more elaborate model for political reasoning is located by Gutmann and Thompson in the democratic practice of deliberation, a kind of discourse that stresses reciprocity elaborated in terms of certain moral norms folded into the rules of successful speech acts. The three process principles in the Gutmann/Thompson program are reciprocity, publicity, and accountability. The content or institutional principles are the familiar staples of liberty, basic opportunity, and equal opportunity. Reciprocity is at the center of this form of deliberative democracy, and it presents the familiar norm of mutual respect. This is a norm that testifies to an acceptance that one's adversaries in a dispute are moral agents, with arguments formed from moral convictions and not just stark self interest. Another norm, moral integrity, slides into the grammar of discourse. It includes consistence of speech, consistency between speech and action, and the integrity of principle (the application of principles consistently across a variety of cases).[9] Following close on the deployment of these norms, and close also to Gutmann and Thompson's norm of moral integrity, are the more specific rules of language use in discursive contexts. Grice, for example, has outlined them as *quantity*, which specifies that agents avoid over-informing and under-informing in the offering of information, *quality*, which urges truth-telling in the requirement that what is said should be the case as much as possible, *relation*, which requires that utterances be relevant to the subject under discussion, and *manner*, which urges clarity and precision in communicating.[10] Various principles like charity toward the statements of others and sincerity in speaking annotate this process.

The signature statement, the sign of reason in these accounts, is not neutrality but a variation on dispassion, an emotive distance from issues represented by the disinterested observer coupled with the expectation of reciprocity in conditions and outcomes. It is a model of conversation, debate, and discourse that resembles the objective science of civic lore as this practice might be taken into political settings (or a good university seminar), and corresponds to the attitude toward disputes/arguments of the responsible and impartial (fair-minded) citizen of the liberal state as shaped by content-driven principles. It is also presented in a variety of liberal political philosophies as the *sine qua non* of political management and resolution.

To variations on this conceptual package of forms and techniques (in some adumbrated form) Rawls added the variable of scope, which opens the journey from private to public reasoning. It is a special sense of scope since he resists the observation that the political conception of justice is just another comprehensive doctrine of the sort that he dismisses as a basis for political authority. But this resistance is curious, and more than a little important. It turns in part on a careful and partial rejection of the argument that a political conception of justice for the basic structure is impossible without incorporating one or more of the comprehensive doctrines in the political society. Rawls pointed out that comprehensive doctrines are spread across a pluralist setting, and that while a political conception "includes a large family of nonpolitical values" (presumably drawn in part from doctrines that include the religious), the fact of multiple comprehensive doctrines requires that the political conception not be a variation on any one doctrine's nonpolitical values. So the scope of the political conception of justice is defined by its political standing, meaning (one supposes) its capacity to move across and address different comprehensive doctrines, and not exclusively by the logic or values of comprehensive doctrines (which presumably are general but unable to extend successfully to other, rival comprehensive doctrines).

Rawls recognized a distinction between "general and comprehensive views and views that are abstract." The political conception of justice "is abstract in the same way that the conception of a perfectly competitive market, or of general economic equilibrium, is abstract; that is, it singles out certain aspects of society as especially significant from the standpoint of political justice and leaves others aside." The political conception, as an abstraction, is able to roam over a wide range of disputes, but it is a conception realized in the context of these disputes, and the particular, and one would think, rival nature of any dispute prevents the conception from being general and comprehensive as it is used. Then, "A political conception is at best but a guiding framework of deliberation and reflection which helps us reach political agreement on at least the constitutional essentials and the basic questions of justice." But the guidance is what we must call firm given that political values trump nonpolitical values. The scope of the political conception is also modified by its restriction to the basic structure of society, meaning a democratic society's main political, social, and economic institutions, and the unified system of social cooperation in which these institutions cohere from one generation to another.[11]

It is never easy to say with confidence what Rawls means. But the practical scope of an authoritative political language, the freestanding political conception found in his account of public reasoning, seems to be lodged in the following considerations and restrictions. The political/legal frame for managing disputes is freestanding in the sense that it is outside the many and often contradictory values and preferences (some comprehensive) found in a pluralist democracy. It is not entirely clear why this frame is not general and comprehensive since the essentials of a constitution certainly aspire toward generality, at least in the modest sense that a legal system driven by the common law rules not for particular cases but for all relevantly similar cases. But Rawls is surely right to stress the abstract standing of a political conception, in the sense that it is a frame specified as it engages the disputes that the state is to resolve or manage. The definition of an abstraction in this process depends on the political conception assuming a form only as it is brought to bear on particular cases, which are the instruments to define it. (This seems to track in reverse the insistence in quantum theory that electrons have no form in the sense of position and velocity until they are observed. It would be as if we say that the concepts in quantum theory are undefined until they encounter the electron, rather than the reverse.) In this sense a freestanding political conception is both logically unlike the comprehensive doctrines informing many religions (some of which are preconceived independent of cases) but also general only in the loose sense that the political frame houses and adjudicates doctrines that can be comprehensive on content and ideologically rigid in confronting experience. Rawls modeled this form of reasoning, which seems to be a kind of public reason of state, in terms of the judicial model of reasoning represented by the U.S. Supreme Court (which is the exemplar selected by Rawls). The legal model appears as the dominant venue for public reasoning. For example, Rawls saw the office of citizens as analogous to that of judges.[12]

The two most important components in this version of public reason are "reasonableness" and "public." The first of these terms insinuates itself into both personal attitudes and the political structures of a just society. In distinguishing the reasonable from the rational, Rawls proposes that "Persons are reasonable in one basic aspect when, among equals say, they are ready to propose principles and standards as fair terms of cooperation and to abide by them willingly, given the assurance that others will likewise do so." Note the close links between the attitudes or psychology of the person and the structures in terms of which this subjective frame is realized. Also note how reasonableness fits into the concept of reciprocity ("assurances that others will likewise do so"). Generally, "Reasonable persons . . . are not moved by the general good as such but desire for its own sake a social world in which they, as free and equal, can cooperate with others on terms all can accept. They insist that reciprocity should hold within that world so that each benefits along with others."[13] Gutmann and Thompson fold reasonableness into reciprocity. Citizens respecting reciprocity must be civil in not pressing sectarian ways of life on each other, which would be unreasonable.[14]

The "public" dimension is a bit less subtle (if that is possible). Public reasoning for Rawls was reasoning that is marked off in part by three traits: it is the reasoning of the citizens as opposed to private persons (practice dualism all over again); its subject is the public or (one supposes) the greater or common good, or justice; and its "nature and content is public" (part of a society's conception of political justice) and so is open to general scrutiny.[15] One might think that the invocation of the U.S. Supreme Court is odd once these traits are accepted since the deliberations of the justices are private, famously shielded from public scrutiny. But the point here is that public reasoning is conducted in terms of rules of inference, evidence and argument that can be understood by a wide range of persons. Its logic, its processes, are accessible, not arcane or in principle remote. When the Court publishes its reasoned opinions the reasoning of the Court is there to be studied, interpreted, and made sensible to all who take the effort to understand the deliberations. (This is what is normally meant by transparent reasoning.) Public reasons, then, are reasons crafted on open forms of reasoning that resolve disputes on fundamental political matters in terms of reliable methods of justification that are or can be shared by all citizens.[16]

3

Does this package of form and scope represent the political type of reasoning that can resolve or manage disputes in the liberal state? Setting aside most of the ways in which almost all parts of the package are corruptible in everyday politics (the roles of power and advantage in distorting deliberations, etc.) on the grounds that all models are corruptible, it is hard to see how the model of deliberative democracy can succeed even as an uncorrupted theory without representing more directly the collective considerations and practical influences that mark off political reasoning. Current versions of deliberative reason are especially apt targets for this observation since most of the terminology in these accounts is derived from individual discourses. The problem with such a starting point is that the need for a model of reasoning begins on the expectation that practical reasoning differs among practices and communities, in the direct sense that rules of inference, evidence and argument are local to sectors of the political society. When these sectors are in dispute in democratic settings a public form of reasoning or deliberation is required. This practice is the management of disputes at and among the collective levels of a political community. Rawls acknowledges collective settings and references with his definition of the political conception in public reason. But the model of reasoned dispute management in deliberative democracy is typically drawn up from an idealized discussion between individuals, in spite of the self-evident fact that collective references abound in politics and in the face of Rawls's caveats that public reason must attend to constitutional or structural matters. It is ironic that one of the alternative approaches to reasoned dispute management in politics is pure structural or institutional change/maintenance. As good post-Marxists (all of us) we know the telling effects of social/economic conditions on attitudes, meaning that the views brought to the public table are often the products of backgrounds, of the locations of individuals in the distributive arrangements of a political society. One of the revered ways to manage political disputes on this understanding is to forego reasoning and directly alter the backgrounds that are complicit in the formation of values and beliefs.[17] The first objection to deliberative democracy is simple enough: at the very least political reasoning must insinuate itself into the collective setting of politics, and into the deliberations of opposing political actors in the reasoning process.

Second, it is easy to conclude (as several critics have) that all versions of the liberal model of reasoning are unreasonably exclusive (or "preclusive"). Exclusionary clauses are not unusual. It is common for practices to have a position on what data are admitted as evidence for rational decisions, and it is not atypical to bar certain views (in science, religion, politics) from the deliberative table on grounds of both intelligibility and morality. But we would expect independent justifications for these exclusions, and an explanation for how the exclusionary provisions accord with the practice at hand. In courts of law, for example, the exclusionary rule for evidence often follows one or another depiction of a legal trial, and the evidence admitted and kept out is roughly regarded as necessary to meet the purposes drawn up from these depictions. In the oft-cited example, if we see a court of law as a kind of contest between defendant and the state, and if we tack onto the depiction the thought that the state has a disproportionate advantage (as U.S. Supreme Court Justice Brennan believed), then the strict exclusion of illegally acquired evidence is justified (fruit of the tainted tree, etc.). On the other hand, if a trial is depicted as a search for truth, even illegally acquired evidence might be admitted if it bears on the guilt or innocence of the defendant.

The exclusionary provisions of deliberation in democratic politics, however, rarely attain even these metaphorical levels of justification and explanation. Mainly, the provisions of inclusion are wrapped in the well-known package of reasonableness. Players are required to be reasonable, meaning (in the most general sense) that they have respect for each other and also maintain views that fall within the overlapping consensus that Rawls celebrates, will introduce to public discourse only those of their views that others can accept, and/or are willing to contract or even amend their views to secure an accord so long as these efforts are within the terms of fair cooperation. Why? Rawls gives the best answer. Citizens are resigned to their limited intellectual fates. They are willing to recognize and accept "the burdens of judgments," which means that they acknowledge the difficulties that we all have in assessing evidence, in part due to the differential influences of our life experiences. We see the glass not as half full or empty, but through it darkly. We are denied certainty of judgment and the confidence, let alone the arrogance, which might come with it. This melancholy state of mind is thought to be conducive to reasonable actions (a thought that certainly makes sense).

The reasonableness package is typically specified with admittance tests (since marking off the reasonable means that there must be unreasonable persons or views). Gutmann and Thompson, for example, have two such provisions: a moral test and an intelligibility test.[18] On the first, certain views, such as racism and sexism, are not admitted because they fail the moral test. On the second, positions formed on unreliable methods of inquiry are excluded from deliberation. These two tests understandably fold into each other on more than a few occasions, but they do present different types of thresholds. The first excludes views on a definitional criterion (they are not really moral positions, not supported by "moral reasons"). The second excludes poorly argued or unsupported views (unreliable methods). On the first test, certain views cannot be admitted no matter how well they are argued. On the second, views that are implausible (beliefs in an intercessory God, for example) are excluded on evidentiary and argumentative grounds even if they are inoffensive on moral grounds.[19]

As many critics have noted, these tests are hardly fair. What is morally repugnant in one community may not be in another, so the tests simply elevate a community standard (based on liberal principles) to dominance without argument or, well, deliberation. The concept of reliability is also widely contested, even within scientific communities. The long line of literature trying to define a critical test to falsify hypotheses is itself testimony to the difficulties in agreeing on reliable methods of inquiry.[20] The chronically contestable state of moral perspectives and reliable methods raises questions about dissent. On the surface, the program seems tolerant of dissent. The right to dissent follows almost inexorably from the contours of public reason and the norms of deliberative democracy, and seems to be in an especially tight accord with public accessibility and mutual respect. The nonviolent resistance of Martin Luther King is a virtual exemplar of principled dissent on the basis of democratic deliberation. But note that King saw the white moderates, the liberals of that time, as his primary antagonists in counseling him to go slow, to be moderate, to be more deliberative and less confrontational in his efforts at racial desegregation. The point is that the deliberative and necessarily slow pace of the liberal model of engagement may be hostile to movements aimed at securing justice in the here and now, especially when the temporal is marked by religious sensibilities.[21] It is telling that Rawls has to invoke extraordinary considerations (a society that is not well ordered) to admit comprehensive dissent on fundamentals, and history tells us that often only in retrospect can we say with reasonable certainty whether a society is not well ordered at a given time and a pattern of support or dissent is morally justifiable.

The phenomenon of moral relativism that haunts all versions of liberalism is well known, and suggests the importance of both a pragmatic and more systemic frame in addressing critical issues in politics. As illustration, look at the Lincoln–Douglas debates. In these debates, Lincoln saw the evil in slavery, but not so clearly in political terms that he supported the Abolitionists. Instead he resisted the extension of slavery to the new states. In retrospect he argued the better moral case in the debates, though not as fervently as we may wish from today's perspectives. But the figure presenting the most interesting deliberative exercise is Stephen Douglas. On reliable methods of inquiry [including the invocation of the U.S. Constitution and the Supreme Court in *Dred Scott* (1808)], and on reasons acceptable among reasonable persons at the time, Douglas deliberated and made arguments in support of a position that we acknowledge now as morally wrong and even unreasonable. Douglas saw no political path to agreement in the country on the morality of slavery. On this observation he concluded that the government should remain neutral and let the people in the new territories decide the issue for themselves. At the time Douglas made arguments that meet the conditions of reciprocity in Gutmann and Thompson's program, but at a later time these same arguments fail to meet reciprocity conditions.[22] A measure of caution and modesty, and appreciation of a more robust scope for comprehensive dissent, might reasonably follow an acceptance of this moral relativism.

The possibilities of disruptions in continuities severe enough to modify forms of reasoning and deliberation that fare well in orderly times are part of commonsense expectations in political understandings. Thomas Kuhn's paradigm shifts have entered the lore of the social sciences and understandings of science in general. But also political inquiry has generously documented critical realignments in American politics that shift the balances among even basic rules and principles, and provide new equilibriums for constitutional stability. Walter Dean Burnham, for example, describes six punctuated upheavals a generation apart.[23] In Bruce Ackerman's second volume of *We the People: Transformations*, his epic study of American constitutional law and history, the author identifies "constitutional moments" in which constitutional reconstruction occurs, where the foundations of the regime are redefined for the next period of stability.[24]

Burnham explicitly appropriates Stephen Jay Gould's idea of "punctuated equilibriums" as a depiction of these theories. In Gould's definition of punctuated equilibrium, a theory (in this case of evolution) must include three concepts: stasis, punctuation, and dominant relative frequency. The relatively abrupt event of a punctuation (a geological moment) is transforming, a shift to a different equilibrium that is then sustained for a (prolonged, geological) time.[25] In social systems theory we might say that a critical alignment, a constitutional moment, is a punctuated upheaval in which a system is reflexively transformed and then maintained for a (more modest) period of historical time. Politics, including public reasoning, deliberation, and accommodation, occur in these periods of upheaval. But these political actions and events may have to succeed in conditions so morally and legally turbulent that even the fundamental ingredients and backgrounds of political reason may be in flux. A form of reasoning that can absorb these movements from a synoptic perspective is a desirable and necessary part of political reasoning. The time-based and constrained thinking outlined in the currently dominant versions of deliberative democracy and public reason will not do this job.

Two lessons from this more historical perspective should be obvious. First, it may be impossible to identify with reasonable certainty the moral courses of action at any given time and place. We are encouraged, on this acknowledgment, to ensure that our gaze is framed within a pragmatic *and* comprehensive perspective containing the recursive powers needed to evaluate claims that exceed even the reasonable (itself located in historical context). The second is that some of the formal rules of reasoning may fail when background conditions dominate reasoning and deliberation. For example, a transitive ordering of moral claims may be impossible with the changes in conditions that seem chronically to mark historical periods. If a is better than b at time t_1, and b is better than c at time t_2, it does not follow that a is better than c at time t_3. The conditions for defining and ordering the claims may have changed across time. (In tranquil times a community may assign dominance to free speech over community welfare, and fix community welfare over state authority. But the same community might grant a trumping power to state authority over free speech if crisis replaces tranquility.) Views of slavery changed as historical conditions changed, bracketing the logical axiom of transitivity (and other axioms as well) as devices to negotiate political reasoning. Again, a frame sensitive to these kinds of inversions on conditional shifts, one not wedded to the strict and simple rules of formal and well-ordered deliberations, may be vital in negotiating the kinds of divisive and synoptic disputes occasioned by differences among political and religious communities.[26]

Here is one key to understanding what is happening here. Moving through all of Rawls's arguments (there is no doubt about this) is a fear of discord and instability. In well-ordered societies (much the favored kind) disruptive views are tabled: "Faced with the fact of reasonable pluralism, a liberal view removes from the political agenda the most divisive issues, serious contention about which must undermine the bases of social cooperation."[27] Unfortunately for this view, politics is a practice occasioned by divisiveness not harmony, and negotiated often enough through confrontation. The more important developments in political morality may be compelled to rely not on deliberation and reason but on confrontations (peaceful and otherwise) and political machinations. Martin Luther King needed and cannily used the violence against blacks (in the South especially) to rally the conscience of the nation. (Absent Bull Connor and the violent confrontation in the first Selma March, for example, and the movement might have been less successful in a tight time frame.) Very little in the way of mutual respect or reciprocity in general influenced these struggles. Yet the Civil Rights movement stands as a successful forging of a moral conscience in the political culture of the United States. These more complex patterns require more complex systems of thought to handle the fallout from rules and principles that always seem to be limited and local in addressing the welcome unruliness of democratic politics.

Third, there are also certain dispositions in the model that raise questions about its effectiveness even in secular contexts where disagreement is tepid and easily handled. The strong reliance on attitudes while distrusting emotions, for example, is odd. It is a commonplace in game theory that we might not always know intentions, and so might be wrong about exactly what game an individual is playing.[28] Worse, since all of game theory elaborates the rationality of deceit in various forms as an instrument for success, sincerity (or any attitude) is often indeterminate in calculations of advantage. Given this literature, mutual respect might be best approached not as a condition of mind but only as it is revealed or encouraged in the strategies of reason, or, maybe better, as guaranteed in the structures or practices of the reasoning game. Requiring it as a conditional attitude or intention for playing the game is superfluous, and probably misleading. It also introduces an avoidable fragility to deliberations given the ease with which individuals can disguise true intentions and co-opt reasoned beliefs. The entire deliberative package (which includes moral integrity, remember) seems to require sincerity among the players without any justification for the assumption. A century of game theory welcomes inquiries into the possibility that individuals may be playing more than one game, that players may be *rationally* feigning sincerity, even integrity, and presenting a bogus tranquil *or* frazzled mind set. Ruth Grant, in a study of Machiavelli and Rousseau, has argued persuasively that hypocrisy may even be more constructive than strictly principled behavior, with the consequence that rationality and integrity in politics may be mutually antagonistic.[29] So we would expect some intellectual skepticism for the naïve expectation that persons divided along fundamental lines are playing, or even can play, a transparent game of trust in political deliberations just because the conveners stipulate the requirement as a condition of the process.

Nor are game theoretic sessions irremediably bad. Many deliberations have mutated into successful resolutions built from tactical interactions. Why are these metamorphoses rejected in favor of an idealized sincerity? The harder question, however, is why the expectation of sincerity is part of the deliberative process given the strong possibilities unearthed by game theory that both particular and general interests may be best served in tactical or strategic interactions, and perhaps (in the arguments that Grant develops) with a measured use of hypocrisy. This objection can be stretched to an even more critical perspective. Leo Strauss maintained that the classical political theorists wrote in a kind of code, with the conclusion that the real meaning of a text must be deciphered by a theorist in command of the right techniques to decode the hidden secrets of the text (Strauss, of course, and his disciples, but not everyone and certainly not the many). The implication of this conviction for many of Strauss's students is that deception is the key feature of political discourse, and anyone who assumes differently is naïve and, really, deluded.[30]

Then there is the suspicion of emotion represented in the importance assigned to the disinterested observer. The ideal person in this sanitized version of politics seems to be dispassionate, guided with excellent and serene attitudes clustered under integrity. This skepticism toward unruly or intuitive or emotive states of mind is part of a distinguished pedigree that maintains true objectivity as cool intellect devoid of subjective distractions. But this view finally is a cranky artifact from a contrived scientific reasoning that is not even an accurate portrayal of the practice of science. First, recent work on mind raises doubts that we can even sensibly demarcate the emotive and cognitive.[31] Second, even if we succeed with a demarcation, the most lucid intellectual achievements and practices can easily be products of intuition and unbridled passion, which is certainly the case in science, and in politics of a compassion that can extend understanding to the views of the other. Why place the disinterested observer in a preeminent position? Even the model of extended sympathy in economics seems better than models distilled from civic science, since sympathetically entering the mindset of the other, *understanding* the adversary on her own terms, would seem to be the good first step in resolving disputes. This extension of sympathetic identification across adversaries is a staple of communitarian literatures, and has worked its way into some views of law. The thought here is that the natural alienation characteristic of adversarial practices, in which law students are taught "a detached, unfeeling, analytical mode of rule application" can be mitigated by encouraging an emotive introduction, an extension of identity across persons, "a connection that would allow us to see each other as the source of each other's completion" as a way of framing and resolving disputes.[32]

4

How can a religious community be addressed with these models of reasoning? As a start, note that the core entry on the lexical menu accounting for differences among religious and political practices is *divinity* (an orientation to a realm beyond nature). Of course there are religions that emphasize various social matters over any sense of divinity, an observation found in many treatments of religion, analytic and empirical.[33] But the crucial demarcation of the secular and the sacred throughout modern Western history (when the demarcation is most commonly made in the way the terms are used here) is precisely an orientation to the temporal in secular life and an acceptance of the supernatural (beyond nature) in religious life. Religions without divinity are not so clearly distinguished from other practices, and cannot easily yield a variety of cohort terms, like conscience. Also, however, when the religious is little more than the social the hard issues of church and state are muted and not so interesting. A quest for the hard issues in relations among the religious and secular forms of the political inclines us toward a reliance on divinity as a core term in religion even in the face of diversity *on this measure* among practices. In this sense an adequate study of religion in politics might accept a strong version of religion while conceding the existence of weak versions that often blend into political practice without contradiction or divisiveness.

The main difficulty in reconciling religion and the politics of liberal democracies is exactly that religion is sometimes not just another social practice, and its distinctiveness is in its allegiance with divinity. It is in fact this belief that makes sense of Locke's observation that religion is different, clarifies his thought that "every church is orthodox to itself; to others, erroneous or heretical," and also begins to explain why the relationships between religion and secular democratic states is so complex.[34] Put in more direct terms, divinity helps explain *on conceptual grounds* the obvious and much discussed fact of church–state disharmonies in Western political cultures. On these distinctions alone it appears that political and religious discourses are, and perhaps must be, radically different in interpreting the break points of power and authority, in conflict when religion (as it is alleged to do in solemn moments) speaks truth to power, and the rational arrangements between church and state may be intelligible only in terms of a language independent of the main assumptions of either practice.

One is obligated at some stage in this discussion to acknowledge a skeptical solution to these difficulties. The allegiance with divinity provides an obvious and especially tempting way to reduce the normal incompatibilities between religious and secular practices: dismiss the source of the distinction, the concept of divinity, with the practical result that the main incompatibilities between religious and secular practices are collapsed, and shown to be illusory. Distinguished literatures aim at such a dismissal. The attempts in post-Darwinism to absorb religion in adaptation accounts that fit any social practice, for example with the view that religion's origins can be found in its contributions to group survival, are prominent reductionist attempts.[35] These efforts may be both true and persuasive on their own terms, even though to be complete explanations of religious beliefs and practices they require citations of the particular features of religion that contribute to survival. But whatever features are cited, and however successful the efforts, the attempts are consistent with a definition of religion in terms of beliefs not in secular matters but in the supernatural. Absent the grammar of the religious game crafted from divinity and one silences religious–secular conflict, but only at the cost of dismissing that which marks off strong versions of religious practices. Locke's proviso that religion is set apart is best explained by the religious tendency to invoke the supernatural as a source of authority.

The special standing of religious beliefs is recognized in many secular cultures. In the U.S. legal system the recognition takes the form of the occasional grant of exemptions to groups from the obligations of law on the basis of their religious beliefs and practices. The recognition is easy to understand if we monitor the particular effects of religious beliefs in any of the thought experiments current in political theory. Imagine, for example, the choices of individuals in Rawls's original position (OP) if their deliberations are dominated by religious beliefs. Tracking the exact principles the OP agents would select, and the ordering they would assign to these principles, is complicated, but it can hardly be thought that they would choose liberty and a binary principle of combined equal opportunity and the difference principle arranged in a lexical ordering. One would expect more attention to forms of authority rather than liberty, for example, and a primary concern with spiritual as opposed to the economic goods targeted by the difference principle. This shift in emphasis would likely follow even on the expectations that religious pluralism is the order of the day in the community entered after OP people make their choices. Even religious minorities, requiring religious liberty to protect their beliefs, might still prefer liberty elaborated in the frame of a rigid social order to arrangements that celebrated liberty as a dominant first principle. The likelihood of different selections would follow an understanding of reality as exceeding the boundaries of the human community, with some expected revisions of secular versions of the good and the right emphasized in Rawls's theories. It is not even assured that a religious orientation would settle on fairness as the driving term for a theory of justice. A concern for a higher order sense of rightness might figure into the background concepts of justice from a religious perspective.

Suppose that we are working with that strong sense of the religious in current understandings of public reason and deliberation. Then, on this grammar, certain distinctions and common themes are evident on the arguments developed here. As summary, there is first the difficulty of ever finding a common value or first principle as a resource to resolve secular–religious disputes. The ability and willingness of so many individuals with religious orientations to submit doctrines that encapsulate the entirety of human experience make a common value to trump disagreement almost unintelligible. Second, the sources of authority differ as we move from the strong version of religious belief to the secular. A strong religious sensibility depends on a wide and deep realism, in truth and existence. One way to phrase this is to say that religion depends on realist truth and ontological experience. Truth is external, in that the presentation of the object in experience refers to a reality outside sense experience. The adjudicative powers of this dependence yield distinctions that a simple scan of jurisprudential scope cannot. Look for a brief moment at ideology and religion. Orthodox Marxism is comprehensive in explaining social experience and in prescribing reform. As an ideology it also has a protective belt ensuring against simple and perhaps any falsification. In these senses one can argue successfully that ideology and religion are identical. But Marxism is oriented entirely to the material organization of a human community, and its sources of authority derive from an influential map of this material domain. Religious authority originates outside the boundaries of human experience. The divine in religion is not reducible to the material because its source is another world. This difference in sources of authority helps demarcate secular and religious thinking. The protective belt that retains core statements, for example, does not vary across these ways of thinking in its thickness so much as its material, meaning the criterion that determines what is allowed past the belt. A secular theory yields under some conditions to falsifying observation statements. A religious doctrine may also be falsifiable by intuition, revelation and pure textual exegesis.

Third, these different sources of authority yield differences in the ways in which religious and political communities can be arranged schematically. A religious community in the strong sense is thought to be located in an unknown and unknowable realm, which is a source of meaning and value for human experience. All religions attest to the truth and goodness of this realm, though its scope and importance is stressed in what I have called here strong religions. In Buddhism human experience is an illusion created by the senses, and access routes to the external realm take one to a reality which is both ultimately good and indivisible. Christian versions of the realm allow for a merger of individuals with God that maintains individual identity. But in all strong religions the external realm is the locus of primary experience. A political community can also be presented as a core center surrounded by an external realm. In political discourses this external realm can contain especially mixed moral possibilities, from dark to light. For example, the assertion of hidden power elites with pernicious effects on the body politic is common enough, as is the inventory of principles of justice that enlighten the political system. This wide variance on a moral scale, however, is fixed by the uncertainty conditions characteristic of politics, where the unknown is accommodated by decision rules that are considerably short of the ultimate in any sense of that term.

Fourth, the connections of the individual to the community are different across religious and secular discourses. A religious community can absorb the whole person in ways that are illicit in the property and practice dualisms of a liberal democracy. An individual can be a good citizen, a model citizen, by a measure of behavior that does not require compliance in thought. But a religious commitment is unintelligible without the right beliefs, an observation that might be made of many practices other than secular political arrangements but is rich enough in religion to extend across both the action-oriented Aristotelian/Aquinas and belief-driven Luther versions of Christianity. One difference that marks off the religious from the secular is that at least some core beliefs in a religious community are intertwined with the identity of the individual. Membership goes deep into core understandings of the self and, on the whole, is difficult to negotiate successfully by any democratic system in terms of the pragmatic forms of reasoning characterizing such political arrangements.

5

The customary approach in secular democracies that more definitively recognizes the special and separate standing of religious beliefs yields three prominent models to address these difficulties, all drawn from legal approaches in the United States to state–religion orientations: the strict separation interpreted by neutrality (and imperfectly expressed in the Establishment clause in the First Amendment to the U.S. Constitution); impartiality, which requires that religious and secular communities be treated in the same way (thus offending the separation thesis with regulations, supports and denials commensurate with secular treatments); and the exemptions in U.S. law that recognize the special standing of religious beliefs (which in turn may be seen as a form of impartiality in treating unlike cases in unlike fashion).

Now, the standard view is that these three models are inconsistent when taken as a cluster on their own terms, but they can all be subsumed under a form of political liberalism. In Rawls's account, religious communities in conditions of pluralism can be in a state of harmony with the political system as sources of support and standards for politics, so long as these communities subscribe to the overlapping consensus required in a well-ordered political system. Rawls famously disallows comprehensive doctrines in public space except when essential political principles are being contested, meaning that order has broken down. In these conditions, where societies are not well ordered, religious doctrines may enter public space with the aim of restoring public reason.[36] But in a well-ordered society comprehensive doctrines are to be kept on the sidelines (in private space), with one exception. The public language of the state is allowed in the game as a kind of comprehensive framework that extends in umbrella fashion over the political domain in well-ordered societies. Religious communities can dissent from liberal principles within their communities, but they must be morally paid-up members of the one comprehensive doctrine accepted in political liberalism: the political conception of justice.[37] This political consensus is the source of political stability, and reiterates the entry test of reasonableness that Rawls locates at the center of his political system. It follows that the public language of the state is privileged, and is the main resource to govern religious communities. As Ronald Thiemann phrases it:

> For such a consensus to form, the conception of justice must be *distinguished from* all comprehensive schemes and *be accepted by* persons who hold those schemes. Thus, the notion of justice developed within political liberalism must both *separate* religion (understood as a comprehensive scheme) from politics and *relate* religion to politics, if an overlapping consensus is to be built.[38]

The burden placed on public language is considerable in this approach to church and state. It certainly requires sustained attention to the logic of public discourse and to the concepts of truth and objectivity. The boundaries between religion and state are due in part to a difference in understandings of objectivity and subjectivity that separates the two. Thomas Nagel has defined an objective fact as one that can be grasped in the same way from many points of view, and a subjective fact as one that can be grasped from only one point of view.[39] The starting condition for the liberal state is a plethora of subjective facts that occasionally leads to disputes. One purpose of public reasoning is to subordinate subjective facts by types of objective facts, but not to adjudicate subjective claims on the basis of truth criteria. The point is to tolerate and even respect the diversity of subjective facts, and manage disputes on criteria of the sort found in Mill's harm thesis. Public reason is the initial frame for liberal governance and the subsequent justification for coercion when talking does not succeed in dispute management.

Both religion and politics can be, and typically are, concerned with truth. But the truth in religion is not congenial with the consensual objectivity sought in public reasoning. The kind of objectivity that helps demarcate the two practices is closer to Nozick's (second) understanding of objective belief (not fact): "A judgment or belief is objective when it is reached by a certain sort of process, one that does not involve biasing or distorting factors that lead belief away from the truth."[40] Religion and politics seem to rely on different types of processes in reaching objectivity. The type of truth and the importance of process also differ. Religion in the strong sense indicated here is oriented to a discovered truth, which provides certainty, and political reasoning is notoriously preoccupied with process itself, which offers the conditions of uncertainty and risk that come with epistemic truth. Conceded: a text can be interpreted in different ways according to rival methods of textual analysis without an assumption that the text is, or is not, true. Postmodern views often seem content to think of texts as no more than artifacts of the reader's interpretive powers. Neither truth nor the concept of truth is needed to complete these views. If, however, truth is a consideration in constructing a secular text through interpretation the truth must be epistemic. On the standard account, any inquiry is epistemic if its principles, theories and claims are defined as constructions, maps for example, rather than statements that correspond to a mind-independent reality. A statement is true in this sense if it is the product of consensus, meaning that it is accepted as true on certain conditions.

Disputes over the meaning of a text do not establish that the text is or may be false, contradictory, vague, confused, or even unclear. The problem might reside entirely with the disputants and their methods for approaching a text. But the assumption that the text is true in a realistic sense frames disputes over meaning. Then the dispute is a deficiency that in principle will be resolved through a correct ordering of the rival claims once the truth of the text is evident. Now suppose that the truth of the text is entirely epistemic, meaning that it is an artifact of agreement under certain stipulated conditions. Then the dispute over meaning must be viewed differently, perhaps as a healthy inquiry that will produce an interpretation that can survive critical scrutiny. This difference in understandings of truth, robust by any standards, goes to the center of distinctions between religious and political discourses, and sets out how we must organize a public language if religious and secular political practices are to be brought into a harmonious order.

6

A more aggressive intellectual approach to religion and politics dwells in the regions of substantive moral resources. The dream of a content-driven device that can adjudicate disputes from a position outside the disputes begins with Plato's arguments for the Form of the Good, and is refreshed in different ways by John Stuart Mill's reliance on a hierarchy of goods and Rawls's use of primary goods. The legendary problem for liberal theory is that the human community is dense with rival claims for content in moral and political reasoning, and it is illicit for the liberal state to hijack one of these claims to dominate the others on the terms set out for the impartial or fair governing that liberalism seeks. One response in liberal theory to this problem has been to offer the thinnest content possible in order to avoid too clannish an affiliation between state authority and community beliefs. In genuinely interesting ways, liberal theory has filled the formal appeal of moral reasoning with minimal content, one might even say a spare form of naturalism, that aspires to universality on the basis of its spare (and agreeable) nature.

One of the more persuasive versions of such minimalism is Martha Nussbaum's list of central capabilities as a legitimate source of moral constraints. Her arguments are among the strongest and more impressive attempts to reconcile religious freedom with liberal values, with the implication that any important failure at such a high level of accomplishment speaks to certain core limitations in liberal theory.[41] Nussbaum recognizes at the outset one of the more troublesome dilemmas of liberal political theory:

Modern liberal democracies typically hold that religious liberty is an extremely important value, and that its protection is among the most important functions of government. These democracies also typically defend as central a wide range of other human interests, liberties, and opportunities. . . . Sometimes, however, the religions do not support these other liberties.

In this way, a dilemma is created for the liberal state. On the one hand, to interfere with the freedom of religious expression is to strike a blow against citizens in an area of intimate self-definition and basic liberty. Not to interfere, however, permits other abridgments of self-definition and liberty. (Nussbaum, 2000, p. 168)

Nussbaum describes two extreme feminist positions on the dilemma. One, which she labels secular humanist feminism, denies that the dilemma is a dilemma by allowing other human interests to trump religious freedom. The other position, which she calls traditional feminism, also regards the dilemma as a non-dilemma by accepting the dominance of the religious value. The second position employs the familiar arguments that indigenous religious practices will in the long run be the best guarantee of human interests, including those that are vital to women. But it does seem clear that the conflict in values (or dilemma) unavoidably compromises the promise of a neutral state and requires for its resolution some substantive reference to justify either forbearance or regulation of the religious beliefs at issue.

Nussbaum, in *Women and Human Development*, presents the dilemma as a real dilemma, meaning that she acknowledges "the weight of the values on both sides" (pp. 187–8). For her, a solution to the dilemma must respect religious beliefs and a range of human capabilities outside religions. The capabilities approach is "based on a universalist account of central human functions, closely allied to a form of political liberalism" (p. 5). The subtle force of Nussbaum's strategy is that she initially presents the capabilities approach as necessary to religion itself. The first principle in the approach is the intrinsic value of religious capabilities. This principle expresses the importance of religion in human life, especially the need among individuals to search in their own way for the ultimate good. It requires the state to allow free expression for individuals in realizing their religious capability or opportunity. The second principle is respect for persons. To a degree this principle is contained in the first. It supplements the view of the intrinsic value of religious capabilities. A third (guiding or orienting) principle more directly assigns capabilities toward individuals. Nussbaum endorses the principle of each person as an end and requires of religious groups that they "promote religious capabilities (and other capabilities) of the group's members, taken one by one" (p. 188). A fourth (and second orienting) principle is the principle of moral constraint. This principle is directed primarily at religions and sets limits on state tolerance. The state is to grant deference to religions only as they promote moral conduct in terms of the list of capabilities and refuse deference when they go outside of these moral understandings. "We should refuse to give deference to religion when its practices harm to people in the areas covered by the major capabilities."[42]

The capabilities approach is a curious mix of respect for indigenous religious beliefs, which is the mark of political liberalism, and the urge to shape religion toward liberal values, which is the sign of comprehensive liberalism. The strong respect for religious values in the capabilities approach, expressed most strongly in the recognition that religion is a vital part of human life, moves against the tendencies in liberal theory to denigrate religion as superstition or worse. Still within the spirit of tolerance for religious beliefs is the "respect for persons" principle as it is interpreted to grant discretionary authority in the matter of religious beliefs to members of a religion. This spirit of deference is contained in all genuine expressions of the free exercise clause of the First Amendment. But then the capabilities approach slides into a legislative function. The respect for persons is stipulative toward religions. The state's deference toward religions must be matched by a religious group's deference toward their members. Capabilities are not group properties but powers assigned to individuals, and these individual powers must be respected by groups. Sanctions quickly follow for noncompliance. The moral constraint principle requires the state to decertify those religions that do not cultivate individual capabilities. In Nussbaum's tough-love program, religions are not really religions that offend the capabilities orientation: "We may and do, however, judge that any cult or so-called religion that diverges too far from the shared moral understanding that it embodies in the core of the political conception does not deserve the honorific name of religion."[43]

The scope of the moral constraint principle overrides the generality requirement established by Locke. The majority decision in *Employment Division v. Smith* is based on the generality test in Locke's solution to church–state relations. In this case the Court refused to grant an exemption from a criminal ban on peyote to two members of a Native American religion who used the drug in religious ceremonies. The Court ruled that the right of free exercise does not release an individual from compliance with a "valid and neutral law of general applicability on the ground that the law proscribes (or prescribes) conduct that his religion prescribes (or proscribes)." The *Smith* decision was unpopular enough to produce a counter movement that led to the passage of the United States Religious Freedom Restoration Act of 1993. This act prohibited the state from "substantially burdening a person's exercise of religion even if the burden results from a rule of general applicability" unless the state can demonstrate that this burden "(1) is in furtherance of a compelling government interest, and (2) is the least restrictive means of furthering that compelling governmental interest." One might see this Act as a legislative reenactment of *Sherbert v. Verner* (1963), which introduced those considerations of compelling state interest and least restrictive means that were ignored in *Smith*. The Act, however, was ruled unconstitutional in 1997 because it was said to exceed Congress's powers under the 14th Amendment.

Nussbaum elaborates the capabilities program in terms of a hypothetical expansion of the RFRA, in two parts: "first, that the principle of RFRA be accepted as the guiding principle in dealing with the religious dilemma. The state and its agents may impose a substantial burden on religion only when it can show a compelling state interest. *But*, second, protection of the central capabilities of citizens should always be understood to ground a compelling state interest: this is the way we interpret the principle of moral constraint and give content to the otherwise vague and amorphous notion of 'compelling state interest.' "[44] Nussbaum's proposal is hostile to the *Smith* decision in its shielding of religion from the generality requirement. A more generous interpretation of the free exercise clause might be expected, including the occasional exemption of religious believers from the normal burdens of secular law. But the shield is odd indeed since it assigns its protective belt only to those religions that pay tribute to the capabilities program. The state is to have a compelling interest in shaping religions toward a capabilities test that looks remarkably like a condition for liberal democracies.

The capabilities approach is an appealing program even as it fails. It is appealing because it offers support for those values that Western democracies regard as the highest mark of civilized life. The capability test is especially desirable to Western cultures whenever a religion is especially cruel and hateful toward some or all of its members, or endorses morally despicable policies such as racial discrimination. But the capabilities approach fails because it pretends to be a program of political liberalism when it actually is a progressive and proselytizing movement to extend liberal values into the domains of religious communities. Political liberalism, whatever else it does, tolerates illiberal values outside the parameters of the political system. The problem of church and state in political liberalism is how to regulate religions while respecting their values even when these values are illiberal.

One of the special attractions of Nussbaum's approach is in its awareness of the complexities and subtleties of religious communities. She is right to stress the heterogeneity of religious life and its capacity for change. She is also right in pointing out that religious extremism is often inconsistent with a religion's own traditions and just as often blatantly in the interests of powerful religious authorities. Nussbaum tells us (in *Women and Human Development*) that "a given form of immorality may at one time have been absolutely central to the beliefs and practices of the religion" (p. 197), but "that what makes religion worthy of a special place in human life (and of special political and legal treatment) is something having to do with ideals and aspirations" (p. 198), and, later, that "(t)he principle of moral constraint suggests to us that nothing of value is lost when we tell people that they cannot lord it over other people in immoral and harmful ways" (p. 235). But the problem is that it is also true that some religious traditions just are, in some legitimate sense, at odds with liberal values, often for good reasons drawn from the differences between religious and secular orientations. These traditions often cannot accommodate the capabilities program of values. One of the more important sources of genuine resistance is a view of the individual as subordinate to the community, and even as fused with collective states, with the consequence that meaning and value are thought to come from external structures (thus individuals are inspired by reality) rather than internal powers (instead of imagination). Classical Greece, and the Roman and Catholic traditions, stress the authority of institutions over the individual. The capabilities program seems post-Reformation in elevating individual over institutional authority, and accordingly biased toward the Protestant view of religion. It is also an approach opposed to the vast majority of collectivist orientations that have filled the world's religious cultures, now and throughout history.

On darker and more practical grounds, many religions do not endorse the values celebrated in liberalism. Two particularly vexing matters are the absence in religious practices of any form of sexual equality, or freedom of choice and/or equity in religious matters. But Nussbaum's program does subscribe to these values and requires that religions follow suit: ". . . nothing in my approach militates against separate systems of personal law, so long as these problems are solved: so long as (a) there are guarantees of sex equality in each . . . and these are enforced; (b) there is adequate provision for individuals who wish to define themselves as nonreligious or to change religions; and (c) there is a continual effort to ensure parity among the religious systems so that individuals do not lose out in basic matters because of the accident of their religious membership."[45] In short, good religions are very much like good liberal states. The capabilities program (there is no other way to view it) is an approach to religion which coercively extends admirable liberal values into religious communities that do not typically accept these values as a matter of religious belief and practice. Also, the state is to dominate religions in areas deemed vital by the state when religions and these particular state programs are in conflict. One may say, the capabilities approach to religion is excellent in terms of substantive values and acceptable priorities in political units, but still a failure as an equitable program for church and state.

7

The special standing of religious communities occasions the type of dilemma found in liberal approaches to non-liberal convictions. I will call it the dilemma of reverse image. It begins with the projection of the core of the liberal program, including especially the values of impartiality and fairness, on all others, and leads to the liberal impasse in dealing with religious beliefs and practices when the projection fails, represented most strongly in an asymmetry of values. Begin with the fact that the liberal perspective is very much influenced by the version of science emerging from the Enlightenment, particularly in the enshrinement of method as a prior origin of content. The political side of this approach elevates a blend of impartiality and tolerance to a privileged standing, and holds this felicitous combination as an instrument to understand and regulate the diversity of beliefs celebrated in the Reformation and the liberal version of a human community. The counter narrative in this account is the presence of beliefs that do not accord with the liberal vision of experience. The dilemma occurs as the liberal image is inverted by these beliefs. The liberal view is compelled to respect diversity, which requires accepting the standing of views contrary to liberalism. But the priority standing of liberalism also compels a judgment that illiberal values cannot be as good as liberal values, and certainly cannot be used to organize (or even influence—see the rejection of Creationism by liberals) a community because such views are regarded as inferior organizing devices. No liberal, for example, can accept a religious principle as a source of political authority. The standard result is a tension between tolerance and the moral privileging of liberal values.

The dilemma is this: in facing non-liberal views the liberal program can become just like any other ideology, bracketing a respect for diversity when beliefs exceed the program's boundaries of tolerance, or it can abandon its uncompromising belief in the superiority (established by impartiality and fairness) of the liberal program. The dilemma is that the forced choice of either of these alternatives has the same result: one contracts and perhaps compromises what it is to be a liberal, either in rejecting the genuine beliefs that emerge from the free exercise of choice, or in ceding authenticity and political standing to beliefs hostile to the core liberal program. It is worth noting that the superiority of liberalism is almost never a casualty in navigating these polar choices. The usual resolution of the dilemma, after the customary conversion pleas to non-liberals to be reasonable, is to contract the toleration part of the liberal program until it applies mainly to liberals. Board the train or remain behind on the platform, seems the tough-love liberal message that always rests on a hope for a world consisting of liberals. That this approach will not do in crafting church–state relations should be clear by now. But it is also important to see the more general point that the liberal program of impartial and fair treatment is possible, even with all of the *ceteris paribus* clauses in place, only if everyone is on message.

Another way to see this overriding need for liberal beliefs is in the expectations for good citizenship threading through most liberal tracts. When all of the arguments for adjudicating or managing hard disputes have been made, accepted, critiqued, it is an unassailable fact that liberal political theory requires a certain type of person in the political system. In Macedo's view, public reasonableness requires two virtues.[46] One is that "good citizens should seek to discern and abide by fair terms of cooperation" (p. 11). The second is "a willingness to acknowledge the fact of reasonable pluralism" (p. 12). In this shared framework, individuals respect each other's beliefs and practices, and rely on a public reason that is authoritative to the degree that citizens of the state can bracket their divisive views in the spirit of fairness and civility. The liberal person is much enchanted with the importance of mutual respect among adversaries (taking the other's arguments seriously by agreeing to disagree), prepared to look carefully at her own evidentiary base and rules of evidence and argument, always willing to subject her beliefs to the critical dialectic of another's arguments and to be persuaded away from one's deepest convictions if the counter arguments are good enough, and capable of dwelling comfortably within the judicious perspectives that define a fair and impartial surveyor (and vendor) of the right goods. This persona characterizes the good liberal citizen. It is a role widely recognized and generally welcomed in secular communities since discussions of the sort familiar to the Western scientific temperament are the choice of resolution for the liberal. Talk things through is the message, be fair to the other's point of view, and seek truth and fairness even when the pursuit and conclusions go against one's own interests.[47]

This intellectual style blends modesty and smugness in a strangely pleasing arrangement, and a sense of comfort and safety often follows its employment, especially among congenial thinkers. The political invitation which adorns the model of reasoning appears as the very essence of reasonableness: If persons want to be members of a liberal democracy, they must accept and work with certain rules and standards definitive of liberal thinking. But if sacred texts mean anything, they mean that there are certain religious matters that are utterly inaccessible to this mindset. A summons from the religious mission may require a whole sense of self with no residue for balance and impartial surveys among competing values. When the management of religious beliefs and practices is strictly liberal, it should be clear that the religious among liberals may not be able to buy into the complete set of regulatory mechanisms. Then the issue is whether tolerance for these different ways of thinking can be consistent with political liberalism, and, if not, whether there are other forms of dispute management, of governance among radically different communities, that can represent liberal values without the oppressive effects of liberal versions of reason and deliberation.

Infinite Regresses, Recursions, and Public Reason

One of the main conclusions of all of the arguments developed and presented here is that influential approaches to church and state in liberal democratic theory are wrong in most important respects. One source of the liberal error is in supposing that there is always a shared or common set of reasons that can be used for governing both religious and secular communities if only people are rational and reasonable. There can be a shared *framework* (not reasons) crafted by the universality of recursive systems, meaning that both religious and political practices are or can be forms of complex systems. But the differences between religion and politics can be substantial enough to divide and subdivide the languages in current versions of public reason and deliberative democracy into partisan portions, reducing all efforts at impartial or fair treatment to the very factions that the state is trying to manage. The secondary conclusion following the dismissal of a quest for reasons is that a form of governing must be found for religion and politics that depends not on the consensus seemingly required in the integrated democratic state, but on arrangements that fulfill more modest goals. It should be no surprise then that theorists might rationally choose avoidance paths away from the *intellectual* divisiveness that any deep heterogeneity in thought introduces to dispute management.

But these bracketing tactics cannot work. The Rawlsian tendency to keep out views because they are comprehensive and, as a consequence, divisive, and the exclusionary practices of deliberative democracy, are both self-defeating on many of the same grounds, perhaps of most importance that the state is then restricted from addressing exactly those issues that may be most in need of adjudication or mediation. Nor can a political program succeed that attempts to reduce religion to politics. Rawls's proviso, again, that religious languages can be useful if stated (in due course) in terms of political languages must be wrong even if true. We might, as Rawls does, assert as hypothesis that the religious rhetoric of Martin Luther King could have been reduced to political languages without loss of meaning, but the hypothesis would fail in missing the distinctive language of religious discourse as presented here (and elsewhere in religious studies).[1] The issue is how to manage religion without reducing it to another social practice, meaning that the interesting and more important problems of state–church occur as religion is ceded its preoccupations with divinity.

It is precisely these more radical differences illustrated by the gulf between divinity and the bounded forms of reason negotiated in liberal democracies that chart a need for different forms of public and deliberative reasoning appropriate for addressing communities that subscribe to divinity as an organizing concept. It is certainly plain that political disputes intertwined with divinity and the discussions that negotiate these disputes do not fit within the types of reasoning and deliberation elaborated in the main parts of liberal programs today. This much is also plain from the discussion here. The current programs of public reason and deliberative democracy are detached from political discourse. Political talk is infused with power and interests, and often dominated by rhetoric and persuasion. The ground rules of an objective inquiry are not the governing standards of such talk. The reasons are familiar: what we might call deliberative talk, found, for example, in a good university seminar, is often talk about ideas without much at stake, at its best an impartial inquiry into forms of truth. Political discourse is filled with partisan heat and high stakes. Everything can be at stake in politics, and the players are often driven by the need to make the case, guarantee the interests of the position or constituents. Dispassion is a lovely artifact that doesn't quite fit the heat and light, meaning the advocacy, of heightened political talk. In these conditions successful forms of political discourse may have to fuse coercion with argument, admit the controlled obscurity of game-theoretic conditions, and acknowledge that a successful political process must rely on a freestanding language that can include the most repugnant moral positions, the most unusual and idiosyncratic methods of thinking and talking, and exclude only those who will not seek a settlement, regardless of their standing as moral partners or even participants in a common way of reasoning and deliberating.

Let's put it in the form of missed opportunities. The vision of the state expressed in political liberalism suggests a form of reasoning demarcated from community languages and presenting opportunities to govern without the partisan vocabularies that frame community disputes. These free-standing languages of state represent the ancient dream of a public space in which authority finds judicious applications on the basis of justice or the common good. This space can also be the locus for a modern domain of reasoning, recursive and collateral, which offers the possibility of accommodating even those communities that may be morally and intellectually distinct, and, like religion, claim universal scope in the face of rival claims of universality. The independent and governing logic of such languages also can give practical force to the abstractions of first order languages, in both secular and sacred manifestations. Reason of state, drawn up as a benign discourse from actual political practices, is much in evidence in both politics and political theory from antiquity to the present. It may also be the key to managing the hard differences between religious and secular political cultures.

2

The search for a distinct political language, a form of practical reasoning that can adjudicate or at least manage radical disputes, begins with dialectical examinations of language. The origin tracks to classical philosophy, and perhaps even earlier. Plato frames the *Republic* with a dinner party scene in which the participants introduce a series of definitions for justice into the public space of the conversation, and these definitions are subject to a critical scrutiny that moves the discussion toward an essential definition of the term at issue. The truth sought by the conversation is secured through a reflexive interrogation of language. These types of recursive inquiries (though without the essentialist conclusions) are presented and negotiated in a wide range of intellectual traditions.[2] G.E. Moore's (1903) "open question" argument and H.L.A. Hart's (1961) secondary rules of law that address primary rules are more recent and standard examples of complex (though contracted) recursive systems with sustained powers to examine and re-examine themselves. The political reasoning shaped by these literatures is inclined to subject claims entered into political discourse to a sustained dialectical inspection, an exercise much in evidence in managing encounters between radically different claims, cultures or ways of life. The "bottom-up" pragmatism of these examinations differs from classical inquiry in its comfort with regresses as testimony for the tentative and provisional standing of truth.

One of the main sources of recursive logic is the existence of regresses in our patterns of thought. We *do* seem able to challenge statements endlessly as part of our linguistic grammars. The child's repetitive *why* question signals the beginnings of a philosophical inquiry that invites recursive examinations to move outside linguistic or system boundaries. An awareness of exit routes to levels of discourse outside a present, any present way of thinking and talking may be as old as language itself. All self-reflection seems, at least eventually, to inspire movements to external interpretations of words and things as we interrogate meanings and explanations. The limitation introduced by Gödel (and refined by Turing), that a consistent system is always incomplete, with the implication that the system will contain statements not provable with its rules and axioms but which can be proved within another system external to the first, is a modern and more severe expression of an ancient awareness. The human desire for coherent wholes, defined by consistency and completeness in Gödel's theorems, may be futile yet still demand an ascent to positions that are exogenous, located beyond particular and perhaps all modes of thought, an external realm of truth only partially accessible to the human intellect (a view that Goldstein, 2005, attributes to Gödel in depicting him as an unrepentant Platonist).

The most exacting route to external levels is the oldest, most puzzling, and traditionally thought to be closest to the divine. In Romantic perspectives infinity represents the ultimate transcendence in providing a concept without closure. Aczel (2000) reports that the Greeks discovered the concept of infinity between the fifth and sixth centuries BC.[3] The concept was immediately mysterious. It emerged from and elucidated some of the more enduring paradoxes in logic and mathematics. Zeno's paradoxes, darlings in logic discussions then and now, depend on an infinite divisibility of space and time. The Pythagoreans worked with the concept of infinity in number theory. In accepting one as the generator of all numbers they understood that numbers are sequentially infinite. There is no ultimate number since one can always be added to any number, no matter how large. The concept of infinity was assigned a mystical standing and absorbed into religious movements in the medieval ages, though it has always been studied in lucid terms by mathematicians and philosophers (including Augustine, Aquinas, Galileo, Cantor, Newton, Leibniz, and Gödel).

Among the more intriguing expressions of infinity are the infinite regresses indicated in algebra. As metaphor they present the ultimate speedway away from any point in discourse by identifying an exit route without an end point. Regresses without an end also suggest limitations of the human intellect in coping with concepts of infinity. The prospect of infinite movement is almost unthinkable, sometimes paradoxical when manageable categories of thought are brought to bear on it. Infinity has always been the rocket fuel for both the promise of transcendence and our most unbearable insights into the limitations of human thinking. One can understand how infinity has been assigned to the realm of God in so many religious movements. But the introduction of divinity also reverses the infinity path for many religions. An infinite regress goes from a lower to a higher (and endless) area, but in divinity the infinite area provides the text that extends as a form of dominance to the lower realm. A strong sense of religious transcendence can require that primary meaning in the temporal originate in the higher reaches of the infinite.[4] One consequence of infinite regresses is that the voice of religious conscience may be impervious to appeals crafted within bounded forms of reason.

Political theorists have provided some of the more prominent braking systems in social thought in addressing infinite regresses, and usually the halting devices are separable according to whether they are a part of the political process or external to it. Hobbes, for example, presents and resolves a type of infinite regress. In rethinking the concept of authority lodged in law he points out that "all laws, written and unwritten, have need of interpretation" (*Leviathan*, pp. 205–6). The need for interpretation takes us to an interpreter, who then as sovereign provides ultimate, meaning final, authority, which the law cannot supply since interpretation *simpliciter* can be endless. This proposition, a standard disclosure in any beginning study of the *Leviathan*, leads to Hobbes's state-of-nature arguments for the establishment of a sovereign power, an individual (or group) who will halt the infinite regresses of interpretation anticipated in a system of authority based on law. The dominance of process, of *politics*, in these conditions is critical. The absolute sovereign is a halting device originating in the internal logic of Hobbes's view of the political process. It is roughly the method used by H.L.A. Hart in presenting a rule of recognition as a device drawn from the legal process to set parameters for what counts as law.

Much of political philosophy, however, is devoted to halting devices that are external to the political process. In classical and medieval periods the primary concerns in political philosophy were to ascertain the good, or identify principles of justice, by discovering external references that instruct on the proper ways to organize a human community. Plato marked the form of the Good as the ultimate stopping point in our reflections, providing light and knowledge and authority that cannot be surpassed. It is a transcendent principle that justifies political authority but also is used to make subordinate forms and sense experience intelligible. Rawls's (1971) original position of choice is a hybrid device. It is in one sense exogenous, in another a heuristic construction amenable to revisions according to our moral intuitions. The famous thought experiment that formally expresses liberal perspectives on fairness also halts a regress of justifications by invoking a device external to politics (the OP) as a source of governing principles. The OP just *is* the device that halts a string of justifications with basic conditions of fairness that yield principles of justice, and these principles are not drawn from any description of the political process. In a deviant sense the OP shares conceptual ground with Plato's form of the Good in providing an external reference that will yield principles to evaluate and govern the political process. In its heuristic guises the OP is a frame for reflection, revisable in terms of the "reflective equilibrium" that invites a re-thinking of one's moral premises. But in both senses the OP originates outside political processes, meaning that it is not shaped by politics. It stands as an external device to evaluate politics.

The need for halting devices has traditionally seemed compelling within languages of state, perhaps for the same reason that infinite regresses are troublesome in ordinary languages. The thought is that if every principle or rule generates a higher or alternative version in an endless and seamless progression it would be impossible to govern on other than a provisional basis mired in the briefest of time frames. Throughout its long history political theory seems designed to establish a reasonable and bounded certainty in political rule. A halting device stops the appellate powers of reflection with a device that justifies authority. A finite hierarchy reassures by identifying where repetitive why questions must rationally stop. Closure seems almost the signature statement of a political system, its point of separation from anarchy.

3

The first peculiar and unsettling thing about regresses is that their effects, at least in an epistemic sense, are unlimited. The second is the ease with which these effects are underestimated. One might anticipate that exogenous devices are vulnerable to the appellate powers of language given that the methods for justifying them are typically external to the process they are designed to control. Rawls's OP, for example, is justified with notions of fairness contestable by alternatives drawn from rival theories. The possibilities for a string of contestations over foundations seem themselves to be boundless in this intellectual setting. One would expect that this kind of recursive examination would be more successfully limited by halting devices derived from within the political process. But process fares no better. Hobbes, for example, solves coordination dilemmas not by invoking higher principles but with coercion-grounded guarantees of reciprocity that ensure cooperation among rational agents who cannot live together successfully in the absence of the guarantees. The problem and the solution for Hobbes are political in nature. He stops infinite regresses of interpretation with a final arbiter on political order, the ultimate authority of a sovereign drawn directly from and justified within the logic of the political process itself, not in terms of objective or external justifications. But if Hobbes is right he is also wrong on the matter of epistemic closure for any sequence of justifications. The sovereign can no more stop infinite regresses of interpretation with superior or final justifications than can any other resource. His orders, and even the process by means of which he is established, will be subject to the same interpretive regresses that warrant the establishment of a sovereign power in the first place.[5]

This admission, however, highlights a range of more subtle halting efforts. For example, the methods of binding arbitration that replicate Hobbes's form of dispute management today—in labor disputes and salary arbitration in sports, for example—are rarely opened for the kind of critical interpretation that reintroduces regresses of interpretation. The two readily available and transparent reasons for this are that (a) the parties bringing claims to the arbitrator, while engaged in a dispute that they are unable to resolve on their own, are still part of a community exercise in which the meanings of the controlling languages are shared at some level deep enough to dispel ambiguity over what the arbitrator intends by her decision, and (b) the power to specify meaning and enforce an interpretation are both with the arbitrator, and are also unlimited and not subject to appeal.

The first set of reasons is set up with an acknowledgment that at least some statements in all languages are regarded as having a kind of core standing, beyond radical dispute. The long traditions of naturalism testify to this belief. Classical notions of essence, more recent proposals for nominal essences (Kripke's "rigid designators"), various linguistic retentions, even Mill's acceptance of settled truth claims—language itself in certain conditions seems to provide a kind of inertia that counts against the chronic contestations over truth or meaning that a radical dialectic proposes. Epistemic closure is secured by the resistance of some areas of language to contestation.[6] On the second set of reasons, the appellate chain is closed by coercion, not justification. The regress of interpretation is not so much stopped as bracketed. Individuals may still contest a text within the parameters of discourse, but not for practical effect. This is the approach Hobbes uses with the introduction of a sovereign who ends all political or *public* interpretations shaped and proposed for political effect.

These are two of the ways in which social practices can limit and contain infinite regresses: deep consensus and power, though each seems to require a different societal order. In some ways it is a melancholy polarity. Deep consensus can stultify, with comfort to the participants, the natural openness of language and intellect, the possibility that the interpretation of any statement can be challenged. Coercion can bracket these powers and possibilities by fiat. These two patterns vie with the role of exogenous devices in justifying a halt to regresses on argumentative grounds (e.g., by theorists like Plato and Rawls). In a sense, exogenous principles seek to impose a consensus on the grounds of compelling public justifications, while theorists like Hobbes simply impose a rational and egoistically driven halt to infinite regresses on the grounds of an internal argument that, without a coercive intervention, instruments of closure can always be reinterpreted endlessly.

The reliance on consensus in political philosophy always seems both difficult and promising, often simultaneously. Rawls suggests that a suitable pluralist democracy must rely on an overlapping consensus. If we draw a Venn diagram of beliefs a formal overlapping consensus might be charted on the intersections of the beliefs. But even on an overlap that represents sameness in beliefs across communities the agreement supposed by the intersections might be specious. Two communities, for example, might have identical beliefs (subscribe to P) that are independently derived and justified. This would be an accidental correlation, in no way dependent on any connection between the communities that might constitute a shared consensus.[7] Or is an overlapping consensus a kind of family resemblance pattern with crisscrossing threads of beliefs but no belief shared by all? Then there is the matter of levels of language and thought, and the presence also of multiple practices and discourses that might overlap only as derivatives from each other. Rawls (1997) seems to regard political views as derivable from other views, and suggests that agreement on the political conception can be derived from comprehensive doctrines, including those that are religious. For example, in footnote 46 of "The Idea of Public Reason Revisited" he discusses two contrary interpretations of Shari'a (divine law for Muslims) and observes that the early Mecca interpretation of the text, which favors equality between the sexes, can support some forms and dimensions of constitutional democracy. Or, democratic norms can on occasion be derived even from sacred religious texts. But of course a derivation, unlike a Venn diagram, is not obvious, at least at first, it has to be produced, and both the rules of derivation and the derivation itself may be contestable. We might also expect different derivation rules as we move across contexts, especially across radically different communities.

Even if derivation and interpretation rules are uniform across communities, and an overlapping consensus indicates a genuine agreement among communities on the standing of texts and the rules of derivation and interpretation brought to bear on texts, this consensus might mask a deeper disagreement on the meaning of the items on which there is an agreement. In the case of Galileo and the Church, an identical subscription to the divine truth of Scripture issued by the scientist and the religious authorities did not forestall an acrimonious disagreement on the interpretation of sacred texts, and on the meaning of Scripture and its implications for the physics of the times. All of these remarks parse the widespread view that consensus is complex and remote as a realistic goal in pluralist societies. It is typically contestable on sense and reference, and when a definition is settled consensus typically occurs at multiple levels and is secured by rival procedures. It is exactly the layered demands of consensus that make a full agreement (on the political structure, the rules and outcomes of the political process, the reasons for an outcome) so difficult and a thin version of consent so appealing (agreement on outcomes for private and possibly different reasons).

Yet, in spite of the near legendary difficulties in establishing consensus, here is a clear and curious point about Western societies. A variety of institutions and practices have procedures that do produce consensual outcomes from disagreements or the absence of agreement. Two such prominent practices are science and law.[8] Science may be the most over-described practice in modern history, with all the contestable understandings expected in a depiction of an iconic practice. But one unassailable feature of science is its ability to move from pluralism to at least provisional consensus. The starting condition of scientific inquiry is a set of rival hypotheses on some state of affairs. The successful (and provisional) end point is a consensus on the retention of hypotheses that (in Karl Popper's felicitous phrase) have resisted falsification. In courts of law the starting point is a kind of formal disagreement, a competing set of claims on guilt or innocence, culpability or blamelessness. The conclusion of a trial (barring a breakdown like a hung jury or a mistrial) is a consensus on one or another of the claims that initiate a legal process. In both practices an accepted procedure grinds out a consensus from what might be called pluralism in viewpoints that are at least occasionally quite diverse and even acrimonious.

How do these kinds of practices work? There is no mystery here. They work because they rely on an acceptance *of relevant particulars*, an agreement on the type of text at issue and a formal endorsement of rules of evidence, inference and argument distinctive of the practice. Courts of law are paragons for making these rules explicit. This is not to say that the rules of legal proceedings are fixed. They vary with revised understandings of law and courts, and any given version of these rules is contested and contestable. But even in the most rancorous contests the rules are visible and on most occasions sharply rendered. The same thing may be said of science. Rules of evidence, inference and argument display the working methods of scientists, and disagreements within the practice over the truth or falsity of a statement are adjudicated with these rules. Again, the rules are disputable, but in any given historical period they are in play and on display. Note that the conclusions drawn from these procedures are also contestable, and revisable on changes in (primarily) evidence and fresh understandings of the practices. The legal process arguably has the most organized appellate system of review to overturn conclusions. But science (unlike law) undergoes sea changes in the most comprehensive of its explanations (as Kuhn has argued). What is constant, however, is a revisable but chronically visible set of definitive rules for producing consensus from specific types of dissonance.

The possibility of divisiveness in democratic pluralism obviously limits shared reasons or mutual reasonableness across communities and individuals as a reconciling force in managing disagreement. The easiest and most helpful lesson drawn from this is that the political process is and is not capable of relying on such procedures. It is capable of identifying information relevant to political purposes. This information is predictably attuned to collective action, and drawn up from a concern to rank order frames for beliefs rather than the beliefs themselves. By this is meant that in all political systems, but especially in pluralistic democracies organized on liberal principles, the state is not mainly in the business of governing by settling the truth of competing claims (epistemic or realist) but by criteria that are outside these matters and governed by collective considerations (like Mill's harm thesis). Political reasoning is simply not evidence-based reasoning in the strong sense in which models of practical and theoretical reasoning typically are in justifying beliefs on evidence. The rational exercise of political authority depends on evidence, but not necessarily of the sort used to determine the truth of claims entered into public space. In the abortion dispute, for example, the state would consider evidence for the effects of certain arrangements between pro-choice and pro-life on the collective values of stability, security, efficiency, institutional continuity and change, perhaps equity, and so on, but not necessarily consider evidence to support or deny the validity of the rival claims. These are the great values of politics, and they do not represent just the liberal inventory of values, nor are they necessarily appropriate for individual reasoning. Put another way, political practices at the state level may be required to modify or maintain the conditions in which a practice is located, or directly govern any practice, including law and science, with the implication in either case that the state cannot mimic or replicate any particular practice.

It is not entirely fanciful to see the orientations to composition at collective levels as a rough guide to settling on relevance criteria for information. But the distinguishing point is that state reasoning cannot be completely boxed into a rigid sense of the relevant. It is part of the pragmatic logic of the state that all methods, rules, and criteria be regarded as indigenous, topics for recursive scrutiny. Recursion is a feature of all complex systems, including law and science. But the wide and even vast range of heterogeneous items that can be candidates for political action in a pluralist society seems to invite a thicker set of quick and possible changes in relevance for political action than found in more settled and clearly defined practices *within* a political system. The state, after all, and like a committee of committees, must itself be somewhat outside the practices and communities that constitute the political society. Politics, as an outside game, seems to require recursive powers in the form of complex systems that can examine and re-examine even practices like science and law.

4

A theoretical approach to infinite regresses and recursive examinations exists that does not depend on any halting devices. This third approach is discussed in various literatures, and seems especially appropriate in crafting an effective theory of public or political reasoning that cannot be bounded by the consensual procedures of practices within a political system. Aczel (2000, chapter 2) documents Georg Cantor's work in set theory that presents circles of bounded infinity nested in other circles, the set ascending to higher levels of infinity. It may be one indication of a common strand that the metaphor of ordered circles is found in mathematics, philosophy (with Quine's web of concentric circles), religion (the visual image of the Kabala as nested circles of infinities), and Dante's presentation of the nine circles of Hell in the Inferno in the first book of *The Divina Commedia* (where the metaphor assumes the form of a descent to the center of Hell). Religious senses of conscience, perhaps the most intense form of divinity in experience, present the core problem in secular contacts with the religious, which is the need to forge a relationship between the infinite and the bounded in political practices. The core suggestion in the nested-circle metaphor is that infinite regresses can be managed (meaning presented intelligibly) within bounded levels of language when the levels are ordered in one way or another within a complex system. In nested or concentric circles there is no obvious stopping point.

Something like the arrangement of levels of language, as mediated by the recursive mechanisms in complex systems, can manage political disputes without a halting device. Put more directly, there is no need or possibility of halting points in complex systems. Process is all, and that's a good and realistic thing in systems theory. It works this way. As a starting premise within this third approach, all of the exogenous references offered in political philosophy are regarded as inextricably bound to the political process. The term "reasonable," for example, though a condition for public reason and democratic deliberation, is a political term and so is in play on the field of politics. So too is Rawls's Original Position and Plato's Form of the Good, or any of the languages offered as exogenous standards for politics. The paths of political influence differ among the exogenous candidates. For intuitionists like Plato the influence path toward the Good is cut on a need to interpret a term that is mysterious by definition and open to a wide set of meanings (or closed as a disguised and duplicitous form of interest expression).

The Original Position is burdened with disputes over the characterization of the original agents, the conditions for rational selection of principles, the thickness of the veil, and other conversation pieces. With a more tangible concept like "reasonable" the influence path is carved in assigning the term to ordinary language contexts. For example, what is reasonable in the abortion dispute will be a function of whether one believes or does not believe that abortion is a type of homicide. In the language of the times we can say that the use and perhaps even the meaning of the term "reasonable" are captured by background moral and political beliefs that define the action toward which one measures the appropriateness of being reasonable. In these conditions exogenous references are not the external standards of review (as they are presented by their champions) but simply a different species of a language game within the political process.[9]

In a rudimentary frame for complex systems we might stretch or array parts in a complete account of political reasoning along the obvious fault lines carved by conditions and what might be called sidebar methods. The basic exercise is a familiar one in microeconomics. Segregating conditions and decision rules is a staple approach in decision theory, which in its most standard form demarcates conditions of certainty, risk, and uncertainty, and assigns appropriate decision rules to these conditions. Basically, certainty is established when the connection between an alternative and its outcome is set by a probability of 1. Risk means that the probability between the two is between 1 and 0, and in conditions of uncertainty the probabilities are unknown, and cannot be used. Conditions of certainty assume optimization techniques, those of risk allow the development of Bayesian decision rules that combine probabilities and expected values to yield a utility ordering of alternatives, and conditions of uncertainty require rules of dominance, maximax, maximin, or more esoteric tests like the Savage regret criterion. The point is that what it is to be rational will be a function of ascertaining the conditions in which one is located, selecting the right decision rule appropriate for the conditions, and then choosing the alternative indicated by the use of the rule. When decision theory is joined to theories of games (both cooperative and noncooperative) how other players act also must be part of one's rational calculations. Again, decision theory presents a sequence of three distinct and different decisions in any rational action. One is a decision (determination, judgment) that identifies the set of conditions the actor occupies. A second is a decision (choice, selection) of the appropriate decision rule for the conditions. The third segment in the sequence is the use of the decision rule to select (make a decision on) an alternative.

With this rudimentary account of decision theory in place, we can say that at a formal background level in politics we can locate the mechanisms that survey and order the conditions which fix the appropriateness of methods for managing disputes. But unlike microeconomics the political exercise is not vitally concerned with the probability relations between alternatives and outcomes. Instead the demarcation among conditions will be set according to other matters, like the degree and content of consensus among reasoning actors and the types of issues (whether primary or secondary goods, moral or nonmoral, etc.) in play. A robust set of political methods will contain such items as arbitration, mediation, bargaining, game theoretic tactics, *modus vivendi* approaches, and of course some species of deliberation. What it means to be rational in politics, in this case to reason successfully, will be similar to microeconomics, however, in conjoining the selection of political methods (that manage disputes or secure prudential goods) according to conditions. The arrangement of background mechanism, conditions, and methods describes a systemic approach to state reasoning that allows the recursive powers of reason, its self-reflective capacities, to be in use primarily at the background level, but also in terms of the assignment and modification of methods and even conditions in the process of political action.

Once we allow a spreadsheet on which to arrange the constituent parts of political reasoning, an arrangement designed according to the appellate oversights of a background mechanism, then some intriguing possibilities occur. Many of these possibilities are partially explored in political theory. Rawls, for example, allows the abolitionists a kind of free reign because the political systems of the times were not well-ordered. A well-ordered political system would not, in Rawls's view, provide justifications for this kind of confrontationally inspired change based on comprehensive doctrines. Conditions, in short, dictate the appropriateness of strong and even revolutionary dissent, meaning that at least some part of public reasoning involves a survey of conditions. But this is a tactic only partially successful in Rawls's theories of public reason because, of course, the definition of a well-ordered society is itself a contestable matter. A more robust contestation, one that addresses conditions like a well-ordered society, supports a political system capable of conducting surveys over all items relevant to politics.

It is important to note that, like most theorists who rely on exogenous devices (the OP in this instance), Rawls is reluctant to subject privileged concepts—reasonableness, for example, which typically remains outside the political process—to critical scrutiny. He is also concerned to shape process, for example, public reason, away from unstable influences. In the well-known assertion, comprehensive doctrines that, by virtue of their temerity in attempting to provide a complete account of human experience, are excluded in Rawls's domains of public reason on the grounds that they might be disruptive, offensive or divisive, maybe just intolerable to other citizens, or—unreasonable. In a partial sense the clash between theories oriented to exogenous devices and those to process is a bit similar to the intellectual tension between Lamarckian design supporting the permanence of species (by means of the belief that acquired characteristics are inherited) and Darwinian natural selection. Design approaches to nature regard species as permanent, or, better, corrigible primarily on the terms of genetic laws outside the environmental processes of natural selection that we now know are the primary sources of change in biological variables. Darwinian biology accepts variability for all forms and levels of life with a process orientation that excludes nothing from the environmental influences of natural selection (though these influences are mediated by the natural laws of biology). Hyper and moderate Darwinists might and do argue about the intrinsic logic of the evolutionary process (including its pace) and the rank ordering of process variables, but the parameters of the arguments still maintain the dominance of process (and change).[10]

All of this work is testimony, in different ways, to the high standing of a continuing and critical examination of propositions in public space. In Mill's political society there are no privileged political matters outside public debate, no cherished political concepts shielded from the recursive powers of the dialectic, and no exogenous items relevant to but outside the political process. Nor can matters be held out of politics on grounds that they are divisive, offensive, or impolite. One prominent casualty of a thoroughgoing or systemic recursive inquiry is the stipulation by Rawls that political actors must constrain themselves in presenting comprehensive views to those who could not accept such views. In Rawls's version of the political process the good citizen must restrict herself to introducing views that other citizens could reasonably accept. But a recursive system can allow, and in fact invites and even demands, a range of views into the political process that extends beyond this "reasonable" threshold. It is the political process itself that mediates and constrains competing views, not the self-restraint of political actors.

Mill's justifications for a dialectical examination of opinions in public space are well known and serve as warnings against individual restraint in political speech. The best opinions are those that provisionally survive a critical examination, and, in a rare joining of deontic and utilitarian values, the benefits of free speech affect both the community and the individual (whose nature demands free expression). Like Popper's introduction of falsification in the twentieth century, the system of critical inspection works best when the views introduced to the open dialectic are more not less contentious, and the dismissal tests more not less critical. In vetting even extreme views science eliminates nonsense with tests that dismiss or falsify them. The parallel argument bearing on a political system is that a human community is better able to moderate dangerous opinions that would be even more dangerous if kept out of open scrutiny. Popper urged that hypotheses be subject to the most demanding critical tests, and maintained only if they survive arduous efforts to falsify them. Mill demanded that all opinions enter critical discussions to determine whether they survive. Individual restraint which shields unreasonable propositions from a dialectical examination would undermine critical testing in both science and politics. Rawls's polite and politic version of individual constraint in political discussion is an odd elevation of internal checks and balances, of individual reason, of a kind of *internalized* process, over the same functions that seem better carried out at more external and systemic levels. But a strong reliance on process is also an invitation to leave the box and collapse distinctions between internal and external levels. The synoptic pragmatism of Mill and Popper seems to demand a surrender of internal checks and balances, an extension of self to process in the adjudication of disputes and claims.

5

Recent work in cognitive science and systems theory offers promissory notes for a sea change in the collective vocabularies and expectations of political theory. These shifts in concepts suggest a different frame for mediating disputes involving religious beliefs and practices. We can begin scanning this literature with the thought that at least part of the package of any credible form of reasoning must be contained in the background institutional arrangements that complement thinking and represent the powers of the brain to conjure scripts away from its environment (however defined). A renewed emphasis on institutional arrangements raises questions about distinctions between internal and external variables. It is surely true that we reason in terms of the institutions in which we are located, and these institutions are so deeply a part of our thinking that we cannot completely demarcate mind and environment. It is also true that the mind, our thinking apparatus, can construct representational scripts, images and symbols away from its environment. We have an internal life, in other words, and this ability to conjure internal texts probably is the most important distinction between the computational powers of machines and the human brain (so far as we know).[11] Finally, the arrangements of culture, including the specific differentiations that yield demarcations among practices, differ greatly, so that we reason in different ways depending on the background structures that are our references.

The generic model of reason that is emerging from the biological and cognitive sciences, and meeting these conditions, is pragmatic in the extreme, largely amounting to (in Andy Clark's formulation) "a rag-bag of 'quick and dirty' on-line stratagems." The larger picture is a complex and appealing demarcation of mind and environment coupled with a suspicion that the two could ever be clearly and utterly demarcated. Again, let Clark put the case. "The idea, in short, is that advanced cognition depends crucially on our abilities to *dissipate* reasoning: to diffuse achieved knowledge and practical wisdom through complex social structures, and to reduce the loads on individual brains by locating those brains in complex webs of linguistic, social, political, and institutional constraints." Put succinctly: "Our brains make the world smart so that we can be dumb in peace! Or, to look at it another way, it is the human brain *plus* these chunks of external scaffolding that finally constitutes the smart, rational inference engine we call mind" (citations are in Clark, 1998, p. 180).

The thing is that the scaffolding varies, and presents radically different opportunities and demands to the mind. Clark (1999) gives the example of a task: "to decide on an optimum placement of footpaths to connect a complex of already-constructed buildings (say, on a new university campus)." Clark describes the traditional strategy of "global, rationalist design" in which a plan is formed from data on geography, numbers of pedestrians, building design, and so on. A second strategy is to do nothing, and then, after a few months, check and plan according to the paths formed by pedestrians as they move through the grass and dirt among the buildings. The second is a type of bottom-up approach, meaning that the solution emerges from actions and practices, not from a rational, preconceived plan (Clark, p. 79). A process version of public reasoning may yield to the path development of bottom-up strategies in crafting rules and principles from a posteriori patterns, but also must find a locus for normative languages in using these patterns to govern actions. At some point in reasoning we must be advised about what we ought to do, and why, and this normative component cannot simply be following the paths carved just by behavior. Politics must also be recursive in examining and reexamining the texts that define practices, and contain something like those understandings of the whole society assumed even in incompletely theorized agreements (Sunstein, 1995, 2003) and politically sensitive mutual accommodations (Wertheimer, 1999).

One can also expand any theory of political reasoning by defining rational agency and the core patterns of reasoning in more imaginative ways than found in prevailing literatures. Two types of dualism influence Western democratic theory and practice. One is the property dualism (mind–body) that has superseded Descartes' substance dualism (soul–body). The other is the dualism separating self and surroundings (practice dualism). Recent literatures in cognitive science have extended the self to body and to the external artifacts that make good thinking a possibility (overviews in Damasio, 1994, and Clark, 1999). It is difficult to find anyone today who is prepared to sever mind from body in anything like property dualism. We seem to think and feel in terms of bodily resources, and these resources cannot intelligibly be stripped from our cognitive powers. The harder step is the introduction of external resources to the thinking act and definitions of the self, which would amount to a contraction of practice dualism. Clark discusses the cases of neurologically impaired individuals who get along only by relying on dense layers of support in their environments. He cites the example (proposed by Clark and Chalmers, 1995) of an impaired individual who relies constantly on a notebook filled with cues, instructions, directions, and the like that is a literal necessity in his thinking and acting. The issue is whether the destruction of this notebook is property theft or an injury to the person every bit as serious as an assault. One is inclined to see the destruction as a personal injury to the self, an assault on the mind of the individual. The general point is that the mind is not confined to the physical self. We all use elaborate external machinery, including language itself, that makes thinking a complex form of collective activity that extends far beyond the parameters of the body (assuming we even know what that term means).[12]

The upshot of this recent work is that the standard dualisms of mind–body, and self–environment, are uncertain, perhaps candidates for dismissal. What are the implications of abandoning these venerable fictions? At the very least the discussion is shifted to a different venue that redefines how we talk about political matters. Styles of thinking depend on the external scaffolding of mind, and the self in all cases extends quite naturally to these surroundings. The extension cannot be complete, of course, because consciousness is individually situated in the human brain. But books, texts, the general instruments of navigation— the paraphernalia in terms of which we are thinking selves—are the materials on which we achieve our mental identities. In a looser framework we might see some of these external resources as the background narratives that inform and guide social practices (e.g., Arendt, 1998).

It is on these terms that distinctions between the internal self and the external world may collapse. The sharpest divide in political theory may be between those theorists oriented to external conditions and those concerned primarily with internal landscapes. Marx is probably the prototype externalist, preferring to reform human communities by rearranging the conditions in which we live and think. Rawls is the latest in a long line of political philosophers (dating to Plato and moving through Kant) who stress the reform of attitudes and beliefs as the locus of reconciliation. These literatures in cognitive science suggest that the dichotomy is wrong. If we need external scaffolding to think effectively, then the scaffolding, as an extension of mind and thus *both* internal and external, invites its own shaping and coordinating. We may have to move external resources (like institutions) around to secure proper thinking, and shift mindsets as a way of defining and reforming societal arrangements, all in the spirit of denying the polarity between mind and environment that theorists have long championed. A process orientation to politics and public reason that is comfortable with the recent bracketing of dualisms is also happily free of most of the main distinctions between external and internal dimensions. In terms of public reason, our understandings of how we think suggests that we adjudicate our differences on a conceptual space that is grander than the strictures of conscience and internal restraints required of the good liberal citizen. States of mind are otiose on the terms of recent cognitive studies, a dialectical process of politics much the finer venue for mediating disputes.

If we work with the expectations of cognitive science, the systemic differences between religious and secular discourses are very much in the scaffolding of experience, in particular the ways in which the panoply of mental resources acts on the self. For starters, we might ask how and to what dimensions the nature of a practice summons an extension of the self. The secular (skeptical, pragmatic) state of mind relies on texts that are artifacts of intellectual efforts, and extends mental powers to the limits of achievements that are always provisional maps through experience. The religious state of mind at least occasionally relies on notebooks that are regarded as hand-me-downs from higher levels of reality. On the acceptance of levels of being there is in principle no limits to the extension of the self, and in some religions (Buddhism) the self is fulfilled when absorbed into being itself.[13] The mind of God, in the favorite phrase of some physicists, may even be accessible to, and perhaps within, the higher stretches of the self. This scaffolding teases the self into a cognitive awakening ready for discoveries viewed as illicit and even impossible inquiries from a secular perspective. The obvious parallel in Western religious thought is with the Gnostic tradition in Christianity, especially the Gospels of Thomas instead of John, where it is argued that divinity is within each of us, waiting to be brought out. The invisible but real line connecting the inner and external selves in cognition represents the Gnostic avoidance of religious dualisms separating humans from a higher and definitely external God.[14]

Clark, more cautious from the vantage point of cognitive science, says this: "It is thus only when the relationship between user and artifact is about as close and intimate as that between the spider and the web that the bounds of the self—and not just those of computation and broadly cognitive process—threaten to push out into the world."[15] Think now of a spider whose web is not an artifact constructed by the spider but a discovery of something created or founded by other forms of life, say the owner of the house. The spider uses this web as a fulfillment of its nature, and becomes more than the original spider by allowing the web to absorb its activities in the most symbiotic fashion imaginable. The spider and the web are now one, and also transcendent in representing vistas beyond the spider's powers of creation and even understanding. This is the spectacular stuff of religious beliefs—discovery, intimacy with the distant, absorption, complexity, transcendence, discovery within the self, transformation, mystery. There is no caution needed here in demarcating these thoughts, and the influences on them, from all versions of secular thinking.

6

Ernest Gellner has presented three contemporary practices on which a systems frame can be expressed, each arranged along the (simple and heuristic) axes of bounded and transcendent modes of thought: religion in the form of Islamic fundamentalism, postmodernism, and science.[16] These are broad and sometime coarse distinctions, they cannot be taken beyond their very limited lexical definitions without distortion, but they offer an intellectual spreadsheet for crafting the uses of systems theory in accommodating religion and politics. The identifying features of the Islam that Gellner presents are comfortably ensconced in a strong version of more-or-less standard understandings of religion. Truth is both realist (not constructed but discovered) and revealed, and refers to a particular form of external domain identified as transcendent, meaning in this case a reality beyond and outside the conventional worlds of human experience. It is not clear exactly what world Gellner refers to given that many religious communities accepting transcendence do so literally, believing that access to a higher reality is very much a part of human experience. But we can understand the transcendence of a religious experience to be a partial contact with something other-worldly, perhaps analogous to the infinite, as this world is drawn up from the perspectives of those who do not believe in such limitless alternative realities.

The direct opposite of this sense of the religious is postmodernism, which dismisses realist truth (sometimes also epistemic truth).[17] In all versions of postmodernism reality is a construction of the subject, and truth is one more artifact of the way we live and think. If polar extremes exist in human experience there is no clearer expression of extremes than these two approaches. One would be pressed even to imagine an intelligible conversation about the parameters of human experience between one who accepts the dominance of a higher reality outside human meanings and one who believes that all of reality is some form of human construction. The contemporary world gives daily testimony to the difficulties of such communication.

Gellner suggests a very powerful and persuasive third way between and in some sense outside of these two communities. He calls it Enlightened Secular Fundamentalism. He means modern science insulated from the shaping effects of culture. This version of science is unquestionably one of the great developments in human experience. The story that Gellner sketches is well known. The Enlightenment witnessed the development of methods and assumptions that have produced an entirely different history than any of the discourses prior to modern science. One of the assumptions is that there is an independent reality beyond any culture, but accessible to methods that combine theory and observation. Revelation is not a part of the methodological package. Reality is described and explained (at least ideally) with nomothetic laws which are symmetrical, meaning that they present an orderly nature that is invariant across cultural differences, and no word from a deity is needed to round off the accounts. The scientific approach to experience admits no privileged truth, observation, or fact. Every statement, no matter how precious or important, is (in Karl Popper's phrase) no more than a hypothesis that has so far resisted disproof. What is privileged in science is its method, which, again ideally, deconstructs (sorry) experience to atomistic units, and then provides universal laws that explain how it all works.

Two prominent revisions of this view of science offer a more complex view of Gellner's distinctions. The first is the recent movement away from the scientific reductionism, originating in the late seventeenth century, which breaks items down into constituent parts and then explains events in terms of the properties of the parts and interactions among them. This methodological individualism views wholes as no more and no less than products of individual descriptions and simple (usually arithmetical) composition rules. Contemporary science is more inclined to accept emergent properties that are either holistic properties of complex systems, or the result of exceedingly complex interactions among parts that must take into account holistic properties. In either case reasonably complex systems are not amenable to analysis in the reductionist sense.

Second, it is interesting that modern science offers a kind of transcendence, though not typically (except perhaps in physics) accompanied by the reverence that Galileo and then later Newton, Einstein, and Hawking bestow on the physical universe. Gellner argues, in ways unlike the efforts of postmodern thought to shape theory to the local contours of indigenous cultures, and unlike the religious belief that we can ascend in some way to another world, that science presents an objective reality within the world but outside any given culture. Its conclusions are products of methods that are, at least in Gellner's terms, culture-neutral. But of course the reasonable question raised so often today is, how can any practice be culture-neutral, or even trans-cultural? What we might call a fourth way (not recognized by Gellner) is the version of science that has followed the work of Kuhn and others in recognizing links between science and culture that shape theory without absorbing it in local frameworks.[18] Thus Newton could follow the paths of alchemy forged by his culture and use these incursions into the occult to vitalize his work in physics.[19] Or, more broadly, the grand achievements of science in any age are influenced by the representative and indigenous models of the host culture. As example, consider the mechanical models employed by Newtonian physics at the dawn of the industrial age. Still, Gellner has suggested useful distinctions between religion and science even when science is in some ways controlled by holistic concepts and influenced by culture. We might say that religious truth is available as truth only from the inside, meaning to those who believe, and this internal commitment can be a conduit to the ultimate outside of a transcendent reality. The religious experience is an odd joining of subjective alignment with the highest form of objectivity. Scientific truth is accessible ideally to those who are committed to being outsiders, meaning impartial spectators who take an objective stance. The occupation of a dispassionate space is the ground for the claim that science is generalizable across cultures but within human experience. In this sense, science structures experience in terms of its theories and laws. The version of religion discussed here claims the power to discover a truth that is generalizable across all possible worlds and so is outside human experience. This form of religious truth, for the believer, is a narrative of human experience from the vantage point of another world. It is hard to see how rival (and often independent and sovereign) stories set at this level, as *systems* of thought (which is what they are), can be addressed without a political language that is in some way outside religious domains, and both pragmatic and fixed at very general levels.

7

These observations and arguments—the orientation in public reason to the larger concepts that frame issues, the concern for collective instead of individual levels of experience, the supplanting in public reason of truth-functional evidence in favor of considerations that support conditions like equity, efficiency, stability, and the introduction of ontological matters in human communities along a secular–religious mapping—compel us to look again at the logic of complex systems in rendering the details of a public reason framed by the collective settings of politics. So much has to be resisted in this look. Systems theory provides a collective orientation that rekindles the perennial dream of developing a general theory of human life, a species of theory that compels us to dismiss some of the more revered concepts in social theory. For example the "collision-like" model of causality is a fatality in adopting complex adaptive systems (Juarrero, 1999). But the opening incentive is almost irresistible in providing a link between experience and formal arrangements, especially in view of the notoriously brief shelf life of both content and intermediate structures in social practices. It is just that permanence and transience, generality and boundaries, are among the more complex topics in social thought. The one portable item that immediately and incontrovertibly expands a concept of public reason is the recursive logic of complex systems. It is this logic that allows public reason to adjudicate or mediate not just disputes over goods but also compose and arrange the frames that order and justify claims.[20]

The attractions of versions of systems theory in negotiating the relationships of secular and religious experiences reside mainly in their intellectual power to manage the disparate perspectives of external and internal viewpoints, of infinite regresses and divinity, community unities and divisions, as a function of the fluid architecture characterizing systems. By this I mean that systems theories are consonant with all languages of interpretation in an indifference to truth *or* knowledge. Texts are paste-it notes on a conceptual message board to be arranged and re-arranged according to the flow and stability of the system. Theories of complex systems also offer helpful modifications of the basic concepts in negotiating the challenges and requirements of governing in pluralist democracies, especially in providing a recursive mechanism of interpretation and re-interpretation that can address both political and religious communities. The first upgrade is the abandonment of the part–whole approach to experience. One of the perennial issues in methodological individualism and holism is the definition of parts. Niklas Luhmann reminds us that parts are typically those units of a whole that are homogeneous with the whole, as, for example, rooms, not building blocks, are considered the parts of a house.[21] The problem of course is not only that different concepts of the whole require different units (houses as buildings are constituted more comfortably by blocks, plumbing, tiles, etc.) but that certain wholes do not have homogeneous parts. A human person, for example, is composed of biological units that are not precisely continuous with the concept of the person. Systems theory avoids these incongruities by replacing the part–whole relationship with systems-within-systems and system–environment relationships.

The first binary is easy to visualize. A human body (to take one system) is composed of a very large number of operating subsystems in (mainly) symbiotic relationships with each other. The kidneys, for example, are self-sustaining organs in a functional relationship with other systems of the body. Even at the micro level one can understand the DNA endowment as a set of systems carrying out a wide range of functions. In this binary arrangement all parts are in some important sense wholes. The second binary is more complicated. Here we are to understand a system as a differentiated whole, but the differentiations are not produced from parts but from a set of repetitions (within the system) of the differences between the system and its environments. The number and nature of these repetitions contribute to the complexity of a system since they can occur at any level within the system (the subsystems may refer to other subsystems as one or more environments).[22] Taken together, these two binaries present a system as (a) a collection of active subsystems that may themselves be governed by different local laws and have different functions, and (b) constituted by differentiations. A "part" is no longer the appropriate term to describe the units of the system (or whole), the subsystems may be described from a variety of conceptual perspectives without theoretically abusing the arrangement, and homogeneity between units and whole is not an issue.

The implications of these binaries for social systems are evident in the contemporary world, especially in democracies. Traditional societies were and are typically organized as hierarchies. The medieval arrangement of classes (or strata), for example, represented inequalities codified by the social structure. The historical changes that reconfigured these arrangements into the conditions of modernity are settled wisdom by now. Among these are the extensions of the franchise in the modern world that, when coupled with the Reformation's tolerance of contrary religious beliefs, favored the development of open subsystems and the regional autonomy familiar in democratic practices. The critical perspectives of recursive functions indicated a need for mechanisms to review, interpret, and revise claims. Certain social forms were generated, including the structural constraints of government—opposition, Madisonian institutions of checks and balances, and appellate oversight in legal institutions. One simple misunderstanding must be avoided. Language has always permitted the reflective inquiries characteristic of complex systems. Classical philosophy is known for the Socratic examination and re-examination of texts in argumentative forms of discourse. The modern world is known for its representation of such critical scrutiny in institutional forms.[23]

Now, the advantages of complex systems are obviously in coordinating the sectors that represent religion and politics. So many liberal theorists have reminded us of the partitions typical of liberal societies. In *Spheres of Justice* Michael Walzer continues a distinguished liberal tradition of theory that demarcates ways of life, social domains that receive and develop terms within parameters. Walzer's work is distinctive in denying a prevailing view at the time that the realm of justice is the entire society. For example, the main polar differences between the interventionist theory of justice provided by Rawls and the libertarian account of Nozick can be contained in the view that justice is a term assignable to the whole political society. Walzer, inclined (on his own admission) to anthropological engagement with the social world, does not subscribe to this view but maintains in its place that single-place concepts and principles in normative theory (equality and justice in particular) are local, not generalizable to the whole society. They are found within the practices or domains of a pluralist society.[24] The issue for such work is whether a demarcated public reasoning is generalizable to all of the communities within the liberal settings, in particular those organized on religious and secular terms. What do we use to govern disputes among sharply divided communities if the criteria of judgment are local? And how do we mediate the disputes among communities in which one or more of the disputants invokes realms external to human experience?

One distinctive approach to dispute management is ordinary politics. A conventional expansion of public reasoning provides methods for gauging and managing intersections between radically different systems like religion and politics (at their extremes). The strategy is oblique in its orientation to disputes. For example, the collateral reasoning characteristic of politics is effective as it avoids the main issues in a dispute by focusing on sidebar issues. The Good Friday agreements in Northern Ireland, for example, are among the success stories of this method. But equally good examples of such reasoning are in the ways in which the U.S. Supreme Court has negotiated the abortion cases since *Roe*. The core holding in *Roe* dismantled all state laws proscribing abortion, giving the woman discretionary authority in the first trimester to decide whether to continue or terminate her pregnancy, and allowing freedom of choice on conditions in the next two trimesters. This peremptory decision has been leavened by the Court in a number of subsequent decisions. Ian Shapiro has properly seized on a throwaway phrase in *Bellotti v. Baird*, "undue burden," to depict the shift in the Court's orientation from the core holding in *Roe* to sidebar matters. In *Pennsylvania v. Casey* the Court negotiated a set of issues—consent by a parent for a minor contemplating abortion, a waiting period before an abortion during which educational materials could be provided by prolife, and the rights of the father-to-be in abortion decisions—by accepting those conditional restrictions on abortion that do not unduly burden the woman seeking an abortion. As Shapiro points out, this phrase at least partially reshaped the abortion dispute by allowing states to discuss which if any provisions could set conditions on abortions while not placing such a burden on women (and without touching the *Roe* core holding).

The collateral or sidebar discourses that mark off political languages—the bounded rationalities that restrict disputes to manageable, finite spaces—are also abundantly represented in the democratic practices of constitutional or judicial review, and are especially enlightening on church–state relations in the United States. The examples form a kind of history and display the inevitable variations that practices impose on any theory. One rich and illustrative source (among so many) is the handling of the establishment clause in the First Amendment's famous religious stipulation: "Congress shall make no law respecting an establishment of religion, or prohibiting the free exercise thereof." In understanding the ways in which the U.S. Supreme Court has interpreted the first clause in that sentence it is helpful to acknowledge the obvious meaning, which is that the U.S. Government cannot establish or be a church. But, as usual, the obvious is only a small part of a complex story. Any tracking of the main Supreme Court decisions exhibits a rich array of linguistic strategies in the sequence of establishment clause interpretations. In the first of the line of comprehensive decisions, *Everson v. Board of Education* (1947), the Court regarded the wall of separation between church and state as consistent with the state reimbursement of parents for bus transportation on public buses to and from private religious schools. Five years later, in *Engele v. Vitale* (1952), the Court rejected non-denominational prayer in public schools. In 1971 the Court (*Lemon v. Kurtzman*) devised a test for determining whether a program violates the establishment clause: (1) the statute must have a secular legislative purpose, (2) its principle or primary effect must be one that neither advances nor inhibits religion, and (3) the statute must not foster "an excessive government entanglement with religion." Such interpretations are loose change in the currencies of law and politics. But the line of these decisions (and many more on the Establishment clause) makes the point that the U.S. Supreme Court engages in a fascinating and continuing language game of dialectics. If we look at these kinds of decisions as patterns it is clear that the Court is addressing a primary text and interpreting it with the use of particular cases. So much is common knowledge. So too is the grammar. It is the kind of pragmatism celebrated in politics, and a language game influenced by the well-known interests of competing groups as mediated by the twin considerations of power and collective reference.

But collateral dispute management is unable to address issues whose core standing promises a lasting dispute or more comprehensive resolutions. In this sense it bypasses the main difficulties and opportunities in reconciling secular and religious communities. But a recursive system of argument guided by collective references, no matter what type of collective is at issue, takes us to models of public reasoning that can match, coordinate, and, in general, accommodate institutions and practices that are dissimilar in the extreme sense, in what we normally call divisive or deep pluralism. The operations of complex systems, curiously enough, also correlate happily with the reflexive logic of conscience in religious thought, suggesting that a model of public reason framed in terms of complex systems might be more successful in addressing the acid test of managing religious communities, at least those oriented to an external realm, than is possible with current and bounded versions of liberal public reason. But mainly a recursive organization of political settings, in requiring a constant critical examination and re-examination of claims, offers a kind of pragmatic realism elaborated by a freestanding language of politics driven by political processes. This orientation would seem to be a more promising start in negotiating the grammars of political engagements in pluralist democracies than the forms of deliberative democracy and public reasoning occupying the attention of so many political philosophers today. This promise, moreover, begins with a turn away from liberal principles and values to the cooler logic of collectives as distinct units operating on the terms of complex systems. The reason is that the main references in political languages, from Aristotle to the present, are the larger and even synoptic considerations that represent the concerns of a political system, a set of references missing or buried in the main liberal models of political reasoning.

8

At this point a generous tolerance of language and value must be a part of political governance. Successful forms of public reason will have to accept the logic of political talk, meaning that everything in the way of claims and claimants must be material for recursive examination. This kind of pragmatic realism would certainly be a more promising start in negotiating the grammars of political engagements in pluralist democracies than the forms of deliberative democracy and public reasoning occupying the attention of so many political philosophers today, which seem chronically inclined to support strong criteria of exclusion for participants and views alike (for the most puritan perspectives see Gutmann and Thompson, 1998, Macedo, 1998a, b, 2000, and, yes, Rawls, 1996).

The plea here is for more innovative and open institutional forms.[25] It is arguable that the institutional arrangements that roughly express the liberal and democratic sentiments in Western thought since the contract theorists of the seventeenth and eighteenth centuries are inept in meeting the needs of the current world. The historical linkage of liberalism and democracy to the state has compromised these theories and practices as the state has become a minor, porous, or reconstructed player in politics. It is a familiar type of narrative. Concepts and theories crafted in one set of historical conditions may not be suitable for radically different conditions. The great modern theories of politics in the West broke with the classical model of the *polis* exactly as the medieval system gave way to the sovereign states of the early industrial age. The critical shift from the group to the individual in liberal thought (from Aristotle/Aquinas to Hobbes) set the stage for the derivations of principles based on consent and freedom, and the vocabularies of rights that celebrate the liberal democracies of the modern age.

These venerable principles for organizing a human community are now notoriously limited. One limitation is indicated by the unyielding contestation presented in bioethics when rights to life, assigned originally to fully developed sentient individuals (white males who owned property, to be vicious about origins), are not easily extended to inchoate and sometimes microscopic forms of life. Disputes over this extension (abortion, stem cell research) have determined elections. A second is suggested by the ambiguous state of institutions that are no longer effective on a global scale. The question is compelling. How can the vocabularies of justice, liberty, legitimacy, the common good, power, authority—generally the desiderata of Western liberal and democratic political theory—bear on politics and political theory when these terms of endearment no longer have referential power in the current global setting? The succinct answer is, they cannot. Then the issue is, what reforms of theory and current institutions will take us to the organizational forms needed to address and moderate political and religious communities in a world being transformed by the changes loosely described as the globalization movement?

There are guides. Some recent contributions in systems theory do provide a heightened awareness of what works and doesn't work in human practices. We *must* know now that recursive systems are superior to static or non-reflexive practices, meaning that those practices containing rules which allow a reflexive scrutiny of themselves have competitive advantages, as illustrated in Hart's (1961) demonstration that simple static versions of law are inferior to more complex recursive legal systems organized in terms of primary and secondary rules. Structural reforms that preserve the dominant principles of traditional political theory indicate an unwelcome stasis at institutional levels. They are indifferent to the reflexive and rapid-fire changes that are complicit in institutional success, looking like old-fashioned Madisonian constitutional reforms in a post-Madison age. Also, if the work in cognitive science and complex systems tells us anything it is that any kind of imposed program of reform will be on the cutting room floor before it leaves the room. Nathan Zuckerman, a fictional writer who is Philip Roth's alter ego, meets a master writer, E.I. Lonoff in Roth's (1979) novel *The Ghost Writer*. Lonoff defines the writing profession as turning sentences around. But induction dominates good social science, and structural reforms invented at a conceptual level, by turning sentences around, are dead on arrival given the pace of political and economic change in today's world.

Suppose that the more pessimistic views are true, that our dominant political and economic theories/institutions have expired, their shelf life definitely over when we contemplate the synoptic and rapid changes in the current world scene. More: suppose that the world faces radically different types of discourses today, with secular and religious languages competing within political frameworks ill equipped to negotiate across such divides. (This would be another way of saying that reforming political systems cannot be predicated on the universality of languages.) If these suppositions carry the day, then a genuinely wide version of public reason must cut down to the rules and principles required in coordinating radically different ways of defining the nature of human experience.

The requirement in governing is to modify traditional ways of thinking about religious and secular communities. The property dualism informing Western practices, the discrete self of modern contract theory, even the causality that frames civic participation—all of these concepts can be bracketed and perhaps abandoned with revised variations on systems theory. The invitation is to *see* secular and religious communities as shifting and porous entities, partitions with no stable equilibriums or points of closure, nor privileged grasp of truth, but rather as entries in the fluid arrangements of complex systems. The truly fascinating thing is that the outline of this genuinely wide concept of public reason is revealed by dismissing a longstanding preoccupation with infinite regresses and how to halt them. The better response, on the arguments advanced here, is that you don't halt infinite regresses. You rely on them in depicting public reason in terms of a complex system driven by recursive functions. The form of reasoning presented in this arrangement celebrates the dialectical standing of political languages, which amounts to an endorsement of the practical operations of complete and *sustained* free speech in any era and across any pantheon of legal and political theorists. At a slightly more ambitious level it also suggests that one of the iconic contributions in logic and mathematics, the impossibility of realizing completeness and consistency demonstrated in Gödel's two theorems, sets the terms for a realistic and open account of public reason.

Modeling Public Reason: Political Liberalism and *Realpolitik*

I

The fine tunings, the nuances of political languages drawn from political engagements and the recursive functions of complex systems, receive a blunter assessment when these languages are turned into the models that might serve public reason. The one model that presents the highest pragmatic hopes for the management of radical disputes is political liberalism. It is, after all, a program that modestly and realistically celebrates liberal values in the domains of the political rather than the larger society. As a result it appears to carry minimal conceptual baggage in managing disputes in the divisive pluralism sometimes found in democratic arrangements.[1] To see how dispute management in political liberalism is to work at its best levels, imagine an extreme: a society in which communities disagree all the way down, to whatever one can imagine as fundamentals, and even beyond that. Say that all of the community-oriented devices that might reconcile the parties are exhausted, or futile from the beginning. Imagine now that the disagreement has become a dispute without a resolution, and perhaps without even a settlement method. Add to the stakes the proposition that the dispute is important and must be managed for the political society to continue functioning. What is the answer to this kind of problem?

The answer in political liberalism is to provide a way of thinking and talking in politics that examines and tries to reconcile opposing positions with an impartial settlement based on fair arrangements and mutual respect, one that is careful to treat the rival perspectives equitably, and reasoned through from start to finish with open methods that lead to a public justification understandable to the disputants. This perspective does not deny the truths found in the disputing communities, nor is it to carry its own hard truth. It is presented as a method, a minimalist set of techniques that allows for the careful and judicious exploration of views with an eye toward a fair resolution. This thin and transparent frame, pragmatic and critical, tentative and driven by a permanent state of uncertainty, is the familiar approach of Western modes of thought from figures like Charles Peirce, John Stuart Mill, F.A. Hayek, John Dewey, Karl Popper, Joseph Schumpeter, and, more recently, the arguments for dissent by Cass Sunstein and the pragmatic turns of Richard Posner.[2] It represents exactly the questioning and provisionally skeptical state of mind characterizing discussions like this one, meaning a quest for conclusions that stand the test of rational examination from a dispassionate perspective. For liberals it is a bare and reasonable framework, by no means onerous, that must be accepted as a political form of reasoning by all citizens. It is also a skeletal model, a concise frame for those versions of public reason and deliberative democracy that are currently the mechanisms for the dispute management powers of political liberalism. In this sense it presents a governing model that represents the recursive logic we want and expect in public reasoning. We would also think that the critical test for this model of reasoning is whether it can adjudicate or mediate radical disputes among secular and religious communities since these disputes often add ontological differences to disagreements.

But religion is a notorious non-starter in all liberal versions of public reason. Rawls, for example, always seemed puzzled by religious communities, most notably in excluding comprehensive doctrines from the political table even as (or because?) these doctrines often represent religious beliefs. (The exclusionary tendencies in recent liberal theory have always seemed paradoxical in bracketing those hard cases in which the governing powers of the state are most needed.) J. Judd Owen (among others) has reservations about political liberalism primarily when divisive matters like religious practices are addressed.[3] The general problem is that religion is a wild-card narrative in secular political settings. It intensifies the prospect of widely different reasons for action by introducing override beliefs to political experience. Strong religions support, within the parameters of a human community, narratives shaped by beliefs that some propositions originate in an external reality. This species of text (whose effects on secular political practices cannot be stressed enough) rests on a web of concepts stretching to points that are believed to exceed the parameters of human communities, with inevitably profound implications for the individual's collective identification. Religious discourse is almost painfully recursive within secular practices, leads easily to external standards of review, and quite possibly is inaccessible to any version of the liberal frame of mind.[4]

Of course a number of philosophers have argued that political liberalism does not succeed as a form of dispute resolution across any species of radical difference, or even on moderately divisive issues since these easily mutate into radical differences. Stanley Fish, for example, is generally skeptical about liberal programs, and Jean-Francois Lyotard sees the exclusionary provisions of modern reason as a form of terrorism, which occurs (for Lyotard) whenever one language game claims a dominant universality and credibility that disqualifies other games with different rules that are not reducible to those representing the dominant game. Or Paul F. Campos, who argues that "Political Liberalism's central concept of 'public reason' is empty, and that Rawls's analysis of political issues amounts to little more than the shamanistic incantation of the word 'reasonable.' " If we set issues of intemperance aside, however, the question plaguing all of these critiques still turns on the limits of liberalism in divisive conditions. If political liberalism does not work when individuals and groups are deeply divided, especially when some or all of the players in a dispute are committed to a truth and methods for reaching that truth which are inaccessible to the liberal frame of mind, then (again) the mechanisms of governance are dormant exactly when they should be active. The question then is—what can work as a method of dispute management consistent with the liberal values of pluralist democracies? The real test for political liberalism, in other words, is finally in the management of divisions introduced by radically different takes on experience, and it is arguable that these differences are most strongly and importantly represented in secular communities by religious values.[5]

There is a strategy for managing disputes that exceed the reconciling powers of political liberalism. It succeeds where political liberalism fails by attending to the conditions in which political reasoning occurs. The strategy yields an alternative version of political liberalism by stipulating a more generous view of pluralist democracies, one that extends the concept of democracy to the semi-anarchic conditions characterizing international relations among sovereign states. This inclusive form of democracy accepts *modus vivendi* agreements (those that are provisional and governed by the separate interests of the parties) as alternatives to moral versions of democratic union and, as a consequence, requires a rival account of reasoning to stand in conjunction with the visions of reconciliation along moral dimensions that currently under-write political liberalism.[6] This more comprehensive form of democracy invites a type of political reasoning driven by the logic of reason-of-state (*realpolitik*) in conditions of deep pluralism. This species of reasoning, found in the languages of state depicted in some realist accounts of international relations, will be presented here as appropriate for communities that do not share the understandings required for the use of liberal terms like reasonableness and civility. Included in the case for a complete version of political reasoning, which must be robust enough to contain both the liberal and *realpolitik* models, is a mechanism that adjudicates the appropriateness of these competing models as conditions differ. The expanded version of democracy and the types of reasoning it supports are more successful in fulfilling the expectations of classical liberal theory. This success is secured with what might be called a col-lective pragmatism that avoids current liberal appeals to be reasonable, reciprocity controlled by moral criteria, and the quest for common rea-sons. It is a success story that offers a much more comfortable fit between political and religious discourses than the critical and cautionary tales related in standard accounts of political liberalism.

2

One productive way to introduce a version of liberal democracies different than expressed in recent influential literatures, and the models of reasoning that these literatures support, is through a deeper explo-ration of what might be called background (assumed, unexamined) concepts. Inquiries into background concepts follow a distinguished tradition in a wide range of theories. In a famous exchange between Einstein and Heisenberg in 1926, Einstein uttered what Heisenberg later described as a terrifying sentence for his own orientation toward observable entities as the foundation of theory: "Only the theory decides what one can observe." Einstein had entered his state of enchantment with rational realism, and was concerned to recognize the rich array of concepts and side theories needed in both observation and sound explanation. He said that, as an example, "one almost unconsciously uses Maxwell's theory when dealing with a light beam that conveys experimental readings."[7] Heisenberg continued to endorse instrumental views of theory, but later inadvertently refined Einstein's approach by pointing out that the uncertainty principle tells us what we cannot observe. Currently the main currents of theory in both the natural and social sciences are acclimated to the thick assumptions that frame and restrict observations, and in general structure theory: concepts, for example, of causality, measurement, time, space, in the natural sciences, additional concepts that include economy, society, the individual in social theory. On occasion the retrieval of assumptions redirects theory. The celebrated exposé by Marx of unexamined assumptions in liberal theory, for example, turned political theory in the direction of political economy and studies of the effects of capital formation on political and legal practices.

The background concepts of political philosophy differ in form and effect. Some background concepts are so well formed that they amount to a model of a human society and its occupants that illuminates particular theories (see, for example, McPherson's arguments for a model of possessive individualism as a core theoretical background in classical contract theory).[8] Other background concepts are more diffuse. George Lakoff argues in his analysis of liberals and conservatives in terms of family metaphors, that there typically are unconscious (in the sense of unattended or unnoticed) metaphors that explain beliefs.[9] For example, and as Nietzsche proposed, morality in the West is drawn from debtor–creditor models, or, in Lakoff's account, financial transactions and accounting.[10]

Rawls offers the original position (OP) as a source and justification for the principles of justice in his theory. But one may ask, what are the background considerations that justify the OP, or the thought experiment itself? We might assert (with others) that Rawls's original position tracks to a mildly acquisitive setting (non-predatory egoists) of disinterested and discrete agents in conditions of moderate scarcity who are wedded to liberty and concerned to distribute those goods that have priority in a market economy. Ronald Dworkin identifies the background concepts of equal concern and respect for individuals as the driving force for the OP, in the simple sense that the thought experiment makes no sense in the absence of these concepts.[11] Once we recognize such background concepts (perhaps combining them) we can evaluate the OP in terms of whether it fulfills the promise of its own design, and we also can locate it on some conceptual map, in Dworkin's mapping as "an intermediate conclusion, a halfway point in a deeper theory that provides philosophical arguments for its conditions" (p. 26). Or, to put another gloss on the OP from the perspective of background concepts, Dworkin states that it is not a foundation of the argument or an expository device, but "... is one of the major substantive products of the theory as a whole" (p. 25).

The component of political liberalism most in need of clarification is the possibility of a freestanding political language, which addresses disputes among radically disparate communities. Can background matters clarify this component? In a background exploration of political liberalism targeting this issue we might ask this question: What is the proper depiction of the social contract that inhabits so much of liberal political theory? Here are two possibilities drawn up from an inspection of theory and the good use of metaphors. One is a contract fashioned on the basis of self-interest. In this type of contract competing parties bargain for an arrangement that meets their preformed interests. The metaphor is a business transaction. The other is a contract that creates agreeable conditions in which the parties can cohabitate and nurture each other. The closest metaphor is a marriage contract consummated on the basis of romantic love. In the former, agreements based on a provisional correlation of interests, independent of emotive ties or even moral obligations, and dependent on an active and persisting convergence of interests for compliance, are the order of the day. In the latter, contracts driven by the romantic metaphor, norms of fidelity and trust, integrity in commitments, betrayals and shared beliefs, certainly overlapping consensus, are natural features of the arrangements (discussion in Freeman, 1990).

Both versions of the social contract simultaneously illuminate their central claim (that justice is based on a kind of contract) and suggest a middle earth territory of mixed concepts (of political reason). Business contracts (elaborated in bargaining-game models) start with individuals motivated by considerations of self-interest, not an antecedent and governing morality. Morality is a derivative concept, appearing as a secondary item or consequent of the agreement that promotes the interests of the contracting parties. In the romantic contract, characterized by morality-driven agreements, the parties are moved by moral concerns. In Rawls's refinement of the romantic contract they have a concept of justice, and they are motivated to enter the social contract to craft institutions that will realize this sense of justice. In the first type of contract, the parties can and must consider not entering an agreement, much in the way that Hobbes allows the choice of no political authority, or anarchy, to individuals in the state of nature. In the second contract the prospect of no agreement is incoherent, as Aristotle could not even contemplate the absence of political authority. The setting is different in each case. The first version describes a contract entered by fully formed egoists with ends and interests, the second by social creatures who must create, through free choices based on a shared point of view, the institutions that will allow them to develop as reasoning and moral individuals (again, Freeman, 1990 for an elaboration).

These rival depictions roughly express divergent understandings of liberal democracies. The business transaction metaphor stands for the classical liberal view that the beliefs of citizens are not the primary concern of the state, and that individuals can subscribe to democratic arrangements for their own reasons so long as they meet the behavioral terms of a contract that meets their shared interests. This metaphor even allows for the prospect that the political system may be defined in different ways by different citizens, which permits the postmodern stance that there is no single objective construct for any institution or practice, that there may be multiple political systems corresponding to the many world views of the citizens in the system, and these circumstances amount to a perfectly satisfactory state of affairs. The romantic marriage metaphor is more demanding. In this form of democracy beliefs and reasons are important fixtures of the state. Democratic polities are successful only if people comply with the terms of the contract for the right reasons. Like good romantic marriages the polity is more than a coordination of behavior that meets the interests of the contracting parties (though it is that). It is a bond among citizens, based upon democratic norms, that deepens as the arrangement continues. Its stability and coherence, certainly its legitimacy, is as much a matter of deep consensus as matching behavior.

There is much that appeals in each of these forms of the social contract. Both are conceived to meet the interests of the contracting parties. But the nature and interests of the parties differ, and the practical difficulties and possibilities are different. The appeal of the classical depiction is that it relies on a palpable and crucial item, what people do, rather than what they profess. In this tradition the key consideration is that individuals and groups comply with the law as they behave, and the reasons for the compliance are outside the purview of the state because (in part) of the difficulties in regulating states of mind. (The difficulties in coordinating beliefs and behavior are legendary. Among the problems is that selves are often walking contradictions, much in the way that all of Shakespeare's main characters are living, breathing antitheses, for and against things from moment to moment, yet still functioning humans.) But the normative differences are the deeper cuts that distinguish these two forms of contract. In classical liberalism individuals are free to believe anything so long as they comply with law and policy. This protective belt expresses a view of liberty that respects the powers of autonomous creatures to have beliefs shielded from regulation, a liberty of conscience and thought that must for validity allow the most bizarre takes on the political scene. This is, strangely enough, one of the quintessential post-Reformation convictions. Individuals are permitted to differ on the most fundamental matters (God, religion), and these differences in understandings of experience are cause for celebration, not a condition to be remedied with a convergence toward consensus (the right reasons), political or otherwise. It is a model of democracy that is thinner by virtue of its respectful attitude toward differences while still meeting political needs.

The second depiction represents the alternative vision. It is also post-Reformation in holding (with Luther) that good acts are not enough. Belief must be antecedent to, and in fact embedded in, these acts. The successful polity on this depiction will consist of like-minded citizens. They share the same understandings of the political system and the reasons offered to justify the actions of the state (especially those acts that are primarily coercive). Moral integrity and common democratic norms thread through this version of a political system like a lubricant of good will. Its original legacy is Aristotle's proposition that the polis should be grounded in friendship (though not his views that good works are the locus of ethics), and Rousseau's conviction that we become moral through membership in the state. This account sees the democratic system as transforming, bringing individuals closer to shared understandings by virtue of membership in the political culture. Civic education must be a primary practice in this view of democratic arrangements. To let citizens go their own way is a normative flaw correctable with education in citizenship (Macedo, 2000, for the summary arguments). This does not mean or suggest that this second account justifies a contract that is utterly stultifying in its demands. As Rawls points out, "Justice as fairness honors, as far as it can, the claims of those who wish to withdraw from the modern world in accordance with the injunctions of their religion . . . ." But then note the condition: ". . . provided only that they acknowledge the principles of the political conception of justice and appreciate its political ideals of person and society."[12] This version of the contract stresses the need to forge a deeper consensus, framed primarily in moral terms, as a condition for a viable democracy. It is the contract model assumed in Rawls's political liberalism and the background concept today in the main versions of public reason and deliberative democracy.

3

There are multiple forms of reasoning in democratic political systems. Juries, draft boards, hospital ethics committees—the landscape is filled with forums that rely on different rules of practical reasoning according to the tasks they undertake and the problems they are designed (or evolve) to address. These differences lead to the adoption of diverse exclusionary rules and modes of argument. The physician, attorney, mechanic, assembly worker—all practitioners occasionally use different rules of evidence, inference and argument if purposes and contexts differ among the practices. Now recall that the defining mark of the state is the negotiation or coordination of a system of authority and power over a region populated by otherwise sovereign or autonomous units. It follows from this and the usual formation patterns of practical reasoning that the language games of the state will have rules and principles crafted from the practices that manage this type of system. The terms found in communities will be present in state languages, but their meanings may differ. It is precisely in these semantic differences that the state finds resources to address disputes among communities, which can neither control nor understand one another, and it is at this point that the individual oriented liberal model of public reasoning must be modified and in part abandoned. The reason is that the main references in all of these political languages are the larger and even synoptic considerations that represent the concerns of a political system, a set of references missing or buried in the main liberal models of political reasoning. In a sense languages of state are a type of meta language in occupying conceptual space outside the communities that the political system is to govern.

It is at this point that the languages of diplomacy, of state-to-state negotiations, and realism in international relations can come into play in offering substantial alternatives to the features of these liberal models. Proposals for an international language of state reasoning that is in some way detached from private or nonpublic languages annotate the texts of political theory past and present. The practical correlates of one type of such reasoning, state reasoning as *realpolitik*, are found throughout the entire span of political history and are the inspirations for realism in international relations theory today.[13] Reason of state is sketched in the Melian Dialogue by the Athenians, an argument replicated by Thrasymachus in Plato's *Republic*, discussed in the Athenian assembly and Roman forum, elaborated by Machiavelli and his statecraft, but especially sharpened in the calculations of modern figures like Cardinal Richelieu and his *raison d'état*, Metternich's and Palmerston's alliances among states, Bismarck's even more complex and stable (for a time) balances-of-power, the pragmatics of George Kennan, Henry Kissinger's state-interest principles, and the corps of professional diplomats in all eras of international politics. Generally, the venue for *realpolitik* is in political systems where authoritative decisions are negotiated among sovereign or autonomous units for a political region. The language games in this history are not identical, but in general they are presented as distinct from the reasoning characterizing other social practices and seem to be at odds with the influential languages of public reason and deliberative democracy found in liberal theory today. Languages of state appear with a grammar and vocabulary oriented to power, authority, and collective reference, seem guided by skills of composition and balance, and typically address political settings where no common principles of adjudication can be found. Their champions describe various practice rules, constitutive and summary, arranged in complex ways by the demands of real world politics.[14]

Certain caveats precede the uses of these languages. International relations theory is currently arranged across the poles of realism and various alternative theories. Realism itself is a collection of views, a set of family resemblance concepts. But its main variants constitute a tradition of thought that has venerable standing. Michael Doyle: "Realism is our dominant theory . . . our most distinctive theory that, for some, promises an explanation of international politics grounded in nothing below or beyond the anarchy of international relations itself . . ." (from p. 1 of the Introduction).[15] But, venerable standing or not, the reader should understand that the proposal shortly to follow is not an endorsement of realism as a superior account of international relations. The exercise in this chapter, restricted to the blunt approaches of liberalism and a limited realism, does not require an adjudication of longstanding intellectual disputes over realism, constructivism, liberalism, Marxism, various post-positivist and post-realist approaches from Wittgenstein-like language-game subscribers (Karin Fierke, 2000), constructivists (Nicholas Onuf, 1989), feminist theory approaches (Cynthia Weber, 1994), discourse analyses influenced by Foucault, Derrida, Laclau (Roxanne Doty, 1996), and other orientations.[16] In this rich intellectual setting a language of *realpolitik* is decidedly and unabashedly old fashioned. This quest does rely more closely on language games than other theories (and thus on Wittgenstein's

Philosophical Investigations)—on the assumptions that *realpolitik* languages do imperfectly exist among practitioners, have arguably existed for some time, and these ancient/modern languages are the resources invoked here to attend to certain failures in the liberal model in particularly divisive conditions in domestic politics. But the issues generated by rival linguistic theory in international relations are limited here. It may be asked of this invocation whether realism is better than its alternatives in providing languages that can establish civil relations between secular and religious communities, but not whether realism is the best depiction of international relations or even (strange as this sounds) whether such a language exists in strong form within political realities. The aim in this chapter is merely to find and describe, and perhaps construct, a form of reasoning with properties derived from scales of cultural and political anarchy, and proffer this reasoning form as a strategy to avoid the failure of the liberal model in the deep pluralism occasionally encountered in political democracies, whether this language has robust standing or not in other venues.[17]

The version of realism adopted here is also a thin theory, meaning that it does not present the full set of views normally attributed even to core realism. Doyle sets these views out as a skeptical attitude toward schemes for international order, an assumption that state interests should and do dominate class interests and can be distinguished from individual rights, and (of most importance) that anarchy, uncertainty, and warlike situations are the conditions of international politics. It is the latter definition of the international scene that makes power or force the main reliant and core feature of international politics in realist perspectives (Doyle, 1997, p. 43). The transfer here of the languages of state reasoning from international to domestic politics carries no realistic expectations about chronic states of war, the dominance of state interests or states, the preeminence of power or force (though see below for observations about power as a missing variable). The disparities presented in democratic public space by radically different communities (secular and religious) are tantamount to a limited intellectual and moral anarchy. This anarchy, a kind of adversarial relationship among quasi-sovereign communities, can be managed on the terms of liberal democracies only by models of reasoning drawn up from languages framed in condition of state sovereignty. These models are part of the family of realisms, certainly at some distance from liberalism in international relations, but without the entire conceptual baggage that realism typically carries in any of its variations (for a range of variations on realism, Doyle (1997, pp. 41–160).

4

The salient observation now is that the main assumptions and working methods of political liberalism are not continuous with the languages of realism. We can start elaborating this point with the thought that rational agents in politics are typically representatives talking for others (their constituents) and amassing perspectives that will speak for a collective of some form. These layered arrangements for reaching outcomes, including the national standing of representations and the legendary (and graded) autonomy of nations in a sovereign state system, may help account for what might be seen as the presentational feature of international negotiations. In presentational talk no one needs to be persuaded or convinced of anything, no minds need to be changed, for a successful international settlement. The intellectual conversions required in academic seminars do not dominate presentational negoti-ations (though they might on occasion). Settlements can be reached through adjustments of interests that are typically known prior to discussion. We would expect that the protective belts securing core values held by the rival cultures/systems will govern adjustments of interests. But argument, persuasion, convincing or proving—these staple features of intellectual inquiry are not necessarily prominent parts of interest-adjustment sessions. If the staple features are present it is eminently possible that they are directed at third parties rather than the adversary.

Consider, as several examples among many, the recent (and ongoing) mediated settlements in Northern Ireland. Each side in these particular mediated sessions were burdened with egregious views of the adver-sary, regarding the other side as morally corrupt, murderers and worse. Arguments were largely rhetorical, framed for public consumption. The tenuous settlement depended on establishing the conditions nec-essary for peace, sensitivity to time and timing, an ability to find innocuous terms to replace a language dense with the semantics of past conflicts, and, primarily, a balancing of interests, an accommodation free of the burden of mutual respect, that served the combatants in securing peace and stability.[18] Very little of the reason and deliberation in liberal models can be found in these proceedings and settlements. This mediated model of reasoning is found in different forms in a variety of negotiations, for example, the various conferences on the reunifica-tion of Germany before the event occurred, or the Geneva conference that settled the Indochina War, or the Geneva Four-Power Conference in July 1955, or the Geneva Conference on Laos (1961–62).[19] The summaries of these conferences do not suggest the dominance of rational persuasion, even though arguments are part of the proceedings. The participants are mainly presenting pre-formed positions and attempting to adjust interests to reach a settlement.

Publicity is also not a dominant feature of diplomatic talk, where confidentiality is often prized over and above transparency in reasoning. It would be more accurate to say that diplomatic reasoning is public in the sense in which all languages are public, but even this sense of the public is often limited in diplomatic talk to representatives of the participating communities, not to the communities themselves. The logic and opportunities of communication sometimes depend directly on restrictions in accessibility. In a story told in the Hebrew Bible, Book II of Kings 18, the Assyrians attack Jerusalem and, from their camp outside the city walls, shout the terms of surrender to the inhabitants within the walls, enveloping these terms with threats, taunts, scornful references to Yahweh, promises of horrors of the most severe sort. The Judean leaders come out to speak to the Assyrians on the other side of the walls and reply—"Speak to us in Aramaic." The Judeans wanted to communicate in a language that was not understood in the marketplace or the streets, for only then could they strike deals that would avoid a disaster.[20] The language of diplomatic settlement has long had the power to redefine the meanings of actions that would appear to the ordinary citizen as a compromise or defeat, and the success of the redefining efforts is often a function of restrictions in the public dimension of political languages.

Moral integrity and mutual respect in diplomatic sessions are also often extraneous since the terms of these verbal commodities typically are lodged in criteria indigenous to the rival communities. Even summitry, the diplomatic meetings of state leaders, is frequently governed by position papers drawn up prior to meetings, and mutual respect is an add-on condition in even this more nearly person-to-person-diplomacy [where the governing adage is still the old thought that great states (we could add, all states) do not have friends or allies—they have interests].[21] Unlike both the expectations of extended sympathy in some communitarian models, or the dispassionate figure in deliberative models, the grammar of the encounter in international politics can at least occasionally trump the mindsets brought to the interactions.[22] The goals of diplomacy can be secured, the sessions can be successful, without deliberation, or reasoning on shared values. The actions at issue can be an exploration of interests to reach an accommodation on rules recognizable from centuries of practice.

Exclusionary tests and reciprocity also are different in these settings. There are exclusions in diplomatic talks, and they may appear to follow some set of moral guidelines along the lines of legitimacy. The famous post World War II exclusion of what was then known as mainland China in favor of Formosa was usually presented on the grounds of legitimacy. Mao's government was rejected as a candidate representing the authentic Chinese state because it originated in a civil (read: illicit) war. But this exclusion is now widely regarded as a canard, a product of Cold War rhetoric and anti-communist fervor. Nixon's opening to China in 1972 is acknowledged today as inspired by the same power considerations that excluded China. Any such inspection of exclusionary rules in international politics will easily conclude that moral tests are often frontal decoration, that the criteria of admittance to the reasoning table is parallel to the use of viability in medical treatment: if the agent can respond productively from the encounter, then the treatment is administered. Criteria designed (as in the liberal model) to judge the moral standing of attitudes as a condition for participation in public reasoning or political deliberation are irrelevant. The point of diplomacy is to engage states in the interests of some international order. A moral membership test for such engagement is often no more than a cover for strategic calculations. The logic of this model of reasoning is much more compelling than the high ground taken by the liberal model. Disputes are often most in need of management when some or all of the parties are morally flawed or especially divisive (read: unreasonable). To exclude the more difficult adversaries in a dispute admits that political reasoning is less effective exactly when it may be most needed. Again, this seems the inverse of what is required.

Reciprocity in international politics may also be exempt, or at least separated, from moral obligations. Look again at Rawls's take on reciprocity. It is, he asserts, a relation between citizens on the fair terms of cooperation "in which everyone benefits judged with respect to an appropriate benchmark of equality defined with respect to that world."[23] Diplomatic negotiations can proceed even if the parties do not share fair terms of cooperation. Imagine a world populated by reasoning agents who occupy radically diverse communities (say, secular and religious) that absorb all senses of fairness in their differences. There would be no reciprocity on common benchmarks of any sort, but there still would be reciprocity on the terms of an agreement defined in different ways by the rival communities. One of the truly intriguing and offensive features of the transformative version of liberalism is that it violates the longstanding liberal distinction between thoughts and behavior. The demands of law in a proper liberal community do not require that citizens agree on the reasons for a statute, only that they behave as if they do. This fragile equilibrium, the regulation of behavior on the recognition that agents might have widely different reasons for compliance and may even define the law and its justification in different ways, might even be seen as the true source of genuine pluralism. But the dominant liberal models of reasoning and deliberation require the right moral beliefs for membership in the reasoning game, and, naturally, a reciprocity measured by these common beliefs.

The international arena is sometimes pure relief by comparison in allowing (because it often must) divergent understandings of accords, of different criteria for cooperation, and in this almost paradoxical sense comes closer to traditional liberal ideals than stipulated in recent versions of public reason and democratic deliberation. That sovereign states act in ways that maintain the interests of participating members as they each define and calculate these interests is enough. Fairness need be no more than just another concept without a shared foundation, understood differently by the players. Reciprocity may be similarly defined and measured by private not shared standards. These differences, represented in the approaches developed in international politics, may yield better devices in managing disputes among domestic partisans when the stakes are high and the divisiveness is foundational enough to yield radically different forms of reasoning. A thin theory of realism in international relations theory, in short, may provide a more effective set of guides for managing hard or extreme in-state disputes than anything proposed in political liberalism.

5

Scanning the disparities between the listed features of management strategies in political liberalism (deliberation, public reasoning) and those in international relations is a lineup exercise that yields an alternative schedule of dispute management techniques. Two items on this schedule speak at higher volumes about the limits of political liberalism and for alternative models of political reasoning. One is *modus vivendi* arrangements, which are among the main transfers from international relations to domestic politics. These arrangements are (notoriously) resisted in Rawlsian traditions and the resistance tracks in yet another way the influence of the romantic contract model. Arguments against the political settlements represented in such arrangements are often framed with glum concerns, sometimes warnings, of instability in such arrangements.[24] But these jeremiads represent confusions in liberal theory over stability, which are especially pronounced in Rawls's work. Rawls seems to desire not just stability for its own sake, but certain types of arrangements that are stable in part due to their normative standing, evidence for which is that they can be justified by public reasons (1996, pp. 390, 392). The full thought is that the most reliable and legitimate stability is grounded in an overlapping consensus on democratic fundamentals. Establish the consensus and one will have genuine stability in political arrangements. This is a different proposition than that an overlapping consensus yields stable political systems of various types. The first thought is a kind of tautology; the second is empirical and may be false. Most of the time, however, Rawls seems to be saying that a political system based on a *modus vivendi* is in some way less stable than one based on an overlapping consensus even if the *modus vivendi* is a rudimentary democracy. If we grant a conventional and independent meaning to stability, that, for example, it denotes consistency over time in the maintenance of basic rules and principles (whatever they might be), or, more generally, of a social practice, then there is at least some evidence that this statement is false, at least on occasion. There are many other sources of stability and instability than the differences between a *modus vivendi* and an overlapping consensus.

Stability per se is a mixed blessing since one might prefer some forms of instability, such as the moderate chaos of progressive populism with a cacophony of voices to the artificial stability of entrenched interests. Instability of various kinds and at various levels is sometimes a good thing. But the main point in the discussion cuts across mixed blessings and good things. Whether any set of arrangements is stable or unstable is an empirical issue, not settled by glib theoretical declarations, and there is at least some evidence that *modus vivendi* arrangements can be remarkably stable, at least in international relations. The alliances crafted by Bismarck after the Austro-Prussian and Franco-Prussian Wars of 1867 and 1870 lasted for decades, finally succumbing to the clumsy machinations of Wilhelm II that led to World War I. It is at least arguable that a more adept maintenance of these European balances-of-power would have sustained them for even longer periods of time. But the general empirical case for linking stability to an overlapping consensus is a subject for field work, not the pronouncements of political philosophers.

Moral failures complicate matters. Egregiously bad outcomes can follow a rejection of *modus vivendi* arrangements. According to Peter Kornbluh, in November 1970, shortly after Salvador Allende had been elected and the Chilean Congress had overwhelmingly ratified him as the country's president, Henry Kissinger dismissed the option of a *modus vivendi* with the new Chilean government. He told a special meeting of the National Security Council on November 6 that the United States would not initiate any arrangements with Allende and instead would pursue a covert hostile policy designed to subvert the Chilean head of state. On a ranking of possible U.S. approaches to Chile at that time in history, a full cooperative relationship was not an option given political realities. But a choice could have been, and was, made between *modus vivendi* and hostile opposition. The rejection of relations with Allende led, as we now know, to support for the coup that produced the brutal Pinochet regime and arguably the worst abuses of human rights in the history of the region. I am not suggesting that the choice the Nixon administration made was for evil instead of *modus vivendi* arrangements, but it is clear in retrospect that *modus vivendi* would have been a feasible and better moral choice given the realities of the time. Or, more generally, in certain divisive conditions, *modus vivendi* might be quite the more desirable alternative.[25]

A darker and more totalitarian interpretation of political liberalism is also close at hand in the consensual tests that Rawls scans into stability assumptions. Listen again to Rawls on why a *modus vivendi* is a poor substitute for consensus. It is unstable, he believes, but also not deep enough in its failure to represent beliefs. An overlapping consensus is much preferred to a *modus vivendi* because it is deep, it "goes down to the fundamental ideas within which justice as fairness is worked out."[26] So even if stable, a *modus vivendi* is flawed in not securing stability for the right reasons, that is "by a firm allegiance to democratic society's political (moral) ideals and values."[27] Political liberalism is a program that joins disagreements on fundamental ideas with consensus on a political conception. But in spite of the acceptance of strong pluralism in the society at large it is clear that, for Rawls, heterogeneity in or for the political conception in a well-ordered society is second best and definitely transitional, a movement toward practical ideals of mutual trust and public confidence, and a political society in which citizens support the form and outcomes of public reason on shared and transparent moral grounds. The great values of politics for Rawls are liberal values, and the use of these values as a kind of test for identifying good reasons, especially when coupled to the ambitious arguments by other political theorists to extend these values to social practices, is a thickening of political liberalism that moves it proportionately back to the more thoroughgoing liberalism of *A Theory of Justice*.[28] This process is also assigned to societies that are not well ordered. Rawls believes that the abolitionists and the leaders of the civil rights movement are authorized by the divisive state of their societies to support political values on the basis of distinct and rival comprehensive doctrines, but the goal of these movements is a society in which the political conception, defined by the values of liberalism, is widely realized and accepted for good political reasons.[29]

Even when citizens vote, in the privacy assured by the secret ballot, Rawls requires that they must be sincere in voting for positions that they can in good faith justify, presumably on political criteria that are public.[30] J. Judd Owen sets out (a bit uncharitably) the strong demands in this program of political liberalism: "Rawls is not satisfied if a citizen obeys the laws, respects the rights of others, serves in the military when called, etc. He is not concerned with outward acts only. Rawls is concerned that citizens do what they do 'for the right reasons.' "[31] Now listen to Steve Macedo in a remarkable and revelatory declaration of welcome for the transforming effects of liberal views: "(i)t is in this sense that liberalism might be said to 'silence' the 'religious voice': not through direct censorship and the heavy hand of state oppression, but rather through a wide array of sometimes subtle expectations about appropriate forms of speech and reasoning which amount to a system of unequal psychological taxation sufficient to drive out certain patterns of deeply held belief and practice, not all at once but over the course of generations." And: "We should, therefore, preserve liberal institutions, practices, rituals, and norms, that psychologically tax people unequally, for if that has the effect of turning people's lives—including their most 'private' beliefs—in directions that are congruent with and supportive of liberalism, thank goodness it does. This is what transformative constitutionalism is all about."[32]

No comment is needed to see the destructive effects on religion from an integrative liberalism organized on uniform reasons and the transformations this uniformity would require, or the hostility toward religion represented by the expression itself. A deep moral consensus on political principles is almost unintelligible when required of all religious communities in a secular democracy. If the money shot in liberal theories of church and state is in settling on the basis for regulating church when toleration limits are exceeded by religions, then the proposal that people have the same political reasons seems itself to exceed a political understanding of tolerance. How close are we in this program to saying that the right political thoughts are being summoned as a condition for good citizenship? The only justification of this version of the social contract is a belief in democratic exceptionalism. Democratic norms are not like other norms. They are superior, and their superiority resides in the fact that they allow a freedom that is denied in alternative norms. So we can require that all citizens accept and absorb these norms because the norms are not really restrictive. They are testaments to freedom. But of course to a religious community the acknowledgment may be hostile to the reasons for accepting citizenship in the first place. Like a bad romantic marriage, the vows may offend those understandings that do not meld with the expectations of either the marriage partner or the now demanding terms of the contract.

The difficulty is that liberalism is often championed with a pluralism that extends to foundational beliefs, the many voices of the modern scene that Nietzsche indemnified with internal objectivity (as many eyes as possible), accompanied by the conviction that no belief can be demonstrated to be absolutely right.[33] But then look again at Dworkin's classic (and uncompromising) stipulation of constructivism for political morality: "political decisions must be, so far as possible, independent of any particular conception of the good life, or of what gives value to life," and made by a state that must maintain equal concern and respect toward the members of society.[34] This stipulation raises the usual questions. How can any form of political liberalism even vaguely indicated by this stipulation manage a dispute when some or all of the disputants assert truth-functional claims based on different, exclusive, and rival criteria of truth that absorb politics? And, especially, what does it mean for a liberal state to respect communities that assert true, overriding, permanent, universal, and sectarian (anti-liberal) conceptions of the good life?

It is easy to forget that much of democratic culture is defined by common behavior, not common reasons, and this subscription to privacy in the matter of reasons is arguably one explanation for the stability and desirability of democratic systems. The longstanding liberal acceptance of private thoughts and public accord is on continual exhibit in voting by secret ballot. There is no attempt anywhere in a genuine democracy to require citizens to vote on anything for the right reasons, even as reasons are used to persuade voters to support a proposal or candidate. In fact reasons in voting are in general shielded from public scrutiny, and typically there is no entry point to add reasons on a ballot. Rawls prefers the reasoning of the U.S. Supreme

Court. Of course, since it delves into Constitutional essentials and, unlike the electorate and legislative bodies, is required to provide its reasons and forms of reasoning to the public. But voters and members of legislative assemblies are not so required, either by tradition or law, and these are remarkably stable institutions without the requirement that members act for the right reasons. It is arguable that one source of their stability is the fact that while their members may share and exchange their reasons with one another in the good and often volatile political talk (not just deliberation) that precedes and follows a vote, they may also keep their real reasons for voting private in expressing their political opinions. Even the most avid precinct worker and legislative whip are satisfied if their members vote the right way. Getting them also to vote for the right reasons would be rightly seen as oppressive, and very strange.

6

The second item is power. It is not entirely fanciful to import alternative models of reasoning from the languages of international politics. Some communities in pluralist democracies present a heterogeneity familiar in relations among sovereign states, and with differences that cannot always be settled by the dominant, integrative forms of liberal reason and deliberation. Such communities may be separated by zones of moral and political anarchy that testify to their intellectual autonomy. These differences are exhibited sharply in the practices of religion and politics, where connections between the two practices resemble cultural encounters and relations among sovereign states. Many political systems have quasi states within the state. Lucas Swaine has argued that theo-cratic communities do not receive appropriate treatment on the terms of legal standards within liberal democracies, and proposes that we view these communities as semisovereign entities, meaning as a type of community that "has a significant measure of political or legal auton-omy, with respect to some greater political order, but its sovereignty is not entire."[35] In these settings, the semi-anarchic conditions of sover-eign states (conditions referring here to both cultural distinctiveness and the absence of political authority) may be the richer source for models of political reasoning.

But it is important to acknowledge that the import also brings undisguised possibilities for coercion. The complex terrain of semi-anarchic conditions within political systems, with the attendant need to balance tolerance and regulation, liberty and order, yields two well-known strategies, both employed by Hobbes and each supporting the view that he drew up the state of nature as analogous to relations among sovereign states.[36] First is the expectation that even the most diverse communities have an interest in a set of prudential goods if a cooperative arrangement is to be successfully established. In the *Leviathan*, individuals have to share a certain commitment to a peaceful order, and subscribe to life and its continuation, if their disputes are to end in an orderly fashion. Hobbes presents these goods as part of a package of natural laws. In addition, individuals have to accept the fact that no side can win decisively. (Toleration for diverse views is often a result of stalemate and the rational calculation that one's views have a better chance of flourishing in mutual toleration enforced by a sovereign authority.) Given these conditions and postulates, the classical liberal approach is a political solution that recognizes as much as possible the higher endorsement of order as a condition for securing common goods.

Second, and almost as part of a natural setting in classical liberal theory, is a recognition and justification of power in a variety of situations. Hobbes prominently argued for a sovereign with the power to kill his subjects as sanction for noncompliance, an incentive eminently rational and compelling in Hobbes's rudimentary theory of a human nature that prioritizes life above all other conditions.[37] The logic of Hobbes's strategy also implies that the credibility of such a prospect attests to its disuse, since all players in the civil society would prefer to be in conditions of guaranteed reciprocity rather than the no-authority conditions of the state of nature. The neutrality of the state is superfluous. Reasoned settlement gives way to an agreement based on the need to secure this deeper common interest. In fact, the classical liberal state was committed to those values that would secure this interest in a timely and reliable fashion. It was not presented as neutral.[38]

Very little of this type of discussion—of the possibility of anarchic patterns in community relations, the imposition of the goods of peace and stability as premises rather than choices, the allied introduction of propositions on human nature, the role of coercion in politics—is part of those contemporary political theories that rely on liberal versions of dialogue, deliberation, and reasoning. One of the prime missing items is a rationale for force. The failure of talk, and the compelling case for coercive intervention that sometimes follows a failed discussion, is not seriously entertained in contemporary liberalism. It is no accident that rational choice theorists call dialogue "cheap talk," meaning that is has no implications for politics and typically proceeds with nothing at stake.[39] But it should come as no surprise to say that politics, finally, is a contact sport, and if the adversaries are radically different on the axes of reasoning and roughly equal in power, an accommodation may be the only type of settlement possible short of conflict. Of course if they are not, if the state, say, has a monopoly of power, then a coerced settlement (not a reasoned or deliberative resolution) is not a counter-intuitive outcome. But in neither case is the outcome a "talk-it-through" solution to disputes on liberal rules and principles, nor is it a case of power in dialogue. The international language of reason-of-state is finally a discourse that tracks and responds to conditions of differential power outside talk, not to intellectual requirements. This discourse is very much at home in divisive domestic politics. It differs from "transformative" liberalism (Macedo, 1998), especially in its explicit commitment to power and its reluctance to transform anything but behavior (and that on genuine, not psychologically taxed, consent).

The neglect in political liberalism of what was once the obvious in political theory is puzzling. The concept of power has been at the center of political theory since its inception, and political discourse has always tried to temper the hostility between power and the normative vocabularies of politics. The earliest discussions in the history of theory negotiate opposition between these two dimensions of political discourse, usually enlivened with references to justice. In his *History of the Peloponnesian War* Thucydides cites the Athenian declaration in the Melian Dialogue that "the standard of justice depends on the equality of power to compel and that in fact the strong do what they have the power to do and the weak accept what they have to accept" and the Melian response that this declaration forces them "to leave justice out of account," a response that supposes justice is different from self interest and power.[40] Plato, in *The Republic*, tries to refute the argument (which he attributes to Thrasymachus) that power dominates and perhaps absorbs reasoned conclusions on truth and justice. Modern theorists in liberal traditions (Locke, for example) distinguish external power and internal persuasion, and inevitably favor the intellectual powers of argument over brute coercion. The rightness of a claim must depend on thinking through arguments shielded from those coercive powers that can force compliance but can never determine who is right or wrong. It may be this longstanding assignment of merit to the best arguments rather than power that makes the failure of the shields between the two so disturbing. Yet even as all of our instincts separate the force of argument from the force of swords and guns, the separation does not require the dismissal of the latter. And of course contemporary theory has persuasively maintained again and again (with arguments that are themselves subject to the same assertions) that there is no best argument in a variety of commonplace situations concerned with the management of disputes, and that all arguments are intimately connected in one way or another to power.[41]

The topics of power, coercion, and force occur naturally once the full intellectual and behavioral differences in some forms of divisive politics are catalogued. Any model of international negotiations recognizes the ways in which exclusions from the deliberative table, and the differential influences of those at the table, track distributions of power among the players and the potential players. The paths to international settlements are strewn with power issues that affect and sometimes compromise the very sovereignty of states, and result in *modus vivendi* arrangements that acknowledge the limitations of power. The influence of power in politics stresses again the sharp differences between the accounts of public reason and democratic deliberation in liberal political theory and a set of realities of the political world. Let's accept, for purposes of this discussion, that the uses of power provide the locus for generalizable moral discussions on the exclusion of participants and issues. Then the thickness and timeliness of the parameters that recognize legitimate issues and limit the scope of discussions are crucial to all justifications of power. Nozick accepts moral side constraints that keep certain matters out of the libertarian framework.[42] In mediation some positions are illicit, nonstarters in the pursuit of a settlement. Settled moral issues, like slavery and torture, are not fit topics for any form of talk. They are acknowledged as wrong. The cases are closed. But notice that such items are typically not closed with the instruments of talk in any form. They are put to rest with adjustments of interests, modifications of political conditions, the actions of dominant coalitions, attrition of the disputants, certainly the judicious and sometimes aggressive use of force.

The recognition that some alternatives are outside the parameters of political discussion and reasoned settlements is not equivalent to the tendencies in liberal theory to keep certain positions from the deliberative table on the grounds that true (read: successful on liberal terms) deliberation must have a moral base and reliable methods, and not address issues that are too divisive. It is rather a gate keeping function drawn from the limits and failures of talk in general, and certainly efforts at accommodation. It is also a moral acknowledgement of the barbaric edges of rational thought, and perhaps recognition that some actions qualify as evil, that explain why force must occasionally be used.

Alan Wertheimer (1999) reminds us that we accommodate one another when we do not think there is a right answer to an issue. It is a form of dispute management often linked to deliberation as a method to find out how to contain rival preferences. But in the case of issues closed on moral grounds, even accommodation may be an affront. *Realpolitik* has traditionally extended a (different) forum to rational agents and issues excluded from public reason and deliberative democracy. But not all matters are talking points. The turn to power follows the natural recognition that closed issues are sometimes unfortunately reopened, the parameters of licit political relationships are occasionally and perhaps frequently breached, and the need to intervene forcefully becomes testimony to the limits of political discussion. It is a testimony that both enriches and deprecates the spheres of international politics, and is the great silent matter in so much of contemporary liberal political theory. It also sketches, like nothing else, a particular set of boundaries for talk as a method of managing disputes, and instructs us once more on the moral inadequacies of talk for the sake of talk, without a mechanism for power when talk is ended and action must be taken.[43]

7

There may not be a single form of public reason or deliberative democracy, and no form that effectively meets fairness tests generalizable in the robust pluralism reasonably expected in liberal democracies. But the arguments here favor at least a partial restoration, across the full and varied scope of public reasoning, of that background model drawn from what I have called the business contract metaphor and its affinities with *modus vivendi* arrangements among sovereign states.[44] This contractual form is found in the origins of liberal thought, for example in the theories of Grotius and Hobbes. The sanctions of the business model are oriented to practices rather than free choices, to arrangements rather than emotional ties. P.S. Atiyah provides a close analysis of different forms of a contract. He distinguishes among contracts binding on benefits attached to a promise (borrowing money, say, and promising to repay the sum), those binding as others have acted in reliance on the promise, and those that are "wholly executory" and so binding only as promises. Atiyah observes that promise-based liability, grounded in freedom of choice, is the paradigm for philosophers and represents ordinary discourse in contemporary times. I want to say that both benefit-based and reliance-based liabilities (and Atiyah asserts that while both are hostile to free choice, the latter is more so) are practice-driven, and that the sense of a contract on these grounds is more consistent with classical liberalism in rejecting contracts relying on correct beliefs. For example, such contracts are, in keeping with an orientation to behavior among sovereign entities, enforceable with reference to collective considerations rather than just the free promises made by autonomous individuals. States of mind are not decisive.[45]

Liberal principles begin with these two latter types of business contracts, benefit and reliance-based, and it is exactly these origins that put into relief the slide of the Rawlsian program to a romantic perspective that tracks free choice to a kind of belief-convergence. This more recent coalesced individualism finally undermines the original assumptions of liberalism (and compromises any preparation for the divisiveness of religious and secular differences) and is arguably more menacing for individual autonomy than practice-driven sanctions. But the restoration suggested here is definitely partial, requiring contemporary theory in the uses of complex systems as resources to rank order alternative models of political reasoning. The task is familiar enough. Liberalism emerged as the Aristotelian concept of individuals, elaborated in collective arrangements that crafted identity, gave way to the individualism of post-Reformation history with its emphasis on liberty and individual choices. Community became a deliberative construction for these pre-existing persons modeled after the sovereign states of that era. (Paradoxically, community now seems a moral imperative in the collectivist demands of transformative liberalism.) I am arguing that the classical sense of a contract must be both restored and revised, and suggesting that the restoration/revision be within the logic of complex systems as influenced by the calculative rationalities displayed in cognitive science, in this way yielding a political reasoning informed by recursive methods guided by collective languages. Like all revisions in political philosophy these proposals carry the intellectual weight and inertia of the past while responding to persuasive theories found in the present.

If one looks at the current (and probably lasting) disagreements among international relations scholars on the appropriateness and efficacy of realist and liberal depictions of world events, a curious three-part phenomenon presents itself. One part is the scholar's reality that the intellectual dispute among these competing factions is missing on the scenes of domestic politics in liberal democracies since the liberal model dominates in these arrangements. The arguments I offer here are efforts to break this pattern by suggesting the anarchic similarities between domestic and international politics when communities differ in fundamental ways. The second part is that critical takes on the liberal model, its much discussed limitations (especially in handling religious beliefs and practices), are reified in international relations theory. One result of this reification is that the intellectual disputes among realists and liberals (or idealists and constructivists) can be assigned to both political domains. This assignment provides intellectual insights into both levels of politics. Third, the recognition of domains suggests that some of the intellectual dispute surrounding realism can be ordered and perhaps resolved by employing a well-known tactic from both the natural and the social sciences: identify the parameters of a theory within which it is valid, outside of which it is not. In the form of a question, under what limiting conditions within political systems does the realist model of international relations theory dominate, and what are the conditions that make versions of the liberal model effective?

The more obvious answer to the questions on limits is that the liberal model (by which I mean now the integrative version of liberal reasoning) can be effective in any domain where there is an overlapping consensus on the rules and principles of political reasoning, and on fundamental liberal expectations of the good life. It is not effective when the disputing parties are members of radically different ways of life that influence the proper methods for resolving disputes. But this answer is simplistic. It cannot resolve differences among international relations scholars on the issues of realism versus its alternatives. Yet it does seem that some who write about various aspects of globalization are making arguments that would illuminate the conditional nature of realism versus liberalism disputes. On the efficacy of globalization, these critics say it depends on which sector of economic capital one is discussing. This conditional-dependence view may help in ordering realist or liberal theories: which is the better concept in explaining international relations may be a function of the domain to which the concept is assigned. The decisive influence of conditions, illustrated in different ways in these literatures, is exactly what I am stressing as one of the features of the alternative middle-earth forms of political reasoning that demand a background mechanism to survey conditions in adjudicating the efficacy of liberal versus *realpolitik* models.[46] More interesting is the intellectual strategy the observation requires. If conditions dominate the effective uses of any set of rival models, then some intellectual machinery must be in place to recognize and order the conditions for a proper set of decision rules. This machinery would contain the recursive interpretations that can evaluate both the conditions in which models of reason and deliberation are assigned, and the models themselves in conditions of stasis and transformation. We would expect political reasoning not only to manage claims entered into public space but also to adjudicate among rival models of reason, in particular the integrative liberal and reason-of-state models.

Put another way, the distinctions between domestic and international politics are not as useful as the differences between authoritative and anarchic conditions in any political arena. It follows that a complete theory of political reason would contain both liberal and state reasoning with no privilege assigned to either, and also the intellectual devices that can survey conditions and tell us when to use the liberal model and when to engage in *realpolitik*. Such a theory would then bracket the empirical issue of whether the integrative (or, in Macedo's vocabulary, transformative) liberal model of reasoning is best because an overlapping consensus is likely and perhaps widespread, or flawed because democratic societies tend toward divisiveness or are typically found to be deeply pluralistic. On the arguments here, it doesn't matter. The point is that a complete version of political reasoning must contain both integrative liberal and *realpolitik* models, and the capacity to determine which is appropriate in different conditions. One might even argue that the more important role of political reasoning is to rank order the intellectual devices used to manage claims.

Also, even the best pragmatic accounts of political reasoning are obligated to supply a missing piece of the political setting, the concept of power. The suggestion here is that mediating forms of dialogue drawn from international politics and open to *modus vivendi* arrangements— when needed in divisive conditions—reduce the deleterious effects of internal power by marginalizing the importance of truth claims. But this discussion acknowledges the occasional need to invoke the external force of power as justified by the internal force of arguments. Utterly intolerable actions, for example human rights violations like genocide, are palpable items in the world, and the thought that purely communicative action will resolve all disputes, given the extremes of human action, is misdirected innocence. A complete theory of political reason (only sketched here) will contain a framework for selecting among various models of practical reasoning, an inventory that includes both the liberal (and perhaps even transformative) model, but also must stretch to those *realpolitik* models that can join reason to the justified use of external force.

Stated simply and bluntly (and repetitively), political reasoning must be a binary arrangement constituted by a controlling mechanism and an inventory of political languages proffered as governing resources. For example, among the prominent languages in liberal political theory are (1) the classical liberalism represented by Hobbes (*modus vivendi* arrangements buttressed by theories of human nature), (2) transformative liberalism, as developed by the later Rawls and the recent Steve Macedo (a reformist effort to craft right-minded beliefs), (3) deliberative democracy (where reasoned outcomes are sought among reasonable people who use established procedures), and (4) a state reasoning drawn up from thin realism in international relations theory that operates on *modus vivendi* with minimum assumptions about human nature. Now, on this binary arrangement, one cannot say that political reasoning just *is* any of the candidates listed here (or any plausible addition to the list) for an authoritative political language. The mistake in current accounts of public reason is to assign dominance to one candidate (liberalism or realism, say) when the point is that the mechanism that adjudicates among the candidates is the authoritative venue for political reason.

Hobbes proposed a program of governance in which it is rational to be moral.[47] We might ask of any form of state reasoning that it be crafted on conditions in which it is rational to be reasonable. One can also say that a starting point for this type of political reasoning is a vision of rival cultures or sovereign communities bound together for their own privileged reasons, which is in many ways the more compelling and estimable dream for a divided political setting. No simple and unconditional appeals to be reasonable, arguably an egregious insult to a person of religious conviction, no admittance tests to the reasoning table on moral or intelligibility criteria falsely presented as universal, no inspection of beliefs and reasons, no requirement that citizens bond with one another in some civic mission, just the reasoned search for an accord that will meet the interests of the disputing parties as they define these interests and understand the settlements. That this is vital to the congenial standing of religious communities in a democratic secular state should be self-evident. What is relevant, and should be controlling, is that liberal democracies originate in substantial part from the Reformation acknowledgements of religious freedoms. This historical shift produced the tolerance of religious communities within the democratic state that one would expect in all contemporary political systems.

The arguments here suggest that an authentic tolerance for such radical diversity is more likely to be found in an orientation toward the middle earth of political realism, a respect for the privacy of thoughts (reasons, intentions), a generous acceptance of provisional accords derived from accommodation rather than resolution, an acceptance of coercion as a complement to public reasoning, an orientation to collective considerations, but mainly in a commitment to a recursive form of reasoning that scans and selects political languages appropriate for specific conditions. A *modus vivendi* arrangement is not denigrated in this wide version of dispute management, but often the best that can be achieved and marked with considerable value. One might argue that the background concepts driving liberal programs, especially the prime virtues of tolerance and liberty, are more fully met on such expectations. In a setting dominated by the differences between secular and religious, religious and religious, a model of reasoning drawn up from the realities of politics within and among morally and intellectually sovereign units, based not on the qualifying attitudes or beliefs of the participants but on the rules of engagement that help define political encounters, might even be cause for celebration in the commonplace divisiveness characterizing so much of domestic politics in all political systems.

Political and Religious Practices:
A Case Study Continued

I

Religious scaffolding extending to the infinite provides one of the more powerful marks of religious identity, that forged by conscience. Conscience has a distinguished line of meanings in political and religious thought, and in the latter it complements divinity by bringing the external references of religion into the identity of the self.[1] In contemporary literatures conscience refers to a type of private knowledge, including especially an intimate knowledge of the self that requires loyalty to the dictates of the moral sense. The Greek terms for conscience begin with a knowing of something with another, and the knowing links to the act of bearing witness to evil. Aquinas expands on the judgmental dimensions of conscience in connecting it to acts of witness, and accusation. The Hebrew derivation of conscience is from the compass sense of north, and in contemporary Hebrew is represented by the biblical word for compass. It is also related to the word for hidden. Tom Green takes conscience into a reflexive judgment on the self and "things that matter."[2] I take an act of religious conscience to be one in which an individual follows an internal command, in religious forms of conscience drawn from a divine source but in all instances of conscience framed within the self and reflexive on the self, that carries the sanction of losing or compromising one's identity if resisted. A potential resistance to political authority is built into religious beliefs with the presence of conscience. It is the absorption of an individual in a religious collective that provides for religious conscience, a commitment of the whole self to a higher cause that, if betrayed, can extinguish the individual's identity.

External moral imperatives do not always represent conscience. When Antigone disobeys an order from Creon (the King) not to bury her brother, she invokes a higher law that commands her to act in opposition to the King. But there is no evidence that she internalized the command, or that her identity was at stake in the event. The reflexivity of the command attaches to the tension between the command of the monarch and the laws of the gods. When conscience relies on higher laws the laws are brought into the moral contours of the self and issued as an identity-driven personal command. Conscience can support or oppose conventional laws. Socrates arguably is driven by conscience in accepting the penalty of death from the Athenian assembly, but the reasons he presents in the *Crito* for his decision are grounded primarily in arguments that do not seem entirely bound to the moral law and in fact prefigure in some ways a kind of contract theory (that he has lived in Athens all his life and so has incurred an obligation by virtue of his presence, that one cannot disobey a particular unjust penalty if the main body of the law is just, etc.). Yet in some sense Socrates seems to feel that he would not be Socrates if he acts otherwise, that the decision to die is the result of a reflexive judgment on himself negotiated within his psyche, and that the demands of conscience require an acceptance of the death penalty as a means to preserve his identity by obeying the commands of a legitimate political authority. Socrates said that he was guided throughout his life by an oracle or daemon, a voice of sorts that spoke to him privately. But this exercise of internal guidance is also influenced by higher laws that are brought into the landscape of the soul. The last line in the *Crito* is Socrates speaking to Crito: "Then let me follow the intimations of the will of God."[3] The dictates from higher sources are welded to a sense of conscience that in this instance requires compliance with positive law. No surprise revelations track from this observation to a classical structure of conscience. The Platonic model of the soul stipulates that we follow the dictates of reason under pain of remorse, or a diminution of the self attending the reluctance to reflect on actions contrary to the commands endorsed by our reflective powers.

Any history of conscience displays its complexity, and diverse content. Thomas More and Martin Luther King disobeyed commands and laws that their sense of conscience rejected. More resisted Henry VIII because he regarded God's commands as superseding the commands of a sovereign. King engaged in civil disobedience of a system of law that he saw as unjust. But even as a term that varies with content, conscience-driven actions do yield a form that helps identify some broad hostilities and connections between religion and politics, even to the point of suggesting that the two systems can be sovereign entities with zones of moral and political anarchy separating them.[4] We might also say that the commands falling within the domain of conscience are arranged hierarchically. Socrates reflects briefly in the *Apology* on whether he could have obeyed Athenian law if he had been commanded to stop teaching, finally concluding that no legitimate authority could have so commanded him ("whether you acquit me or not; you know that I am not going to alter my conduct, not even if I have to die a hundred deaths"—p. 62). Legitimacy figures large in the musings of Socrates. He points out that he had resisted as a member of the Council a decision to try ten naval commanders *en bloc* because the decision was illegal ("you should not act unconstitutionally . . . I thought that it was my duty to face it out on the side of law and justice."—p. 64), and disobeyed the Rule of the Thirty, suggesting that the reason was that they constituted an illegitimate governing body doing illicit things (p. 65).[5] On the other hand, it is well known to historians of the Peloponnesian Wars that Athens engaged in what today would be called genocide, a practice that is (from a contemporary perspective) as regrettable as it has been common throughout history. Yet, as Nicholas Smith has pointed out, no dissent from these (and other) practices came from Socrates. Presumably the reason, which guides the *Crito*, is that one does not disobey a legitimate political authority, especially if one's identity has been forged by that political society and consent has been given to it every day by virtue of living in its culture. But such an authority must permit a kind of free speech that allows the citizen to persuade the government of the moral course of action. Otherwise it forfeits its legitimacy almost on grounds of unintelligibility of rule. It is not a stretch to see this proposition as requiring a kind of institutional dialectic, what in systems theory is called institutional reflexivity, recursive functions at the highest levels, and the higher forms of collective terms as conditions for a reasoned subscription to political authority.[6]

The obvious conclusion from a survey of conscience is that individuals do not always choose their identifications with collectives. In the case of religious identification individuals may be pressed into the service of pure or holistic arrangements as a condition of membership, and the collective is regarded, at least in part, as outside the boundaries of the human community. If we revisit the concept of the sacred the demands of religious texts are clearly different from secular arrangements. The strong definition of the sacred delineates its primary standing as an item representing intrinsic or non-instrumental value, and its independent standing in that it (a) is not an expression of human wants, needs, or goods, but a type of freestanding resource that recognizes and interprets these matters, and (b) issues from what I have called an insensate reality (meaning one that is not entirely intelligible to human understanding). Partly as a consequence of this independence, the sacred summons the whole person by providing a reasonably full instruction on the moral life that intertwines with the individual's identity. The type of conscience crafted on this stronger version of the sacred is precisely what opposes the pragmatic state of mind that is the mark of the secular democratic state. Conscience goes all the way through the individual as a link to the divine. It also presents, in especially vivid form, some of the differences that must be negotiated by a freestanding political language when shared reasons among disputants are chronically elusive.

2

Religious experiences that are the resources for conscience, often depicted as transforming events on members, are presented in numerous stories in religious traditions. It's fair to say that these stories are standard fare and still utterly engrossing. Here is a story that illustrates the effects of the core ritual in Santería on those who are its participants. Augusta Del Zotto, a graduate student in political science, took part in the Osha sacrifice ritual just before beginning her work for a PhD. It was in 1998 and she was living in California. She recalls that she was working through a lot of emotional and physical problems at the time, what she now calls "a string of bad luck" that lasted for three years. Her husband had left her and their son, and she was facing terrible and unanticipated financial problems as a single mother. She sustained a number of serious injuries when three thugs assaulted her near her home. Much later a lump was discovered on one of her breasts and had to be removed. She remembers being very, very tired from these and other events, to the point where she believed that if there were a God she was being tested by this supreme being at extreme levels. She wanted to find a way to be more balanced, to bring love and stability back into her life. A colleague at San Francisco State college, Maria, had a godfather named Nilo Tandrón, Olufandeí (his orisha name), who was a well-known priest of Obatalá. Maria suggested to her that she might want to start seeing him.[7]

Augusta began visiting this very elderly man (he was in his nineties) in his apartment in the Mission district of San Francisco. The fee was whatever she could afford, Tandrón told her, and sometimes she and Maria would simply bring the olorisha some lunch. Tandrón's methods began with a general reading using cowrie shells. Then he would give the client a blessing and some oils for ritual baths. In subsequent visits, if he developed confidence in the client, believed that the person was serious and not just playing in the spiritual marketplace, he would invite this individual to participate in an animal sacrifice ritual. He did invite Augusta, and she immediately discovered that, like all olorishas, Tandrón used different animals for different purposes. For Augusta the animal was to be a dove, the animal designated to heal people with a sick body or spirit. The first requirement of the ritual was that Augusta had to bathe for two weeks in water that had special oils and flowers. She did this. Then, a week before the ritual, she and Maria were asked by Tandrón to purchase the dove. They both knew that the Chinese community had been granted licenses to sell live animals in their butcher stores. They went to a butcher on Grand Avenue in the Chinatown district of San Francisco who immediately took them to a back room when they mentioned Tandrón's name. There they picked out a white dove from one of many kept in a box with little holes in it. They took the dove to Tandrón's house where it was fed special foods for a week.

On the day scheduled for the ritual Augusta was taken into a small room at Tandrón's apartment. She remembers that the room was completely white with a multi-layered altar, dozens of smaller altars, and statues of different saints. In a corner, encased in plastic, was the white suit that Tandrón had worn when he was ordained an olorisha back in the 1940s in Cuba. In other parts of the room were different offerings from clients, money and food, occasionally photographs of a sick relative, all part of separate packages requesting certain things from certain gods. Tandrón arranged a space for Augusta in one part of this room, setting out a white cloth in front of an image of Shangó and placing on it collares beads and some flowers Augusta had brought. Tandrón seemed very frail, a diminutive and thin man, and he could barely stand up. Maria, his niece, and her husband, Robert, assisted him. But when the ritual began Tandrón seemed to be energized, transformed, and was able to conduct the prolonged chanting in Yoruba with no difficulty. Augusta felt herself shifting into an altered state of consciousness as the chanting continued. The room seemed to be getting brighter and brighter. Tandrón passed beads around her body.

He put fire water (pure rum) in his mouth and blew the liquid around her. Then he asked her to move several times in a tight circle, telling her to keep her eyes open, that she had to be brave. The invitation was clear. She was to witness the sacrifice of the dove.

She remembers the ritual in vivid detail. At the critical moment in the ceremony Tandrón took a very small ritual knife that is moon-shaped and slit the throat of the animal. (The use of a knife on an animal as small as a bird is very unusual since the sacrifice is almost always conducted with the hands in these instances. Tandrón may have used a knife because of his age and frailty. Also unusual is the knife that he selected since it is rarely used, and then only to skin and carve larger animals already offered in preparing them for cooking and consumption.) Augusta remembers that the death of the animal was slow and painful. The dove was screeching in pain, dying bit by bit, and Augusta could see the desperation in its eyes, a wildness as it struggled to breathe. Tandrón told her that she had to watch this, that she was not to close her eyes. The Yoruba chants continued and at some point the bird's head came off. She estimates that the death of the dove took several minutes, not seconds, and she admits that it was very hard to watch. She believes that she saw the spirit of a sentient being "snuffed out" in great agony. Immediately after the death, with the dove's body still moving, Tandrón and his assistants poured a little bit of the animal's blood on the scarf she was wearing on her head. The chanting continued until the dove's headless body stopped moving. Augusta recalls that at that point everything seemed to go still, all movement halted. She was asked to go to another room to meditate. Tandrón's assistants cleaned up the room in some ritualistic way and placed the remains of the dove inside a white ceremonial cloth. They then placed the head back on the body and wrapped the carcass with the cloth, but without the flowers that are sometimes placed at this moment inside the wrapping. Later they disposed of the remains. Augusta understood that on the West coast the animal carcasses are placed on rocks on the edges of the Pacific Ocean, sometimes with candles and food alongside, a kind of second altar that people occasionally encounter before the setting is absorbed by nature.[8]

Did the ritual help Augusta? She maintains that it did. The logic of the ceremony was to transfer the agony inside of her into the animal and when the animal is sacrificed the human agony dies also. To this day she says that she feels tremendous guilt over the animal's death. She had asked before the ceremony whether it was necessary to actually kill an animal. Couldn't a symbolic ritual suffice? The answer was no. So she went through with it. The sacrifice seemed to her to be a kind of sad duty, a reminder of mortality and the inevitability of death. She did feel a real connection to the animal. She believes that it was not treated as an object but as a being which had to serve this somber purpose. The immediate aftermaths were simple. She was to keep taking her ritual bath for a week and talk with no one about the experience. Not talking was important. The belief conveyed to her by the olorisha was that the power given to her by the experience would be diminished if she spoke about it. Silence was imperative.

Augusta considers herself a member of the urban classes in Western culture. Yet she transferred something in herself to an animal, and in doing so felt that she was taken to a different level of consciousness. That sensing of a change in consciousness remained with her in strong terms for five or six months. The therapeutic effects were permanent. Her spirit was no longer afflicted. Today, when she feels weak and ineffectual in front of other people, she meditates on the experience. The meditation renews her strength.

One might argue that the beginning of moral sensibility is found in extended sympathy, which means a seeing of the world from the point of view of the other. This extension of vision, this entering the head and skin of others, is at the center of Golden Rule morality and the mercy that allows justice to be tolerable. Extended sympathy is a large phrase for empathy, and an umbrella for a family of moral terms like compassion. What is intriguing and agonizing about animal sacrifice in Osha is that it is presented as a transference that carries some sense of the human self to the animal. Not, thank you, the tired liberal notion of "I feel your pain" but a crueler and more demanding invitation to the subject to experience the animal's death, and by this empathetic experience to be cleansed of human pain and illness as the animal dies. It is harder to imagine a stronger and stranger passage to death as transfigured and vicarious release.

3

The Lukumí Church pursued its suit against the city of Hialeah and its officials in two directions and at two levels. One direction was against the city itself and the ordinances passed by the city council that prohibited animal sacrifice. This direction set the course for the later constitutional test of church–state relations since it pitted a religious institution against representatives of the state and, primarily, local ordinances advanced as the expression of secular interests. But a second direction, more private and even primal, suggests the intensity of the dispute. Ernesto Pichardo and the church also brought suit against the city, and the mayor and city councilmen in their individual capacities, on charges of harassment and discrimination.

The two levels at which the first suit was pressed illuminate the distinct constitutional issues. At one level, less complicated and more proximate, the church argued that the city ordinances were not consistent with Florida's slaughter laws, specifically the exemption for ritual slaughter. Even on a generous interpretation one is compelled to see this contest as primarily technical, not advancing or clarifying the relationships between church and state in liberal societies. At the second and more profound level, the constitutional test, the main issues were addressed. The church claimed in its suit that the city ordinances banning animal sacrifice violated the free exercise clause of the First Amendment and deprived its members of their constitutional rights under the First, Fourth and Fourteenth Amendments. The church sought to recover damages for this alleged deprivation and for what the Pichardo group regarded as a process of attempted intimidation, including harassment and threats, by the city. Mainly, the church was seeking with the lawsuit to secure "the right of the Church to perform animal sacrifices on Church premises, and for the right of Church members to perform sacrifices in their own homes."[9]

District Judge Eugene P. Spellman, who presided over the non-jury trial held in late July and early August 1989, was quick (as legal matters go) to dismiss the suit against the mayor and city councilmen in their individual capacities. On the defendants' summary judgment motion, Judge Spellman ruled that the city officials could not be sued as individuals. They were protected by absolute legislative immunity and so could not be held personally liable for monetary damages. It was apparent at that point that the lawsuit was to proceed as a contest between rival institutions and practices, not as a personal dispute between the Pichardos and Hialeah city officials.

The judge also granted the defendants summary judgment on the issue of harassment, finding that the plaintiffs' allegations of discrimination were not supported by the facts. Here it is instructive to compare the court's findings of fact with Ernesto Pichardo's narrative of events leading up to his lawsuit. The judge noted and accepted the facts that Pichardo related to support harassment charges. Waste service was not provided even though a deposit was accepted and a bill was sent to the church for the service. The Florida Power & Light Company shut off existing power to the church after a deposit was made, and would not reconnect the power until after the city issued a Certificate of Occupancy. This certificate was delayed for three days while the city checked the church's tax-free status and its original certificate of occupancy from the state as well as certain zoning regulations. The court also accepted the fact that a cluster of three inspectors suddenly appeared at the church on the Monday following a Friday submission of complete documentation and that the church was found to be deficient in some way by each of the inspectors.

But, in contrast to Pichardo's interpretation, the court regarded all of this activity as benign and procedurally correct. A three-day delay in processing a registration application did not strike the judge as unusual in any way. Nor was he impressed with the failures of the church to pass the fire, electrical and plumbing inspections. The judge viewed the violations as genuine. He noted that faulty wiring in an air conditioner, a faulty disconnect switch outside the building, and an inappropriate electrical meter (the city's descriptions of events) were real problems. He also pointed out that a single bathroom for both men and women violated the South Florida code. Finally, the judge reminded the plaintiffs that the city did issue a certificate of occupancy when these problems were corrected, on August 7, 1987, one day after the final inspection. The court was simply not impressed by events that Pichardo viewed as examples of harassment.

Nor was the court inclined to accept Pichardo's accounts of council influence on the various licensing, zoning and building departments of the city, or the waste service, Florida Power & Light, and Southern Bell (the telephone company). Judge Spellman saw no conspiracy, no coalition of individuals using the powers of the city to intimidate and impede Pichardo's efforts. He even found the charges of undue police activity around the church unconvincing. The judge found insufficient basis for the harassment charges, and dismissed this part of the suit even while accepting the narratives that Pichardo presented to the court.

The court also regarded the city ordinances as consistent with state law. The plaintiffs in the suit, the church of the Lukumí Babalu Aye and Ernesto Pichardo, argued that, since the state law protects the ritual slaughter of animals and provides for civil penalties for violators, the city's prohibition of animal sacrifice with criminal penalties assigned to violators conflicts with state law both as to law and penalty. The judge ruled otherwise. He first cited the State Attorney General's interpretation that the "ritual slaughter" exemption "applies only to religious slaughtering of animals for food" (as in the production of Kosher food). In the opinion of the court, the city ordinances "only prohibit sacrificing animals where the primary purpose is not food consumption." So there is no conflict. Also, the Hialeah ordinances were deemed zoning regulations that at once clarify the exclusion of ritual sacrifice from the State Humane Slaughter Act and specify that all slaughter must be performed in areas zoned for that purpose. The apparent inconsistency on penalties is dismissed with this zoning interpretation of the ordinances. The state law aims at animal control and cruelty. Penalties may differ between zoning laws and animal control and cruelty laws. In addition, a provision of the state law "authorizes municipalities to enact an ordinance identical to the state law 'except as to penalty.' " The judge concluded that no inconsistency had been demonstrated between the Hialeah ordinances and the Florida state law regulating animal slaughter.

Judge Spellman then turned to the constitutional issue raised by the suit. At the time of the District Court decision, announced on October 5, 1989, the controlling framework for ruling on a conflict between the free exercise of religion and governmental action consisted of three tests. First, does the law aim at regulating conduct, not belief? Second, does the law have both a secular purpose and effect? Third, do the secular interests expressed in the law outweigh the burdens that the law places on the religion? The last test was often accompanied by the provision that the regulation be the least onerous action to achieve the state's interests. Judge Spellman used the first two threshold tests in his initial reasoning. The ordinances emerged intact from the application of the tests.

The easier test for the judge was the first. The laws clearly aimed at regulating conduct, not belief, since the practice of animal sacrifice was prohibited, not beliefs in the practice's efficacy or importance. The harder test was the second. Did the ordinances have a secular purpose and effect? Even the defendants admitted that the ordinances were written and passed as a response to the opening of the Lukumí Church in the city. But they argued that their sole motivation was to control a practice of animal sacrifice that was becoming an increasingly serious problem in the community. The proposed church was simply the trigger for legislative action. They maintained that the ordinances were intended as neutral laws to prohibit any killing of animals except in slaughterhouses. Judge Spellman accepted these arguments. He allowed that the prohibition of animal sacrifice "was not meant to single out persons engaged in ritual sacrifice, but to put those persons on notice that the state exemption for ritual slaughter only applied to commercial ritual slaughter, done in slaughterhouses."

The controversial terms were the references to "sacrifice," "ritual," and "ceremony" in the prohibitions, which the plaintiffs claimed were indications that the ordinances discriminated against religion by targeting practices that could only be religious, not secular, and thus were unconstitutional on their face. Judge Spellman disagreed. He regarded the terms as generalizable to nonreligious groups that do not enjoy First Amendment protections, like satanic cults. But, also, the judge observed that the First Amendment allows communities to target religious practices when needed to ensure public health and welfare. The question is whether the regulation serves a secular purpose, not whether it is facially neutral. Judge Spellman ruled that the Hialeah ordinances had only an incidental effect on religious practices. Their main purpose and effect were secular.

The third test used by Judge Spellman—whether the governmental interests expressed in the ordinances outweighed the burdens placed on the religious community by these same ordinances—also yielded a positive answer. The judge accepted the real burdens placed on Osha by the city's prohibitions of animal sacrifice. The practice is not a casual or peripheral activity, but one that is integral to the religion. Nevertheless, the court was impressed by three secular community interests served by the ordinances. One was to safeguard the health, welfare and safety of the community. The court's findings of fact included ample documentation of the health hazards of animal carcasses left in public places. Though the defendants offered no evidence of any infectious diseases originating from discarded animal remains, experts testified on the health risks created by the presence of rats, flies and other animals attracted to the carcasses. The spread of disease was judged to be more likely in a setting where animals that had never been inspected by health authorities were killed and left in public areas. This setting did in fact describe Osha practices.

A second interest was guaranteeing the welfare of children. The court heard testimony that children exposed to animal sacrifice, even when part of a religious ceremony, could be psychologically damaged from the experience. An expert witness for the defense testified that observing animal sacrifice would likely increase the probability that a child would behave violently, both to animals and humans. The judge was not persuaded by plaintiff's witnesses who regarded the causal chains between animal sacrifice and violent behavior as more complex or tenuous. He observed that "the city has shown that the risk to children justifies the absolute ban on animal sacrifice."

The third interest was the protection of animals from cruelty and unnecessary killing. A great deal of vivid and dramatic testimony was provided by expert witnesses for the defense on the suffering of animals who are killed in Osha rites. The conditions in which the animals were held were described as filthy, overcrowded, and sometimes lacking adequate food and water. Defense witnesses described the fear and pain experienced by the animals, including a death prolonged by inadequate and even incompetent techniques of killing. The court found less persuasive the testimony for the plaintiffs by Charles Wetli, an MD who at the time was the Dade County Medical Examiner, that the actual sacrifice is medically humane. Judge Spellman used these findings of fact to support a widely acknowledged responsibility of government to prohibit cruelty to animals.

The court refused to allow an exception to these government interests for the Osha religion. To do so, the judge argued, would be to allow all religions such an exception, with the result that "the exception would, in effect, swallow the rule." Nor would the judge permit the church to practice animal sacrifice openly in conjunction with its own efforts to monitor and control the practice. In this way, the plaintiffs had argued, they could meet the government's interests in less restrictive ways. But the judge was unconvinced that all Osha practitioners would follow any single set of guidelines. Judge Spellman admitted in his decision that the city ordinances were "not religiously neutral but were intended to stop the practice of animal sacrifice in the city of Hialeah." But he added that "the ordinances were not passed to interfere with religious beliefs, but rather to regulate conduct." He saw the ordinances as governed by secular purposes.

The balance of interests was decided in the government's favor. The decision of the District Court was that the ordinances were constitutional. The absolute ban on animal sacrifice enacted by the city of Hialeah was allowed to stand in its entirety.

4

Ernesto Pichardo was remarkably sanguine about the District Court ruling. He remembers that the first reporters to interview him asked their questions with a kind of sad, grieving tone, the underlying theme being that the city had been entirely victorious, the church entirely routed. But Pichardo, courting judgments of madness from his friends and associates, thought the ruling was to the church's advantage. His reasoning was that Osha had been given a first-time historical opportunity to present itself in a court of law. So while the city of Hialeah had (there is no other way to characterize the legal ruling) demolished the church in the District Court, Pichardo was content that the church had established that it was a genuine religion, a faith with ancient origins, and that animal sacrifice was a core ritual in its practices. Of course each time Pichardo tried to explain to reporters his take on the ruling they were more baffled, and remained fixated on whether animal sacrifice was really necessary in this day and age.

Pichardo's main discomfort at this point was with the American Civil Liberties Union (ACLU). They had been in the case from the beginning, after some tough negotiations, and he had the distinct impression that they were taking over. This troubled him because the people they brought on board had strong personal agendas. Many were vegetarians, had strong views on animal rights, and found it difficult to embrace the church's case as a true First Amendment issue. He believes to this day that many of the ACLU attorneys regarded the issues as frivolous in a larger legal context. Also, Pichardo was convinced at this stage that lawyers in general know very little about religion. This meant for him that he was being represented by people who were ignorant or indifferent about what it was they were defending. Since he felt strongly that he and other church officials had to be sitting at the table with the lawyers arguing the case with them, it meant that both the legal and church teams had to educate one another. Finally, there were from Pichardo's perspective a number of conflicts or near conflicts of interests among his attorneys. The father of Richard Garrett, the head lawyer for the city, was a strong financial supporter of the same ACLU from which some of his legal team came. Also, one of the church's attorneys was personally close to the District Court Judge.

An important re-shuffling of the team of lawyers for the legal appeal of the case was the hiring of Douglas Laycock as chief attorney. Laycock, a distinguished authority on church–state, came from Texas, meaning that he joined the legal team without the interlocking and over-lapping networks of local ties that the Miami attorneys brought to the case. He was an outsider, with no binding Florida connections, meaning no favors owed to anyone, and he was and is acknowledged as brilliant. He also had concerns. The main one was the conservative composition of the U.S. Supreme Court. Shouldn't they wait for a more liberal Supreme Court before appealing the ruling? At this point Pichardo prepared a check list of for-and-against points in the case and sat down with the legal team to go over them. He had compiled the points in part from a check-form issued by the Internal Revenue Service for churches seeking tax-exempt status. One of the lawyers had suggested that this form might represent a pragmatic guide for distinguishing a religion from a cult given that the Court had not provided such criteria in previous cases. Pichardo remembers getting to the 21st point against them with only 3 points going for them. He sat back at that point and conceded that the legal case was against them. But he felt that God had started this business and they had to go with God.

The District Court ruling on the Lukumí case had been affirmed by the U.S. Court of Appeals for the Eleventh Circuit. The U.S. Supreme Court accepted the case for review, and Pichardo and his brother flew up to Washington on a Friday to attend the oral arguments before the Court scheduled for November 4, 1992. The church was broke by this time, and Pichardo's main concern was not with the case but with scrounging up the money to pay travel expenses. Also, death threats from animal rights supporters had increased in volume and intensity as the day of the hearing drew near. At the hotel, as Pichardo and his brother walked through the lobby to have dinner with their Miami attorney, he glanced at a news stand and saw that his photograph was on the front page of the weekend edition of *USA Today*, full color, for a story announcing that the hearing on the case was scheduled for the U.S. Supreme Court the following week. Great, he remembers thinking. Any number of people have threatened to kill me if I appear in Washington, DC, and here is a public reminder of my presence. It was at this point that he visited a contact at the FBI. The Bureau quickly checked out the death threats. The District Metro Intelligence also intervened by identifying the animal rights groups who were active in the area and ensuring that their demonstrations were peaceful. It was the Metro unit that arranged for him to enter the Supreme Court building in a secure way. As it turned out, Pichardo and his brother were protected but there were no violent incidents at any point in the legal proceedings. Pichardo remembers one final irony. As he and his brother walked into the U.S. Supreme Court building a friend noticed that the halls were filled with statues of past justices and notables from ancient Greece. Ah, thought Pichardo, ancestor worship and homage to pagan life.

5

The decision by the U.S. Supreme Court, presented on June 11, 1993, reversed the lower court rulings along what might be seen as predictable lines. The legal background consisted of the two familiar interpretations of the free exercise clause in the First Amendment. One is that the state ensures religious freedom if it recognizes the compelling nature of religious conscience by granting some exemptions from the law for religious beliefs and practices. In this first interpretation the state may restrict religious practices only where a compelling state interest is at stake, and the least restrictive means is selected for the regulation. The other interpretation is that the state fulfills the free exercise clause if it treats religious and secular institutions in the same way with laws that are neutral across both sets of institutions. The first interpretation governed in the District and Appeals court rulings on Lukumí. Pending the appeal to the U.S. Supreme Court, however, the case of *Employment Division v. Smith* (1990) was decided by the Court. The rules had changed with *Smith* to a reliance on the second interpretation of free exercise. Hialeah city attorneys, who had argued compelling interest in the lower courts, claimed progenitor with *Smith* in the U.S. Supreme Court on the generality of the animal sacrifice prohibition.

Attorneys for the church of the Lukumí Babalu Aye argued to the Court that the absolute prohibition of animal sacrifice targets certain religions and mainly burdens the Lukumí Church. Even *Smith*, they pointed out, requires that the state treat religions no worse than secular institutions and practices. Yet this rudimentary neutrality is violated, they argued, with city acceptance of a wide range of animal killing, such as euthanasia of pets, hunting, slaughter of animals for food, pest control. In the oral arguments before the Supreme Court, the Lukumí attorney suggested that exemptions had been reversed, with secular practices allowed broad exemptions that effectively targeted an unpopular religion for regulation.

It is not a strange thing for secular authorities to underestimate the differences between secular and religious beliefs. The error in Lukumí originated with the assumption that the city could judge the necessity or appropriateness of religious practices. In a language that breaks every rule of legal prudence the Hialeah city ordinances defined "sacrifice" as the unnecessary killing of an animal in a ritual or ceremony not for the primary purpose of food consumption. The Lukumí attorney, no doubt grateful for the well-meaning zeal of the city fathers, pointed out to the Court that this judgment requires the city to prove that the Osha belief in the necessity of animal sacrifice is false, which is a heresy trial. The city obviously forgot that religious beliefs are drawn from an alternative reality that is not subject to secular corrections.

The Court had several options in deciding Lukumí. One was to allow the ordinances to stand, which would have sent a strong message that the Court wants legislatures, not the legal system, to craft whatever exemptions are granted to religions. Another was to strike down the ordinances, perhaps on the grounds that the use of religious terms in the ordinances (like "sacrifice") and the blanket restriction of all animal sacrifice in the face of widespread animal killing in the community exceed even the generous regulatory guidelines of Smith.

On June 11, 1993, the Court ruled the ordinances unconstitutional, though the ruling did not directly affect the standing of *Smith*. All nine justices agreed that the city ordinances violated the free exercise clause of the First Amendment. In the majority opinion written by Justice Kennedy, the Court found that the ordinances intended to suppress the Osha religion even though they did not state such a goal. The use of the words "sacrifice" and "ritual" was not decisive for the Court since Kennedy admitted in his opinion that current usage of these terms also admits secular interpretations. But the Court did rule that the ordinances, by intending to prohibit animal sacrifice conducted by the Lukumí Church, failed both the neutrality and general applicability tests of Smith. The problem was that the clear objective of the regulation was the suppression of the main ritual of the Osha religion, which effectively targeted religious beliefs for regulation. This "is never permissible," according to Judge Kennedy.

6

Pichardo was at his mother's house early one morning with friends and family sitting at the dinner table waiting for some Cuban coffee to be made when the phone rang. It was a reporter in Washington saying that he had just read the decision, offered his congratulations, and wondered if he could get a statement. Pichardo replied, well, great, you are really on the ball, but please, sir, we will be glad to give a statement if you could first fax us a copy of the ruling right now because even our lawyers do not know what has happened. The reporter did fax a copy, and then Pichardo called the attorneys and said, wake up, people, get on it and tell us exactly what it is we won because we do not know what has happened. The Miami attorneys called their associates in Washington, had them run over to the Supreme Court to get a copy of the ruling, read it, fax it down to Miami. Pichardo remembers that he and his brother quickly swallowed their Cuban coffee and started sending faxes, getting faxes, and then started racing to set up a news conference. Pichardo went home to change his jeans and t-shirt for a suit, canceled his afternoon appointments, then decided to have the press and everyone to his home for a press conference, thinking that it would be better to react to the ruling spontaneously, nothing rehearsed, respond to the information as it came in, call the shots for the media then and there as he and his associates discovered as the morning progressed that they had won decisively in the highest court in the land.

Is it appropriate to offer general observations on political and spiritual domains? We might say here that the maintenance and practice of spiritual beliefs inevitably risk conflict with secular powers. Beliefs in a reality that exceeds the natural world, as this world is drawn up in materialist theories, are by definition antagonistic to secular practices. There is intellectual discord, and often mutually incompatible actions drawn from the moral principles that alternative realities support. These patterns of conflict are found throughout history. Political leaders have persecuted religious groups on the basis of these differences, and, conversely, religious leaders in authoritative positions have often seized on the differences to inflict sanctions on skeptics. The deep issue in the Lukumí dispute is how spiritual and secular communities can live together successfully in liberal democracies, especially those that stress the materialism of Western economic life. It is not at all clear that satisfactory arrangements can be found for beliefs that differ on the scope and content of reality. But the Lukumí case does clarify the social practices that might yield a compatible arrangement extending across the two types of communities.

One practice is the identification of areas of agreement between church and state when they are in a dispute. This was a third way of addressing the Lukumí case. It was not chosen by the city. The city of Hialeah had argued that the health, hygiene and cruelty problems they were concerned to solve are particular to animal sacrifice, and that the only way to solve such problems was through the prohibition of the entire practice. This argument had two strange implications. One was an exclusion. It disallowed the possibility that at least some of the problems the city identified with animal sacrifice could have been attributed to other practices and resolved independent of the religion. A second was that the city had to maintain that it is easier to regulate an entire practice, conducted largely in the privacy of homes, than it is to monitor and enforce a prohibition on the undesirable procedures/rules/rituals and side effects of the practice. If these two implications had been recognized and stricken from the city's reasoning the religious practice of animal sacrifice might have been tolerated within the frame of regulations governing the slaughter of animals in secular practices.

A political solution appeared to be possible from the start. The city could have drafted a law regulating the manner of animal sacrifice, including a total ban on the discarding of animal carcasses in public areas and the introduction of humane standards for animal sacrifice that would apply to veterinarians, pet owners and pest control techniques, as well as to the Lukumí priests. In this way the "compelling interest" of the community could have been more accurately directed at the genuine concerns the city has with the Lukumí Church rather than at the religion itself.

Would the Lukumí Church have accepted the arrangement? At the eleventh hour, on the eve of the District Court trial, the church hastily applied for a license to be able to conduct animal sacrifice as a slaughterhouse in the church, subject to the state regulations governing slaughterhouses. The church attorney, in the oral arguments before the Court, said that his clients were willing to comply with disposal regulations and accept reasonable zoning conditions. These concessions were not surprising. If the prohibition of animal sacrifice had been upheld, then the central ritual of the religion would have been illegal and the religion itself would have been outside the law. This strategy required that Lukumí not receive a constitutional ruling on the thought that mending the edges rather than the centers of issues is sometimes best. The more difficult question—who is right?—could then have been avoided. A political settlement of a religious issue would have been exactly what the *Smith* Court most desired.

But this classic sidebar settlement was ignored by the Court. The Court's ruling took a different direction. In shielding Osha from the city ordinances the Court recognized the traditional wall between church and state. The free exercise clause "commits government itself to religious tolerance," Kennedy observed in the majority opinion, "and upon even slight suspicion that proposals for state intervention stem from animosity to religion or distrust of its practices, all officials must pause to remember their own high duty to the Constitution and to the rights it secures." Justice Souter pointed out in his concurring opinion, however, that Smith allows prohibitions of religious exercise as an "incidental effect" of neutral laws. The problem with the Hialeah ordinances was that they targeted the religion, and so failed any definition of neutrality and any test of state nonintrusiveness.

Pichardo had forfeited economic issues at the beginning of the case. He and his colleagues did not want money from the dispute. Pichardo estimates that the city of Hialeah did have to spend about $500,000 in legal fees that were paid directly to the ACLU. But the church sought no damages. Pichardo reports that he took readings throughout the legal dispute and the message from God was always to keep money out of the proceedings. When the dispute began Pichardo had told the acting mayor, Julio Martinez, that it was a moral dispute, and that if the church won he wanted nothing from the mayor's pocket but a signed dollar bill when it was over. At the end the mayor said, come on, the trial's over, what more do you want out of me. Pichardo replied that it was not over until he got his dollar. The mayor said, I know you're not going to let me live in peace until you get your dollar, so here, and at this point he pulled a dollar bill out of his pocket and said, you won. Oh, no, Pichardo said, you're forgetting the rule. You've got to sign the dollar. Remember, he told the mayor, where we came from things were done this way. We didn't go to trial. Things were settled on a handshake. Sign the dollar bill and give it to me. The mayor signed it and Pichardo said, now it's over.

7

Of course nothing is ever really over. The city of Hialeah and the Lukumí Church are at peace with one another, but Santería keeps evolving (as all religions do), with doctrinal matters framing practical proposals and enactments. Some adherents are arguing for a transformation of animal sacrifice into the symbolic sacrifices represented in religious rituals today. Others (not surprisingly) resist changes in the core ritual. All members and affiliates are interested in the standard efforts of private organizations to raise funds, recruit members, and assist in community projects. This is the social side of religions housing those benign continuities between religious and secular communities, which many sociologists focus on today. But we might say that divinity is the background concept against which the mutable and conflicting interpretations unfold that stand for what we mean by a religion.

The Santería story is one entry in the multiple and utterly enchanting narratives of religious and political practices. As one other example, Christianity has at least two historical trajectories in the West. One is the axis forged by Aristotle and elaborated by Aquinas in which good acts precede and create faith, the other the Reformation-inducing program initiated by Luther in which faith has to precede (and indemnify) good acts. Now, both trajectories attend to the state of mind (soul) of the individual, though from different directions, and in shielding the mental from the regulatory powers of the state help initiate the negative rights of liberal democracies. This concern for the inner self is one important way in which Christianity, along with many other religions, is distinct from the classical liberal state. One could argue that this history is now being realigned with transformative liberalism, which urges the conversion of individuals to liberal states of mind as a requirement for being a good citizen. A sea shift from religion to the secular liberal state, and now to a *proposed* liberal state concerned to cultivate the right beliefs even in the face of religious liberties gives one the rare opportunity to see a historical loop every bit as fascinating as hermeneutical turns in postmodern texts. One possible outcome is the creation of new institutions that bracket the Enlightenment distinctions between religion and politics on which the liberal state was organized. It promises to be an appealing narrative in a time of appealing narratives.

Stories of religion and politics annotate Western history. Rogers Smith has proposed three types of primitive stories blended together in all real-world visions of political membership: economic stories offering material benefits, political power stories that promise protection and shares in collective power, and ethnically constitutive stories that appeal to identity, or who people truly are as members of a community.[10] These stories are primitives in the sense that they originate in the earliest stages of human history, are general across political cultures, and trump other stories that are artifacts of more recent historical change in the conditions of human life. But we also might identify stories that directly address foundational or metaphysical regions of human cultures, and in this sense are constants in all social practices. I have in this work proposed adding to the inventory of narratives such a primitive story, the religious narrative, which attends to questions of a more primordial sort in membership (political and other) appeals.

The three dominant stories of political membership are internal stories. The religious narrative invokes an external domain. In a religious community the basic distinctions assigned to experience can slide easily into familiar differences between the indigenous or bounded and the divine, meaning that religious beliefs present the severe sense of the external represented by a sense of infinity conceptualized as divinity. The divide between living and observing a narrative is unavoidable within the conventional boundaries of human experience. Suzanne Farrell, describing her relationship with George Balanchine, was unable to understand how the choreographer "could have known so much of what was to happen" when their relationship was just beginning. But then she concedes that "Since I was the story, I couldn't see it."[11] A religious sensibility could attribute the inaccessibility of the full narrative of human experience to the fact that we are living it, and so not outside of it in a privileged viewing location. But traditional religions also provide an account of a decisive external observer (God, the creator and teller of the ultimate meta narrative) with full access to the human narrative, and a complete reality presented as timeless, unbounded (infinite), and linear (God's design). Even as a language game strong religious communities are distinguished by a realist truth that originates and resides in an external space.

Intimate and quite natural connections between religion and politics have been crafted from antiquity to the present on the preemptive force of divinity, even in primarily secular communities. The shaping effects of religion on politics in the United States, for example, are legion. The abolitionist and civil rights movements come readily to mind. Each of these movements introduced a different and more robust understanding of the person to contemporary politics that helped upset racist categories. The favors are returned. Legal privileging of religion occurs even on an acceptance of First Amendment walls between church and state. The occasional exemption from the burdens of law granted to religions by the U.S. Supreme Court pays homage to the special standing of religious beliefs and practices, and especially to the compelling force of religious conscience, which is widely thought to be an imperative command to act or not act on pain of losing one's identity.

But the case study and the arguments developed here suggest that it would be a mistake to conclude that the religious and secular are either similar or complementary on these welcome coordinations. The introduction of ultimate matters from divine sources to any dispute invites us always to consider the counterfactuals that haunt any accord between secular and religious communities: what happens if final political or legal decisions on vital matters go against religious communities? Two contrary intellectual traditions provide conjectures for settlement patterns. One is the model of consensus emphasized in democratic theories. Its defining feature is the belief that an absence of overt conflict is evidence for consensual accords. Another is the conflict model suggested by Marx. Here the presence of consensual tranquility might mask a deeper conflict that is prefigured in the background distributions of power and interest represented in institutional arrangements. If we use the first model then we are inclined to devalue conflict between religion and the state when disputes are settled agreeably, and we might view any particular settlement as indicating a general harmony between the two practices. The second model, however, takes us in a different direction. In this model an agreeable conclusion may mask a deeper conflict, and both agreeable and disagreeable outcomes can easily lead to a continuation of a dispute if the underlying interests remain mutually incompatible.[12] The peremptory nature of God's commands in Osha suggests that the second model is the more adequate representation for this case. It would have been impossible for the Church to compromise on the core ritual of animal sacrifice, and opposition between the Lukumí Church and the state would likely have continued in some form had the Court ruled in favor of the municipality of Hialeah. The direction of the legal outcome led to a resolution that was fortuitous in rendering peace instead of conflict, but also misleading if we conclude that church and state are not all that different when they are opposed to one another. It is also reasonable to think that the conflict model best presents the stakes in all strong religious disputes since issues of conscience often lead to nonnegotiable commands from external realities.

The presence of radically different systems of belief is hardly new in human experience, though the sharpness of distinctions between religious and secular communities can be more than a bit profound. The central dilemma that strong religions introduce to secular democratic states is reconciling or managing communities that differ radically from one another on the dimensions that present the identities of the communities. Perhaps the key intellectual indicator of these differences between church and state is that religious and secular political practices rely at least in part on different reasons and different senses of a reason. Secular arrangements at the extreme scale of the postmodern, acquiescing in the by now standard tensions between completeness and consistency, individual subjectivity and theoretical objectivity, are societies that are nonlinear, complex, bounded, and indeterminate states of affairs in which observer and observed occupy polar situations that, in some cultures, oscillate with each other. The dominant narratives in this species of secular arrangements are particular accounts presented in recursive patterns (where subsequent states of affairs are calculated from previous states) crafted, ironically enough, for stochastic events. It is not surprising on this account that religious stories both complement and oppose dominant political narratives. When they are in opposition the prospect of widely different reasons for action among secular and religious communities can be expected. This is the species of division represented in strong religious claims and disputes.

The definitive first step in establishing realistic arrangements between church and state in contemporary democracies is the recognition of these substantial contrasts between the narratives of religion and politics. The second step is realizing that the social arrangements containing religion and politics might be forged not so much on partitions between the two practices, but rather (in the broadest sense) on the basis of contacts among radically different cultures, including the use of pragmatic instruments of accommodation, the mutual effects represented by transculturation, limitations on conflict through collateral reasoning, patterns of syncretism, and more. It is an unavoidable and not entirely unwelcome fact of social realities that religious ambitions for universality compete with the collective orientations and pluralist settings of a democratic political system. At the point of intersection of these two quite different systems the narrower political strategies of arbitration, mediation, deliberation, accommodation, the sidebar focus on peripheral matters and the complementary crafting of parallax views, the languages of transformation, *modus vivendi*, the recursive discourses of complex systems, the judicious use of force—each and all of these items are appropriate or not as devices to address religious problems depending on the conditions underlying the political matters at issue. The third step is accepting a wide view of public reasoning that can survey and identify the conditions yielding proper governing devices. At least a proper survey of historical patterns of cooperation and resistance would lay to rest, permanently, the popular creed of exceptionalism, the belief that secular patterns of thought, grounded in compromise and toleration, can scan and comprehend religious beliefs from some impartial perspective. This prospect is finally unintelligible when beliefs, laws and sacred texts are defined from a religious perspective, perhaps in the same way that animal sacrifice is inexplicable within liberal frames of reference.

Plato thought that the structures of the *polis* and the individual soul are symmetrical. He examined the wider canvas of the state to identify virtue and its attachments. The reconstructions of political theory suggested here offer a wide conceptual field that does not replicate the internal ordering of the individual, as Plato thought the political society did. But this field produces a comprehensive view of public reasoning that can arrange and order the practices of religion and politics. This possibility suggests again that relationships between the secular and the sacred, religion and politics, church and state, are settled by the great political languages of stability, efficiency, equity, and power (among other collective level terms), not the metaphors of walls and spheres.

Notes

Preface

1. Foscarini's proposal and the responses from some of the main players in the dispute are discussed by Jerome J. Langford, *Galileo, Science and the Church* (Ann Arbor: University of Michigan Press, 1992), chapter 3, in an excellent treatment of the issues leading up to and including Galileo's trial (and helpfully cites some of the texts in Scripture that assume a geocentric view, pp. 52–53). Langford documents the confused views of the players, the influences of temperament and politics, and the missed opportunities for a resolution. Especially telling was the unfortunate acceptance by both Cardinal Bellarmine and Galileo of the scientific standing of Scripture when both Augustine and Aquinas (among others) counseled against regarding the Bible as a supplier of theories on the natural world. For insights into Galileo's personal life in the form of letters from one of his daughters, see Dava Sobel, *Galileo's Daughter* (New York: Walker and Company, 1999). On realist and epistemic truth, William Alston, *A Realist Conception of Truth* (Ithaca, NY: Cornell University Press, 1996).
2. Grigoriadis, Vanessa. 2004. "In His Own Hothouse: From Before Sunrise to Before Sunset, Ethan Hawke has never stopped trying to grow. But into what?" *New York* (June 28–July 5), 2004, pp. 38–41, the quotes on p. 41.
3. Mailer, "Evaluations—Quick and Expensive Comments on the Talent in the Room," reprinted in *Advertisements for Myself* (New York: Putnam's Sons, 1959), pp. 463–473.
4. This characterization of boxing from, of course, A.J. Liebling.

Chapter I

1. The observation and comments here are drawn from my paper, "The Free Exercise of Religion: Lukumí and Animal Sacrifice,"

Institute for Cuban and Cuban-American Studies Occasional Paper Series, University of Miami (November 2001). The research for the paper included two long interviews with Ernesto Pichardo and briefer sessions with other principals, as well as (of course) wide reading in written texts.

2. The proper name of the religion is not entirely settled. Santería ("the way of the saints") is a Western term assigned to the religion by the Catholic culture that received the slaves. It is accepted currently by some priests in the religion, but not by others, and often functions as a cluster concept for many types of Afro-Cuban religions. "Lukumí" or "Lucumí" is also used to designate Yoruba practices in the West. It derives from the term "Ulkimi," an ancient Yoruba kingdom, and is considered by some researchers as a transliteration of the Yoruba phrase, "I am a friend." It is also the name of the Church that Pichardo founded. I use the "Lukumí" spelling for the Church because the Church does so, and because the legal case is in the law journals with that spelling. One generally acknowledged term for the religion is the one I am using: "Osha," or, more completely, "Regla de Osha" (or Ocha, initially the Hispanic term for "orisha"). Other acceptable terms include Regla Ifá and, less formally, "orisha worship." Some practitioners say that Yoruba priests in Africa, if asked to identify their religion, would simply say that they are priests of Shangó or some other divinity. This devolution reflects the influence of local organization in the religion. I am grateful to Rafael Martínez for discussing these terms with me. I have also profited in this note and elsewhere from Sara M. Sánchez's discussion in her "Afro-Cuban Diaspora Religions: A Comparative Analysis of the Literature and Selected Annotated Bibliography," (Institute for Cuban and Cuban-American Studies Occasional Paper Series August 2000). My gratitude extends to Ernesto Pichardo for the interviews, of course, but also for comments on an early draft of the paper, and the Rev. Juan J. Sosa and Willie Ramos, who both read late (and different) drafts of the paper and made many helpful comments throughout the manuscript. Ramos was especially helpful in suggesting changes in the paragraph on the initiation ritual (page 18) and the pages on the role and forms of dance in Osha (pp. 20–1). He also made Appendix I of his masters thesis available to me for clarification on the dance rituals in the religion. I have learned much from the "At the Crossroads" program at the History Museum in Miami, Florida, held between February 23 and July 8, 2001, and have

taken at least some of the population figures and terminology from that program's exhibitions and presentations. Steve Stuempsle, the Museum Curator, met both of my requests for oral tapes of panel discussions with an alacrity that seemed boundless. Of course I absolve all of my informal consultants from the errors I know must still be present in my descriptions and analyses of Osha. I am still learning about this fascinating and complex religion.

3. Ernesto Pichardo's narrative is drawn up primarily from the two long interviews I conducted with him in Miami, Florida: the first (in the church of the Lukumí Babalu Aye) on December 12, 1989, and a second interview (in his home) on November 7, 1999. The views I attribute to Pichardo on pages 59–60 are from an email he sent me and the comments he made on the panel discussion on May 31, 2001, as part of the "At the Crossroads program." Others on the panel were José Acosta Santo, Mercedes Sandoval, and Nelson Mendoza.

4. The material on Santería is drawn from the interviews with Pichardo, and from interviews with Lydia Cabrera and Terisita Pedraza, August 5, 1989, also in Miami; and a number of helpful articles and books on Regla de Osha: Migene Gonzalez-Whippler, *Santería* (New York: The Augustan Press, 1973) and *Santería: La Religion* (St. Paul, MN: Llewellyn Publishers, 1999); Joseph M. Murphy, *Santería* (New York: Beacon Press, 1988); George Brandon, *Santería from Africa to the New World* (Bloomington and Indianapolis: Indiana University Press, 1993); Marta Moreno Vega, *The Altar of My Soul: The Living Traditions of Santería* (New York: Ballantine Books, 2000); Mercedes Cros Sandoval, "Afro-Cuban Religion in Perspective," in *Enigmatic Powers: Syncretism with African and Indigenous Peoples*, ed. Anthony M. Stevens-Arroyo and Andres J. Perez y Mena (New York: Bildner Center for Western Hemisphere Studies, 1995), pp. 81–9; Juan J. Sosa, *Sectas, Cultos y Sincretismos* (Miami: Ediciones Universal, 1999); Baba Ifa Karade, *The Handbook of Yoruba Religious Concepts* (York Beach, Maine: Samuel Weiser, Inc., 1994); El Obatala, *Creative Ritual* (York Beach, Maine: Samuel Weiser, Inc., 1996); Conrad E. Mauge and Awo Fayomi, *Odu Ifa: Book One, Sacred Scripture of Ifa* and *Odu Ifa: Book Two, Sacred Scriptures of Ifa* (Mount Vernon, NY: House of Providence, 1994); Raul Canizares, *Walking with the Night: The Afro-Cuban World of Santería* (Rochester, VT: Destiny Books, 1993) and *Cuban Santería* (Rochester, VT: Inner Traditions Intl

Ltd, 1999); Lucumí'ni Lele, *The Secrets of Afro-Cuban Divination: How to Cast the Diloggun, the Oracle of the Orishas* (Rochester, VT: Destiny Books, 2000); Julio Garcia Cortez, *The Osha: Secrets of the Yoruba-Santería-Lucumí Religion in the United States and the Americas* (Brooklyn, NY: Athelia Henrietta, 2000). I have also benefited from Roger Bastide's imposing study of African (Yoruba) culture in Brazil, *The African Religions of Brazil* (Baltimore, MD: Johns Hopkins University Press, 1978). Among the more general articles I have used are Andrew Webster, "Health and Body," *Salon.com* (January 26, 2000), Bess Lovejoy, "World Religions: a Santería Primer," the e.peak/1998–3/issue, Roberto Cespedes, "The Mystical Powers of Elían," *The New York Times* (September 30, 2000), Gustav Nieguhr, "Cuban Church: It's Weak But Unified," *The New York Times* (January 21, 1998), and various information sites on the web.

5. The Lukumí Church has issued two papers on these issues. One, "Syncretism," suggests the distinction between theological and member syncretism. The other, "Rule or Diplomacy," explores the religious mixture of Santería and Catholic religious expressions (by Ernesto Pichardo). See also the monograph by Ernesto Pichardo and Lourdes Nieto Pichardo, *Oduduwa: Obatalá* (Miami: St. Babalú Ayé, 1984) where the authors argue that the African form and structure in Osha transferred to Lukumí remained intact, without blending with Catholicism. The intact thesis is also supported by George Brandon, *Santería from Africa to the New World*. Brandon sees the core of the ritual system in Santería as African, not Catholic. Also important is the work of Fernando Ortiz, who stresses the mutual effects of contact between Yoruba and Catholicism (which he calls "transculturation"). See (among other works) Ortiz, *Ètnia y sociedad*. Selección, notas y prólogo de Isaac Barreal (Habana: Editorial de Ciencas Sociales, 1993). I have taken the view of Lydia Cabrera I cite on page 6 of this chapter from Sara Sánchez's monograph, "Afro-Cuban Diaspora Religions," p. 6. Sánchez also cites Harry Lefever's ambitious efforts to define Osha as a kind of resistance to cultural oppression (p. 6). The full development of Lefever's view of the Lucumí religion as a form of hegemonic resistance is in his article, "When the Saints Go Riding In: Santería in Cuba and the United States," *The Journal for the Scientific Study of Religion* 35 (September, 1996), pp. 3–27. Some recent collateral research also seems to suggest African dominance. See Mary Ann Clark's argument that the similarity of multiple

orisha worship in Africa and the New World indicates the priority of existing African antecedents, in "Orisha Worship Communities: A Reconsideration of Organizational Structure," *Religion* 30, No. 4 (October 2000), pp. 379–89. Clark also argues the point against syncretism on the basis that "Santería altar displays contain few or no statues of Catholic saints or other anthropomorphic figures," suggesting the dominance of African understandings of "spirituality and materiality and the place of the human body in religious practice," quotes from the Abstract, in "No Hay Ningún Santo Agui! (There Are No Saints Here!): Symbolic Language within Santería," *Journal of the American Academy of Religion* 69, No. 1 (March 2001), pp. 21–41. In this article Clark also examines some differences between the terms "saint" and "orisha," and suggests that the emphasis in Osha on the natural instead of the somatic is an invitation to rethink our categories of the material, spiritual, and somatic. I see the ordering in the religion (in parallel fashion) as a challenge to the property dualism that has dominated Western thinking since Descartes. My understandings of the practical effects of syncretism have been broadened by conversations with a number of people in the Miami area, in particular Jackie Rodriguez and Willie Ramos, and by the helpful treatment of these issues in the panel discussions as part of the "At the Crossroads" exhibition. The two panel discussions I found most instructive were held on April 5 and May 31, 2001. The first included Ramos, Mercedes Sandoval and Nelson Mendoza, and the second (again) included José Acosta Santo, Ernesto Pichardo, Mercedes Sandoval, and Nelson Mendoza. I have taken many of the views on syncretism I attribute to Sandoval from the thoughts she expressed in the April 5 panel presentation.

6. This caveat. The Catholic Church, in its doctrine of transubstantiation, maintains that the bread becomes the body, the wine the blood, of Christ in the communion ritual. The implication is that while the ceremony is symbolic it is also in some complex sense to be regarded as literal.

7. When I began my current intellectual journeys into religion and politics I taught a graduate seminar on the topics. At one moment in the class I asked each student to construct and present at the next meeting a typology of state–church relations in the contemporary world. At the next meeting, we acknowledged the impossibility of the task, meaning in lay terms that none of us could put together an adequate representation (including me).

Chapter 2

* I am conscious of the word play in the title of this chapter, and, yes, my memories of Ernest Gellner's *Words and Things* are alive and well, and to the point here.

1. John Stuart Mill, *On Liberty* (New York: Norton, 1975), especially part Four.
2. Roy Rappaport, *Ritual and Religion in the Making of Humanity* (Cambridge: Cambridge University Press, 1999). Rappaport argues for ritual as the main component in religion. Ninian Smart, *Worldviews* (Saddle River, NJ: Prentice-Hall, 2000), provides a helpful (and much cited) overview of concepts.
3. John Hick, *An Interpretation of Religion* (New Haven, CT: Yale University Press, 1989). Hick's list of individuals who have contributed decisively to concepts of human awareness is on pages 29–30.
4. M. Gauchet, The *Disenchantment of the World: A Political History of Religion* (Princeton, NJ: Princeton University Press, 1997).
5. Jonathan Z. Smith, "Religion, Religions, Religious," in Taylor, ed. *Critical Terms for Religious Studies* (Chicago: University of Chicago Press, 1998), pp. 281–2.
6. For example, Schubert Miles Ogden, *Is There only One True Religion or Are There Many?* (Dallas: Southern Methodist University Press, 1992). Ogden combines Tillich (below) with Geertz (also below) to propose a definition of religion with both subjective (a form of self-understanding) and objective (a form of culture) standing, and developed in the context of a discussion of true religion and religious pluralism.
7. Argued most recently by Timothy Fitzgerald, *The Ideology of Religious Studies* (New York: Oxford University Press, 2000). (See especially Part l: Religious Studies as an Ideology.)
8. C. Geertz, "Religion as a Cultural System," in *The Interpretation of Cultures* (New York: Basic Books, 1973), p. 90.
9. Mark Taylor, ed., Introduction, *Critical Terms for Religious Studies* (Chicago: University of Chicago Press, 1998). Not to press the point here, but Tom Green notes, in a private circular, that we do not teach about science and languages. We teach students how to do science, speak languages, so that the insider view of religion would lead to a curriculum synonymous with the way science and languages are taught in secular practices.

10. The famous definition by Paul Tillich, *The Shaking of the Foundations* (New York: Charles Scribner's Sons, 1948), p. 57. Then see Jonathan Z. Smith, General Editor, *The HarperCollins Dictionary of Religion* (San Francisco, CA: HarperCollins, 1995), pp. 893–4 for the emphasis given to a definition of religion as "a system of beliefs and practices that are relative to superhuman beings" (p. 893).

11. W. Christian, *Meaning and Truth in Religion* (Princeton, NJ: Princeton University Press, 1964), p. 61.

12. But see the different version of faith provided by Alvin Plantinga, *Warranted Christian Belief* (New York: Oxford University Press, 2000). After dismissing a harder version of Mark Twain on faith (in this case, "believing what you know ain't true") Plantinga develops a Calvinist version of faith as a form of true belief based on certain knowledge of God's plan as it applies to oneself. See especially pages 246–66. The full Twain quote Plantinga cites is a bit different, and also referential: "There are those who scoff at the school boy, calling him frivolous and shallow. Yet it was the school boy who said, Faith is believing what you know ain't so." In Mark Twain's *Following the Equator and Anti-Imperialist Essays* (Oxford: Oxford University Press, 1996). The quote is from a vignette in "Pudd'nhead Wilson's New Calendar." Heading to Chapter XII, p. 132.

13. M. Weber, *Political Writings* (Cambridge: Cambridge University Press, 1994). The spatial dimension of politics is expressed by Weber's definition of the state as that agency with a monopoly of physical force in a given territory; D. Easton, *The Political System: An Inquiry into the State of Political Science* (New York: Knopf, 1953); Gabriel Almond and James Coleman, eds., *The Politics of Developing Areas* (Princeton, NJ: Princeton University Press, 1960); Harry Eckstein, "Authority Patterns: A Structural Basis for Political Inquiry," *American Political Science Review* (1973); and, for an elaboration of the political as pure amoral force among antagonists, Carl Schmitt, *The Concept of the Political* (reprint edition: Chicago: University of Chicago Press, 1996). For early minimalism, my own "The Structure of Politics," *American Political Science Review* 72 (September 1978), pp. 859–70.

14. Robert Nozick, *Anarchy, State, and Utopia* (New York: Basic Books, 1974).

15. John Rawls, *A Theory of Justice* (Cambridge, MA: Harvard University Press, 1971; 1999). The list of primary goods is on

page 54, 1999 edition. It contains rights and liberties, powers and opportunities, income and wealth, and self-respect.

16. The discussion of conditions in which the difference principle must be interpreted differently, as with the presence or absence of chain connections, is on pages 69–72, *A Theory of Justice*, page citations for the 1999 edition. Rawls has provided a more elaborate interpretation of the difference principle in *Political Liberalism* (New York: Columbia University Press, 1993, 1996). For example, on page 283 (1996 edition) he says that the DP holds for institutional items such as taxation, fiscal and economic policy, public law and statutes, and not for particular transactions or distributions. Still, in all of its incarnations the DP must make a contribution "to the expectations of the least favored." Even in the case of institutional type distributions, however, it does seem that those affected by the DP as the least favored will be situated in particular practices, the criteria for the least advantaged will be at least influenced by these particular identifications, and there may be no general least advantaged persons that an institutional or background reference can use as a focal point for distributions. And, for religious and secular communities, the least advantaged will likely be defined in different ways, suggesting not only that the actual working of the DP will rely on, and perhaps be defined by, particular practices, but (again) that what I have called the break points in theory (in this case, the DP) are interpretable differently by religious and political practices.

17. I argue exactly these points at greater length and, I hope, subtlety in "The Free Exercise of Religion: Lukumí and Animal Sacrifice" (Institute for Cuban and Cuban-American Studies Occasional Paper Series, University of Miami, Novemeber 2001), the paper that is the organizing case study for this book.

18. See Rawls, *Public Reason* (Ithaca, NY: Cornell Univerisity Press, 1999).

19. S. Haack, *Manifesto of a Passionate Moderate* (Chicago: University of Chicago Press, 1998), quote on page 144. The argument appears originally in *Evidence and Inquiry* (Oxford: Blackwell Publishers, 1997).

20. A. Koestler, *The Sleepwalkers: A History of Man's Changing Vision of the Universe* (Cambridge: Cambridge University Press, 1984).

21. Jerome Frank, "The 'Fight' Theory Versus the 'Truth' Theory," in J. Frank, *Courts on Trial: Myth and Reality in American Justice* (Princeton, NJ: Princeton University Press, 1976), pp. 80–5.

22. Karl Popper, *The Logic of Scientific Discovery* (London: Hutchinson Publishing Group, 1968).

23. William Frankena, *Thinking About Morality* (Ann Arbor, MI: University of Michigan Press, 1980) and *Ethics* (Englewood Cliffs, NJ: Prentice-Hall, 1973).

Chapter 3

1. The emphasis in Osha on practice instead of prior belief corresponds with Aristotelian and Catholic orientations rather than Luther's emphasis on faith over good acts. The preoccupation of the Catholic Church with ceremony is well documented. Peter Ackroyd, in his biography, *Thomas More* (New York: Anchor Books, 1999), chronicles the pageantry of pre-Reformation England before Henry VIII and the martyrdom of More. The Ackroyd tour is more than a bit wistful over the post-Reformation abandonment of this pageantry. Andrew Greeley documents the contemporary enchantment of Catholicism, a state of mind typically represented in ceremony, in *The Catholic Imagination* (Berkeley, CA: University of California Press, 2000). The insider story on Arnaz, by the way, is that he was not a devotee and that he took the "Babalu" song from Miguelito Valdez, a friend who was a disciple.

2. My description of the initiation ceremony may not be complete, or consistent with all accounts and experiences. But it is a good faith rendition of a protected ritual drawn from both scholarly works and interviews with practitioners.

3. I was present at a wemilere where an orisha was apparently trying to gain possession of a participant, seeming to move in and out of the man's countenance as he danced. The singer was chanting the African phrases directly into the man's face in what seemed an unusually loud voice. The mounting was incomplete, in part (I was told) because of the ceremonial nature of the afternoon's session. In bembé the mounting might have been completed.

4. Eco's proposals are impossible to describe adequately without reading his arguments (another source of support for the importance of context?) but I think that he is right on the mark when it comes to textual interpretation, even when he changes the mark with continuing reflections.

5. Hercules makes a first appearance in R. Dworkin, *Taking Rights Seriously* (Cambridge, MA: Harvard University Press, 1978), chapter four, and serves again in *Law's Empire* (Cambridge, MA: Harvard University Press, 1986). Dworkin introduces in this latter work the tests of fit (accord with the law) and best (justifiable with

moral principles) as guiding proper legal judgments. In *Life's Dominion* (New York: Knopf, 1993) Dworkin offers the definition of the sacred that I cite in the text. I hope it is clear that I do not regard all senses of the sacred as religious. Sometimes a secular sense of the sacred appears to be even more compelling than the obviously sacred found in religions. When I was traveling through Spain one summer in my youth I took photo after flash photo of altars in churches claiming to have the Holy Grail, with no one among the officials in these churches voicing an objection. At the end of this particular trip I traveled outside Madrid to visit Goya's home. When I started to take a photo of the grave in the courtyard where the artist is buried I was immediately stopped by a caretaker who explained to me that this was sacred ground.

6. These thoughts are drawn from Lawrence Sager's legendary lectures in Constitutional Law at New York University Law School, as communicated to me by my younger daughter, Christina Frohock (who took, and also was a teaching assistant in, the courses).

7. Listen to one of the quotes from Constable that Gombrich provides, this on the reverse of Constable's study of Borrowdale in the Lakeland: "Fine, blowing day, tone very mellow, like the mildest of Gaspar Poussin and Sir George Beaumont, on the whole deeper toned than this drawing." (p. 315) Gombrich shows us again and again that painters see nature in terms of other paintings.

8. The spectacle of domains that cannot be ranked was noted by Justice Blackmun in the beginning of his majority opinion in *Roe v. Wade*. An enchanting discussion of the roles of context in setting precise meanings is provided by Stanley Fish, "Normal Circumstances, Literal Language, Direct Speech Acts, the Ordinary, the Everyday, the Obvious, What Goes Without Saying, and Other Special Cases," *Critical Inquiry* 4, No. 4 (Summer 1978). I am also grateful to Robert Daly, friend and colleague, for triggering this line of thought into the examples of medical domains.

Chapter 4

1. R.F. Thiemann, *Religion and Public Life: A Dilemma for Democracy* (Washington, DC: Georgetown University Press, 1996), pp. 154–64. Also see the (almost unbearable) optimism of Roger Gottlieb in documenting the happy unions of religious and political actions, in *Joining Hands: Politics and Religion Together for Social Change* (Cambridge, MA: Westview Press, 2002).

2. J. Rawls, "The Idea of Public Reason Revisited," *University of Chicago Law Review* (Summer, 1997), the quote is in footnote 46.

3. J. Searle, *The Construction of Social Reality* (NY: Free Press, 1995).

4. Bruce Ackerman, "Why Dialogue?" *Journal of Philosophy* (January 1989), pp. 5–22. The need for a core morality in political reasoning is asserted (and negotiated) by Charles Larmore, *The Morals of Modernity* (NY: Cambridge University Press, 1996).

5. Thomas Nagel, "Moral Conflict and Political Legitimacy," *Philosophy and Public Affairs* (Summer 1987), pp. 215–40, the adumbrated quotation is on p. 232.

6. Rawls, *Political Liberalism*, pp. 16–17. I know, reciprocity, as a relation, is a difficult fit with the idea of a norm. But in Rawls's framework of public reasoning norms, relations, virtues, and principles all seem to be ingredients in the languages of dialogue among disputants.

7. Rawls, *Political Liberalism*, p. xlvi.

8. Amy Gutmann and Dennis Thompson, *Democracy and Disagreement* (Cambridge, MA: Belknap Press, 1998), pp. 52–3. Reciprocity obviously depends on reasons that are public in the sense that they are mutually accessible. Deliberative democracy is sometimes contrasted with liberalism. See Steve Macedo's "Introduction" in Macedo, ed., *Deliberative Politics: Essays on Democracy and Disagreement* (New York: Oxford University Press, 1999). But the two positions are just gradations on common premises.

9. Gutmann and Thompson, "Moral Conflict and Political Consensus," first published in *Ethics* 101 (October 1990), pp. 64–88, and later in R. Bruce Douglas, Gerald M. Mara, and Henry S. Richardson, eds., *Liberalism and the Good* (New York and London: Routledge, 1992), and Gutmann and Thompson, *Democracy and Disagreement*. The literature on deliberative democracy is vast, and growing. Among the interesting contributions that elaborate in different ways the core elements of this essentially epistemic and/or procedural (but non-aggregation) approach to politics are (in no special order) Joshua Cohen, "Deliberation and Democratic Legitimacy," in *The Good Polity*, edited by Alan Hamlin and Philip Pettit (Blackwell, 1989), and "An Epistemic Conception of Democracy," *Ethics* 97 (1986), pp. 26–38; James Fishkin, *Democracy and Deliberation* (New Haven, CT: Yale, 1991); the review essay by Samuel Freeman, "Deliberative Democracy: A Sympathetic Comment," *Philosophy and Public Affairs* 29 (2000), pp. 371–418; the very good insights and

arguments by James Johnson and Jack Knight, "Aggregation and Deliberation: On the Possibility of Democratic Legitimacy," *Political Theory* 22 (1994), pp. 277–96; Joseph Bissette, *The Mild Voice of Reason: Deliberative Democracy and American National Government* (Chicago: University of Chicago Press, 1994); Richard Vernon, *Political Morality* (NY: Cambridge University Press, 2000); David Estlund, "Who's Afraid of Deliberative Democracy?" *Texas Law Review* 71 (1993), pp. 1437–77; the excellent work by James Bohman, *Public Deliberation* (Cambridge, MA: MIT Press, 1996, 2000); and (in addition to the anthologies I use here), the collections of essays in Jon Elster, ed., *Deliberative Democracy* (NY: Cambridge University Press, 1998), Bohman and William Rehg, eds., *Deliberative Democracy* (Cambridge: MIT Press, 1998), especially the papers by Gerald Gaus, "Reason, Justification, and Consensus: Why Democracy Can't Have It All" and Thomas Christiano, "The Significance of Public Deliberations," and David Estlund, ed., *Democracy* (MA: Blackwell. 2002), especially the excellent paper by David Miller, "Deliberative Democracy and Social Choice," pp. 289–307. Then (of course) Jürgen Habermas, *Between Facts and Norms* (Cambridge, MA: MIT Press, 1998), especially chapter 8 and section 8.1. See also the helpful discussions in Colin Bird, "Mutual Respect and Neutral Justification," *Ethics* 107, No.1 (October 1996), pp. 62–96, and Thiemann, *Religion in Public Life*, chapter 6, "Public Religion in a Pluralist Democracy: A Proposal." I have been guided in some my arguments here by Thiemann's analysis. I have also profited from reading Kenneth Baynes's unpublished paper, "Deliberative Democracy and Public Reason," and from talking with him about these matters.

10. H.P. Grice, "Logic and Conversation," in *Speech Acts*, edited by P. Cole and J. Morgan (New York: Academic Press, 1975) and in D. Davidson and G. Harman, eds., *The Logic of Grammar* (California: Dickenson, 1975).

11. Rawls, *Political Liberalism*, pp. 154–8 for the discussion of comprehensiveness, with the first quote in the text (on abstraction) on p. 154, note 20, and the second quote (on the guiding framework) on p. 156. The views on basic structure are on p. 11.

12. Rawls, *Political Liberalism*, (paper edition), Introduction, page lv.

13. Rawls, *Political Liberalism*, p. 49 (for the first quote) and p. 50 (for the second quote).

14. Gutmann and Thompson, *Democracy and Disagreement*, pp. 56–7. For an exposition and critique of these (and other) points, see Leif Werner, "Political Liberalism: An Internal Critique," *Ethics* 106, No. 1 (October 1995), pp. 32–62. Werner sees the Rawlsian project as two-staged, with justice as fairness comprising the first set of arguments and political liberalism as a presentation of justice as fairness in terms of the reasonable as a way to envelop justice in an overlapping consensus. Also see Onora O'Neil's distinction between two interpretations of reasonableness that seem to thread through Rawls's work: the reasonable person offers fair principles of cooperation that others *will* accept, or others *can* accept. In "Political Liberalism and Public Reason: A Critical Notice of John Rawls' Political liberalism," *The Philosophical Review* 106, No. 3 (July 1997), pp. 411–28. That these are quite different takes on the reasonable is indicated by the fact that the first implies the second, but not the reverse. "Can" also implies a moral failure on non-acceptance while "will" obviates that possibility. I have been enlightened on these points by a paper by Roald Nashi, "Reasonableness in Rawls' Political Liberalism" that he wrote for my (spring 2003) graduate seminar on these matters. For a thoughtful and sympathetic treatment of deliberation in politics, more general and complex than the literature on Rawls, see James Bohman, *Public Deliberation* (Cambridge, MA: MIT Press, 2000).

15. Rawls, *Political Liberalism*, p. 213.

16. Rawls offers a later statement of his views in *Justice As Fairness: A Restatement*, edited by Erin Kelly (Cambridge, MA: Harvard University Press, 2001). He emphasizes again the differences between nonpublic and public reason, and introduces the corporate standing of citizens in the exercise of public reason. See Part 3, section 26.

17. Two of the better pieces that develop (in different ways) the importance of institutions are Ian Shapiro's "Enough of Deliberation: Politics Is about Interests and Power," and Russell Hardin's "Deliberation: Method, Not Theory," both in Macedo, ed., *Deliberative Politics: Essays on Democracy and Disagreement*. Shapiro describes the many ways in which interest groups co-opt the deliberative process, leaving us to wonder if authentic deliberation is even possible in a pluralist democracy. Hardin makes a case for developing the right institutions in democratic arrangements

and then letting them run, do their job, to bring about good outcomes over time.

18. This distinction—which I concede is a coarse representation of nuanced arguments—moves through the main critical understandings of the Gutmann–Thompson theoretical package but it was used for special effects by one of my graduate students, Michael McFall, in an enlightening seminar discussion.

19. Gutmann and Thompson, *Democracy and Disagreement*. See also the responses to the essays in the Macedo collection, "Reply to the Critics." In defense of the criticism that their theory accepts only views that the authors agree with, Gutmann and Thompson point out that they allow pro-life into the deliberative process as a tenable and reasonable position even though they disagree with the view. Not to be unkind, but one might want to be careful here. Pro-life bleeds easily into discriminatory economic policies and abortion-preventative measures that liberals might find, well, morally unacceptable, even unreasonable.

20. On the exclusionary effects of the Gutmann and Thompson tests, see Stanley Fish's lucid paper in the Macedo volume, "Mutual Respect as a Device of Exclusion." The literature in philosophy of science on reliable methods is voluminous, and starts with the famous Alan Musgrave and Imre Lakatos, eds., collection, *Criticism and the Growth of Knowledge: Volume 4*: Proceedings of the International Colloquium in the Philosophy of Science, London, 1965 (Cambridge: Cambridge University Press, 1970), especially the classic piece by Lakatos, "Falsification and the Logic of Scientific Research Programmes." A helpful overview of these issues is in Anthony O'Hear's *Karl Popper* (New York: Routledge Kegan & Paul, 1992).

21. "Letter from Birmingham Jail."

22. The relevant text from Gutmann and Thompson, *Democracy and Disagreement*, pp. 55–6. See also Michael Sandel's discussion of the Lincoln–Douglas debates in *Democracy's Discontent: America in Search of a Public Philosophy* (Cambridge, MA: Belknap Press, Harvard University, 1996), pp. 21–4. Sandel questions the bracketing of moral views to achieve a political agreement, which was the view argued by Douglas and the kind of perspective on comprehensive doctrines found in the liberalism that supplanted republicanism.

23. Walter Dean Burnham, *Critical Elections and the Mainsprings of American Politics* (New York: Norton, 1971). See Burnham's review of the second volume of Ackerman's work in the *Yale Law*

Journal 108, No. 8 (June 1999), pp. 2237–77, and Ackerman's article in the same journal.

24. B. Ackerman, *We the People: Transformations* (Cambridge, MA: Harvard, 2000).

25. Stephen Jay Gould, *The Structure of Evolutionary Theory* (Cambridge, MA: Belknap Press of Harvard University Press, 2002), pp. 776 and 765–74.

26. I am indebted to one of my graduate students, Michael McKeon, who suggested the Lincoln–Douglas example and developed some of the ideas in these paragraphs. They are found mainly in his term paper, "Reciprocity, Morality, and Fraud: An Analysis of the Scope of Deliberation," which he wrote for my 2003 spring semester graduate seminar. In an earlier work, *Rational Association*, I proposed similar themes, in particular a version of reasoning that is tiered, preferences supervenient on reasons, with a dismissal of transitivity and universal domain in examining Arrow's theorem, and a rank ordering of conditions as a more robust approach to rational, as, well, *reasoned*, choice.

27. Rawls allows the abolitionists a freer reign to challenge basic constitutional principles, for example, because the political society of that time and place was not well ordered. But whether a society is well ordered is itself contestable, especially in the heat and light of political challenges to basic structures, which places us back in the political process. See Rawls, *Political Liberalism*, pp. 249–254. For the quote on removing divisive issues from the deliberative table, p. 157, *Political Liberalism* (1993).

28. R.M. Hare, "The Promising Game," in *The Is-Ought Question: A Collection of Papers on the Central Problems in Moral Philosophy*, edited by W.D. Hudson (New York: Macmillan, 1969). Also see the more hardheaded views of deliberation collected in Jon Elster, ed., *Deliberative Democracy* (Cambridge: Cambridge University press, 1998), especially the pieces by Gerry Mackie, "All Men Are liars: Is Democracy Meaningless?," Susan Stokes, "Pathologies of Deliberation," and James Johnson, "Arguing for Deliberation: Some Skeptical Considerations." Interestingly enough, Gutmann and Thompson observe that strategy and deliberation "are not mutually exclusive." In "Reply to the Critics," Macedo, ed., *Deliberative Politics*, p. 257. So much stronger, then, is the case for a game theoretic frame on deliberation, with all that this implies for the three process principles and the norms of mutual respect and moral integrity.

29. R. Grant, *Hypocrisy and Integrity: Machiavelli, Rousseau, and the Ethics of Politics* (Chicago: University of Chicago Press, 1997).

30. L. Strauss, *Persecution and the Art of Writing* (Chicago: University of Chicago Press, Reprint Edition, October 1988). The presence of Strauss's students in the Bush administration showcases this view. See Seymour M. Hersh's article, "Selective Intelligence," *The New Yorker* (May 12, 2003), pp. 44–51.

31. Daniel Goleman, *Emotional Intelligence* (NY: Bantam Books, 1995) for a popular summary, though, yes, Goleman falls into the standard view that temperance is preferable to ardor, with much talk about passion hijacking reason and the importance of calming down and controlling emotions. Maybe the paradigm from Plato, the tripartite soul fully integrated only when reason dominates appetite, has had a disproportionate influence in Western history. Where are the Romantics when we need them? Well, in the intelligence of Martha Nussbaum. See her studies of the roles of emotions in deliberation and self-knowledge, and especially her fusion of emotion and intellect in ethical understanding, in *Love's Knowledge: Essays on Philosophy and Literature* (New York: Oxford University Press, 1990). In the editorial review: "Nussbaum investigates and defends a conception of ethical understanding which involves emotional as well as intellectual activity, and which gives a certain type of priority to the perception of particular people and situations rather than to abstract rules." Also, see her massive and passionate *Upheavals in Thought: The Intelligence of Emotions* (Cambridge: Cambridge University Press, 2001). In a more recent book, however, *Hiding From Humanity: Disgust, Shame, and the Law* (Princeton, NJ: Princeton University Press, 2004) Nussbaum explores the meanings and roles, and the danger, of the revival of *disgust* (and its cohort term, shame) in law, including a discussion of Patrick Devlin's famous reliance on the term in *The Enforcement of Morals* (New York: Oxford, 1970) and the use of the emotion in tests for obscenity in *Miller v. California* (1973). All of these works, with their contrary views of the roles of emotions in law and politics, suggest that what counts as emotions and their relevance in politics are contestable in political languages. For a presentation of emotions that has joined philosophy of mind with neurology, see Antonio Damasio, *Looking for Spinoza: Joy, Sorrow and the Feeling Mind* (New York: Harcourt, 2003). Now, having listed the good contemporary works, allow me two famous quotes from Diderot (*Pensées*,

1746): "We are constantly railing against the passions; we ascribe to them all of man's afflictions, and we forget that they are also the source of all his pleasures." And: "Only passions, and great passions, can raise the soul to great things. Without them there is no sublimity, either in morals or in creativity. Art returns to infancy, and virtue becomes small-minded." Gutmann and Thompson, are you listening? I have to say here that the most judicious case for emotions in political arguments is made by James Johnson in "Arguing for Deliberation: Some Skeptical Considerations," in *Deliberative Democracy*, edited by Jon Elster (Cambridge: Cambridge University Press, 1998), pp. 161–84. Johnson is far more civil and controlled, well, less emotional, than most on the issue of emotions in politics.

32. Peter Gabel, "Spirituality and Law," *Tikkun* (March/April, 2003), p. 39.

33. Alan Wolfe, *The Transformation of American Religion: How We Actually Live Our Lives* (New York: Free Press, 2003) is one of the latest entries in the impressive social tagging of religion. But see also David Sloan Wilson, *Darwin's Cathedral: Evolution, Religion and the Nature of Society* (Chicago: University of Chicago Press, 2002), for a dismissal of the supernatural in accounting for religion. Note also, however, that a number of works do rely on divinity in marking off religious sensibilities, including John Hick, *An Interpretation of Religion* (New Haven: Yale University Press, 1989)—from the discussion in chapters 2 and 3—and Abdolkarim Soroush, *Reason, Freedom, and Democracy in Islam* (New York: Oxford University Press, 2000). These two entries indicate the range of work in religious studies that still takes divinity as one criterion of religion, though of course in radically different ways. So much of the excitement here could be dispelled with some elementary distinctions. Belief in the supernatural is not the same as belief in God or gods, nor is it equivalent to belief in an afterlife. In some ways Buddhism is the exemplar with its belief in a reality outside the sensory and cognitive parameters of human existence, a realm without gods and which promises an "afterlife" only in terms of an extinction of the discrete self. But mainly, in the religious terminology used here, the supernatural is a token of limits, part of the acknowledgment that the parameters of human experience may not exhaust the scope of reality.

34. J. Locke, *A Letter Concerning Toleration* (Indianapolis, IN: Bobbs-Merrill, 1950).

35. The evolutionary view of religion is argued prominently by Wilson in *Darwin's Cathedral: Evolution, Religion and the Nature of Society*. See also the impressive account of religion as a product of natural selection in the magisterial and brilliant and one-sided book by Daniel Dennett, *Breaking the Spell: Religion as a Natural Phenomenon* (New York: Viking, 2006). But there are reasons to think that reductionism cannot work its touted magic in collapsing religion in its entirety to biological processes. For openers, that we have explained the origin of beliefs does not invalidate the beliefs. (In an old fashioned reminder, to argue otherwise is to commit a particualrly uninteresting version of the genetic fallacy.) Then there is the intellectual obligation in the social sciencies to inspect and present any social practice at least in part in terms of the meanings ascribed to the practice by its members. The understanding of those who play the language game of religion sincerely is that its grammar and vocabulary are not entirely reducible to biological variables. These indigenous understandings of religion must be part of any full data set in a study of religion, even in those versions of the social sciences that rely on the most naturalistic renditions of the origiin and functions of religion.

36. Rawls, *Political Liberalism*, especially pp. 249–51.

37. Rawls dissents from the thought that the political conception of justice is comprehensive in the way that other doctrines are. See *Political Liberalism*, pp. 154–8. I will take up Rawls's arguments on this point in chapter 7.

38. Ronald Thiemann, *Religion in Public Life* (1996), p. 82. Thiemann's book is a helpful treatment of religion and politics in political and legal theory, with special attention to the U.S. setting.

39. T. Nagel, *The View from Nowhere* (Oxford: Oxford University Press, 1986).

40. Robert Nozick, *Invariances: The Structure of the Objective World* (Cambridge, MA: Harvard University Press, 2002), the quote on page 94. See also the review of the book by Colin McGinn, "An Ardent Fallibilist," *The New York Review of Books* (June 27, 2002).

41. The thoughts and quotes here are drawn from M. Nussbaum, *Women and Human Development* (Cambridge: Cambridge University Press, 2000).

42. M. Nussbaum, *Women and Human Development*, p. 21. The gist of the program described in this paragraph is from the book.

43. Nussbaum, *Women and Human Development*, p. 190. The initial version of this statement, on page 20 of "Religion and Sex Equality," Occasional Paper Series, is harsher: "We may and do, however, judge that any cult or so-called religion that does not contain this conduct-improving element does not deserve the honorific name of religion." Then, later, in the same paragraph: "A moral constraint is applied, then, to the definition of what counts as religion when we protect religion."

44. Nussbaum, *Women and Human Development*, p. 202.

45. Nussbaum, *Women and Human Development*, p. 217.

46. Steve Macedo, "In Defense of Liberal Public Reason: Are Slavery and Abortion Hard Cases?" *The American Journal of Jurisprudence* 42 (1997), pp. 1–19.

47. Among the clearer expositions of these expectations (though unwittingly) is the much-discussed article by Amy Gutmann and Dennis Thompson, "Moral Conflict and Political Consensus," pp. 64–88. Note the frequency of the phrase, "mutual respect," in the authors' close analysis. The stress on "respect" kept me looking for Donald Trump in the examples. For a popular illustration of the frustrating asymmetry that liberals face when confronting non-liberals, see the delicious cartoon strip by Gary Trudeau (July 13, 2002) in which the conservative character points out that "liberals are hung up on fairness . . . (and) actually try to respect all points of view. But conservatives feel no need whatsoever to consider other views. We know we're right, so why bother? Because we have no tradition of tolerance, we're unencumbered by doubt. So we roll you guys every time." When the liberal character replies, "Actually you make a good point," the conservative says, "See! Only a loser would admit that!" Or, if you are more solemn, more of a serious scholar than I am at this moment, see the excellent piece by Alan Wolfe that uses the work of Carl Schmitt to make these points (and make them more elegantly), "A Fascist Philosopher Helps Us Understand Contemporary Politics," *The Chronicle of Higher Education* (April 2, 2004).

Chapter 5

1. Rawls, "The Idea of Public Reason Revisited."

2. I am demarcating recursive and reflexive powers in a direct and simple way: I will use recursive to mean a repetitive application of

self-reflection and reflexive to mean any self-referring action, even one that is non-repetitive. So, in a rough sense, recursive functions as used here are reflexive actions that continue without natural closure.

3. Amir D. Aczel, *The Mystery of the Aleph: Mathematics, the Kabbalah, and the Search for Infinity* (New York: Four Walls Eight Windows, 2000). Other interesting treatments of the history of infinity, presented at different technical levels, include Rudy Rucker, *Infinity and the Mind* (Princeton, NJ: Princeton University Press, 1995) and David Wallace, *Everything and More: A Compact History of* ∞ (New York: Norton, 2003).

4. I have provided arguments for this assertion in "Sacred Texts" *Religion* 33 (2003), pp. 1–21.

5. This problem is discussed by Michael Ridge in a paper that (in part) responds to an article by David Gauthier. The Ridge piece is "Hobbesian Public Reason," *Ethics* (April 1998), pp. 538–68. The Gauthier piece is "Public Reason," *Social Philosophy and Policy* 12 (1995), pp. 19–42.

6. Aristotle's essences were famously revived by Saul Kripke in nominal but still strongly retentive form, in *Naming and Necessity* (Cambridge, MA: Harvard, 1980). Here is a curious quote from Mill which suggests that even the strongest supporters of a critical dialectical treatment of language can countenance a society with a wide range of uncontested truths: "As mankind improves, the number of doctrines which are no longer disputed or doubted will be constantly on the increase; and the well-being of mankind may almost be measured by the number and gravity of the truths which have reached the point of being uncontested." On page 42 of Mill, *On Liberty*.

7. I owe this entire thought on Venn diagrams to Ned McClennen and am only borrowing it for modest purposes here.

8. I take this point from Charles Larmore, "Pluralism and Reasonable Disagreement," *Social Philosophy and Policy* 11, No. 1 (1994), pp. 61–79.

9. And so Jack Knight and James Johnson are right on the mark when they argue that ". . . deliberative procedures subject to the widest possible terms of entry, would make reasonable pluralism, where it were possible, an outcome of, rather than a precondition for, democratic deliberation." In "What Sort of Political Equality Does Deliberative Democracy Require?" in *Deliberative Democracy*, edited by James Bohman and William Rehg (Cambridge, MA: MIT Press, 1997), p. 287.

10. The disputes between strong Darwinists like Richard Dawkins and the moderates represented by Stephen Jay Gould (battles often deployed on in the pages of the *New York Review of Books*) seemed to be about the pace of evolution and whether the process is continuous or lumpy, among other issues within Darwin's framework. No one is a Lamarckian today since (in case it is missed) all of the evidence and the theories in biology support one type of natural selection or another. Are foundationalists headed for a similar burial ground? (Yes.)

11. Overviews in A. Clark, *Being There: Putting Brain, Body and World Together Again* (Cambridge, MA: MIT Press, 1999), chapters 7–11, and Antonio R. Damasio, *Descartes' Error* (New York: Putnam's, 1994). The gorgeous sloppiness of biology is documented in more general (and amusing) ways by David P. Barash in "Why Bad Things Have Happened to Good Creatures," *The Chronicle of Higher Education* (August 17, 2001).

12. Clark, *Being There*, chapter 3 and pp. 213–18, 10.6: "Where Does the Mind Stop and the Rest of the World Begin?" Tort law on occasion does regard property damage as a personal assault. But how can law compete with fiction and film on the extension of the self to things, or vice versa? Negative invasions of technology into human identity have been explored extensively in fiction, in particular the science fiction stories of Philip K. Dick (especially "We Can Remember it for You Wholesale," "Do Androids Dream of Electric Sheep?," "Minority Report," and "Paycheck"— each made into movies, respectively, "Total Recall," "Blade Runner," "Minority Report," and "Paycheck"). In these fictions the self is in part an artifact of mainly hostile "external" conditions, and these connections blur the distinctions between mind and world.

13. The various ontological proofs of God are classic attempts to develop scaffolding that brings a higher order of being into the realm of concepts and their relations to each other. Once the entry route is established, the concept of God is said to provide a proof of God, a proof that offers an intriguing (and contestable) route from epistemology to ontology.

14. Elaine Pagels, *Beyond Belief: The Secret Gospel of Thomas* (New York: Random House, 2003).

15. Clark, *Being There*, pp. 217–18.

16. Ernest Gellner, *Postmodernism, Reason and Religion* (New York: Routledge, 1992).

17. Read again, for example, the influential arguments of Richard Rorty, nicely delineated as a response to discussants in Robert B. Brandom, ed., *Rorty And His Critics* (New York: Blackwell, 2000).

18. Thomas Kuhn, *The Structure of Scientific Revolutions* (Chicago: University of Chicago Press, 1962). For recent overviews see the study of Kuhn and his work in Steve Fuller, *Thomas Kuhn* (Chicago: University of Chicago Press, 2000).

19. Michael White chronicles Newton's intellectual peregrinations into alchemy, in *Isaac Newton: The Last Sorcerer* (Reading, MA: Perseus Books, 1997). See also the more recent book by James Gleick, *Isaac Newton* (New York: Vintage, 2004). It is a remarkable study of both character and science.

20. Probably the best overview of theories of complex systems is the work of Niklas Luhmann, for example in *Social Systems*, trans. John Bednarz (Stanford, CA: Stanford University Press, 1995) and *Writing Science*, trans. William Whobrey (Stanford, CA: Stanford University Press, 1998).

21. Luhmann, *Social Systems* and *Writing Science*.

22. Luhmann, *Social Systems*, chapter 5.

23. These and other themes are developed by N. Luhmann in *Political Theory in the Welfare State* (NY: Walter de Gruyterm, 1990).

24. Michael Walzer, *Spheres of Justice: A Defense of Pluralism and Equality* (New York: Basic Books, 1983).

25. The next three paragraphs contain material from "How I Learned to Stop Worrying and Love the Global System," my review of Andrew Kuper's *Democracy Beyond Borders: Justice and Representation in Global Institutions* (New York: Oxford University Press, 2004), in *International Studies Review* 8 (March 2006), 93–96.

Chapter 6

1. The main advocate here is of course Rawls, *Political Liberalism* (paper edition).

2. Among the better anthologies of Peirce's writings is *The Essential Peirce: Selected Philosophical Writings 1893–1913* (Bloomington, ID: Indiana University Press, 1998), which includes his important

papers and lectures on signs, laws of nature, and pragmatism (including its form as abductive logic). The other cited variations on pragmatism include Mill's dialectical approach to truth in, for example, *On Liberty*; F.A. Hayek's *The Road to Serfdom* (Chicago: University of Chicago Press, 1994); J. Dewey's didactic book, *How We Think* (Toronto, Canada: Dover Publications, 1997); Karl Popper, *The Open Society and Its Enemies* (Princeton, NJ: Princeton University Press, 1971) and (probably) *Conjectures and Refutations: The Growth of Scientific Knowledge* (New York: Routledge, 2002); R. Schumpeter, *Capitalism, Socialism and Democracy* (New York: Allen & Unwin, 1950), with special attention to "Two Concepts of Democracy," pp. 250–83; C. Sunstein, with special attention to law, *Why Societies Need Dissent* (Cambridge, MA: Harvard University Press, 2003); and R. Posner, *Law, Pragmatism, and Democracy* (Cambridge, MA: Harvard University Press, 2003). In this book Posner discusses other theorists, in particular Schumpeter, in an elaboration of pragmatism.

3. Rawls, *Political Liberalism*, pp. 154–8, for a discussion of comprehensiveness, and J. Judd Owen, *Religion and the Demise of Liberal Rationalism* (Chicago: University of Chicago Press, 2000), for the skeptical take on religion. The exclusionary tendencies in recent liberal theory are not just in Rawls's work—see Gutmann and Thompson, *Democracy and Disagreement*, and Steve Macedo, *Diversity and Distrust: Civic Education in a Multicultural Democracy* (Cambridge, MA: Harvard University Press, 2000) and "Transformative Constitutionalism and the Case of Religion: Defending the Moderate Hegemony of Liberalism," *Political Theory* 26 No. 1 (1998), pp. 56–80.

4. I have provided arguments for this assertion in "Sacred Texts," *Religion*, pp. 1–21 (chapter two here).

5. Stanley Fish, *The Trouble with Principles* (Cambridge: Harvard University Press, 2001) and "Mission Impossible: Settling the Just Bounds Between Church and State," *Columbia Law Review* 97 No. 8 (1997), pp. 2255–333; Jean-Francois Lyotard, *The Postmodern Condition: A Report on Knowledge*, trans. G. Bennington and B. Massumi (Minneapolis, MN: University of Minnesota Press, 1984), especially pp. xxiv and 66; and Paul F. Campos, "Secular Fundamentalism," *Columbia Law Review* 94 (1994), pp. 1814–27 (quote on p. 1816). By contrast, moderation may be the guiding light in this book since the alternative models of reason developed here are proposed only for cases of radical dispute.

6. The discussion by John Gray of *modus vivendi* in chapter four of his *Two Faces of Liberalism* (New York: The New Press, 2000) is the obligatory starting point for what I am proposing here.

7. G. Holton, (2000) "Werner Heisenberg and Albert Einstein," paper presented at the symposium, Creating Copenhagen. Graduate Center of the City University of New York, March 27, 2000. The quotes are on pages 8–9.

8. C.B. Macpherson, *The Political Theory of Possessive Individualism: Hobbes to Locke* (Oxford : Clarendon Press, 1964).

9. George Lakoff, *Moral Politics* (Chicago: University of Chicago Press, 1996).

10. Friedrich Nietzsche, *The Genealogy of Morals*, trans. W. Kaufmann (New York: Vintage Books, 1989).

11. Ronald Dworkin, "The Original Position," in *Reading Rawls*, edited by N. Daniels (Palo Alto, CA: Stanford University Press, 1989), pp. 16–53.

12. Rawls, *Political Liberalism*, p. 200.

13. For overviews, Peter Burke, "Tacitism, Scepticism, and Reason of State," in *The Cambridge History of Political Thought 1450–1700*, edited by J.H. Burns (Cambridge, 1991), pp. 479–84. Burke describes the prominent distinctions between false (based on the narrow interests of the ruler) and true (based on the public good) reason of state, a distinction used even today to parse Machiavelli's thesis. Many of the other essays, and bibliographies, in the volume are also helpful, though indirectly, for example, Anthony Grafton, "Humanism and Political Theory" and Nicholai Rubenstein, "Italian Political Thought: 1450–1530." See also Giovanni Botero, *The Reason of State* (1598), trans. P.J. and D.P. Waley (London: Routledge and Kegan Paul, 1956), first published in Venice in 1598 as *Ragione di Stato*, F. Church, *Richelieu and Reason of State* (Princeton, 1972), the discussion in Maurizio Viroli, *From Politics to Reason of State* (Cambridge: Cambridge University Press, 1992), Victoria Kahn, "Revising the History of Machiavellism: English Machiavellism and the Doctrine of Things Indifferent," *Renaissance Quarterly*, 46, No. 3 (Autumn 1993), pp. 526–61, and the intriguing paper by José A. Fernández-Santamaria, "Reason of State and Statecraft in Spain (1595–1640)," *Journal of the History of Ideas*, 41, No. 3 (July–September, 1980), pp. 355–79.

14. In addition to the ancient classics, see H. Nicolson, *Diplomacy* (Oxford: Oxford University Press, 1951–revision of 1939 edition);

Henry Kissinger, *Diplomacy* (New York: Simon & Schuster, 1994); overviews in J.W. Thompson and S.K. Padover, *Secret Diplomacy: Espionage and Cryptography, 1500– 1815* (New York: Frederick Ungar Publishing, 1963); and the studies by J.C. De Magalhÿes, *The Pure Concept of Diplomacy*, translated by B.F. Pereira (New York: Greenwood Press, 1988); D.H. Dunn, ed., *Diplomacy at the Highest Level: The Evolution of International Summitry* (New York: St. Martin's Press, 1996); L. Mark, "Diplomacy by Other Means," *Foreign Policy* 132 (2002), pp. 48–56; D. Davenport, "The New Diplomacy," *Policy Review* 116 (2002/2003) pp. 17–30; A. Sartori, "The Might of the Pen: A Reputational Theory of Communication in International Disputes," *International Organization* 56, No. 1, pp. 121–49 (2002); and the collection of papers in F. Kratochwil and Hannah Slavik, "The Embarrassment of Changes: Neo-realism and the Science of Realpolitik Without Politics," *Review of International Studies* 19, No. 1 (2002), pp. 63–80.

15. Doyle (1997).
16. The references above are: Fierke, (2002, pp. 331–54); Onuf, (1989); Weber, (1994, pp. 337–49); Doty (1996).
17. The contemporary overview classic in realism literatures is Doyle (1997). But see also Stefano Guzzini (1998); Hans Morgenthau (1948); E.H. Carr (1946); Kenneth N. Waltz (1979) for the reinvention of realism in terms of neorealism; and Waltz (1959). For the critics of realism: Robert O. Keohane (1986) in which volume prominent scholars discuss the limits and accomplishments of neorealism; Alexander Wendt (1999) – which is regarded widely as the major recent constructivist statement on international relations; Friedrich Kratochwil (1993, pp. 63–80) and Onuf (1989). The reader will notice that I am particularly assiduous in avoiding a discussion of constructivism, which, at least to me, is a rival to realism (if it always is a rival) on different levels. Whether the world is given or constructed trades into a long discussion scanning most of the history of philosophy, its epistemology and ontology, and seems to address the standing of realism as a theory of international politics only obliquely. For a different view, see the most able theorist and purveyor of constructivism, Onuf (1989).
18. George J. Mitchell (2001).
19. Frederick H. Hartman (1965); Geneva Four-Power Conference July 1955; *Royal Institute of International Affairs Geneva*

1954: The Settlement of the Indochinese War (1969); *The Geneva Conference on Laos, 1961–62* (1968).

20. The story is also in Isaiah 36. Note that Rabshakeh's speech before the walls of Jerusalem differs from Kings to Isaiah. In the first speech he claims the support of the God of Israel, and it is generally thought that God is indeed using the Assyrians to punish Judah. In the second speech the theological course is reversed and Rabshakeh mocks God's power to stop the Assyrian advance. It is the second speech that provokes God to defend Jerusalem. The caveat here is that the shift to a diplomatic language is secondary in Scripture to what God intends for the disputants.

21. See Dunn (1996).

22. A rich set of devices is in place to explain patterns of international negotiations, but the explanatory devices may or may not be employed by the participants. Is, for example, psychology decisive? Perhaps as an account of events, but even the most astute psychological explanations can succeed without cross-over assumptions that the explanatory framework is part of the mindset of the actors. See, among other able works, the study by Peg Hermann and Charles Harmann that compares the psychology of participants in foreign policy with external influences on decisions that are not part of the knowledge base of the decision makers (1989, pp. 361–87).

23. Rawls, *Political Liberalism*, p. 17.

24. See Patrick Neal, "Vulgar Liberalism," *Political Theory* (November 1993) 21, No. 4, pp. 623–42, for considerations in support of a Hobbesian stability based on equality of power rather than a Rawlsian dependence on the beliefs of citizens.

25. P. Kornbluh, *The Pinochet Files* (New York: New Press, 2003). The Kissinger testimony is cited on pp. 80–1.

26. Rawls, *Political Liberalism*, p. 149.

27. Rawls, "The Idea of Public Reason Revisited," p. 781.

28. For example, Susan Okin's arguments that the principles of justice elaborated by Rawls in *A Theory of Justice* cannot successfully address issues of family and gender inequality, while persuasive in some ways, are movements toward a reinstallation of the comprehensive liberalism that Rawls abandoned in *Political Liberalism*. See Okin, "Political Liberalism and Gender," *Ethics* 105 (October 1994), pp. 23–43.

29. Rawls, *Political Liberalism*, pp. 248–9 for the use of comprehensive doctrines to support political values in well- ordered societies, and pp. 249–52 for the use of such doctrines in societies that are not well ordered.

30. Rawls, *Political Liberalism*, p. 226 and p. 771. Rawls does not say that the voter must disclose these reasons, only that the citizen must be in the right state of mind when acting as a citizen. See the helpful discussion in D.A. Reidy, "Rawls's Wide View of Public Reason: Not Wide Enough," *Res Publica* 6 (2000), pp. 49–72. On Reidy's arguments that the incompleteness of Rawls's version of public reason justifies a wider role for comprehensive doctrines, see the dissent by A. Williams, "The Alleged Incompleteness of Public Reason," *Res Publica* 6 (2000), pp. 199–211.

31. J. Judd Owen, *Religion and the Demise of Liberal Rationalism* (Chicago: University of Chicago, 2000), p. 125. The inner quote from Rawls is from the 1997 article. For a more measured response to the immeasurable excess of the Rawls/Macedo package, David Estlund, "The Insularity of the Reasonable: Why Political Liberalism Must Admit the Truth," *Ethics* 108, No. 2 (1998), pp. 252–75.

32. Macedo, "Transformative Constitutionalism and the Case of Religion: Defending the Moderate Hegemony of Liberalism," *Political Theory* 26, No. 1 (1998a), p. 72. Also see the response by Richard Flathman, "It all Depends. . . . On How One Understands Liberalism," *Political Theory* 26, No. 1 (1998), pp. 81–4 and Macedo's "Reply to Flathman," pp. 85–9 (in the same journal, same issue). The transformative view of political liberalism pushed by Macedo is well developed by the time of his book, *Diversity and Distrust: Civic Education in a Multicultural Democracy* (Cambridge, MA: Harvard University Press, 2000). Macedo's hostility to religion, indeed to any views that do not fit the liberal way of thinking, is clear throughout the book and really not at issue as to interpretation. One of Macedo's virtues is that he says what he means, clearly and without reservations. At issue is whether his program is consistent with the best traditions of religious tolerance and liberal visions of the just society.

33. F. Nietzsche *The Genealogy of Morals*, trans. W. Kaufmann (New York: Vintage Books, 1989).

34. Dworkin, *A Matter of Principle* (Cambridge, MA: Harvard University Press, 1985), p. 191.

35. Swaine, "How Ought Liberal Democracies to Treat Theocratic Communities," *Ethics* 111, pp. 302–43. The quote is on p. 327. Also see Swaine's use of conscience to justify the assignment of semisovereign standing to theocratic communities, in "Institutions of Conscience: Politics and Principle in a World of Religious Pluralism," *Ethical Theory and Moral Practice* 6 (2003) pp. 93–118.

36. Richard Tuck, *The Rights of War and Peace* (Oxford: Oxford University Press, 1997).

37. This is the time to admit that it is fashionable currently to deny liberal standing to Hobbes. See, for example, Alan Ryan, "Liberalism," in *A Companion to Contemporary Political Philosophy*, ed. by R. Goodin and P. Petit (Oxford: Blackwell, 1993), pp. 291–311. But it is also easy to go wrong in understanding Hobbes. He is a liberal theorist in the most general and important sense in deriving institutions from pre-existing individuals, even as he avoids the values of liberalism in the derived state. Also, second, his framework can be delineated with a different psychology of risk aversion. One can, for example, cede credibility to friendly persuasion in a culture where moral argument trumps coercion as a guarantee of compliance. Hobbes just happened to subscribe to the popular Western conviction that the threat of violent death is the best guarantee of cooperation. But different guarantees are consistent with Hobbes's main arguments. His main, portable argument supports the establishment of those background conditions, the arrangements of security, that allow individuals to pursue their own beliefs free of collective irrationality and domination by others, including the sovereign. The state guarantees this security through an imposed order that can be restrictive in scope.

38. On the early (particularly American) liberals and the historical emergence of current liberal philosophies, see Michael Sandel, *Democracy's Discontent: America in Search of a Public Philosophy* (Cambridge, MA: Harvard University, Belknap Press, 1996). Sandel disparages the shift away from communitarian views of liberty and the moral commitments of the liberal state to the contemporary endorsements of state neutrality.

39. On bridging some of the gaps between one form of talk and one apparently disparate area of theory, James Johnson, "Is Talk Really Cheap? Prompting Conversation Between Critical Theory and Rational Choice," *American Political Science Review* 87, No. 1, pp. 74–86. But then see the later Johnson piece, "Arguing for Deliberation: Some Skeptical Considerations," in *Deliberative Democracy*, ed. Jon Elster (Cambridge: Cambridge University Press, 1998), pp. 161–84. See also the interesting assignment, by Gavan Duffy, Brian K. Frederking, and Seth Tucker, "Language Games: Dialogical Analysis of INF Negotiations," *International Studies* 42 (1998), pp. 271–94, of a dialogical method to the Intermediate Range Nuclear Force (INF) negotiations in the 1980s.

The assignment is intriguing in its imposition of a second language game (the dialogical analysis) on the primary language game of the negotiations, which imposition is (among other items) an effort to reproduce power relations in dialogical form.

40. The Melian Dialogue is in Book Five of the *History of the Peloponnesian War* (New York: Penguin Books, 1972), trans. Rex Warner, the quotes on page 402.

41. Luigi Pellizzoni, "The Myth of the Best Argument: Power, Deliberation and Reason," *British Journal of Sociology* 52, No. 1 (March 2001), pp. 59–96.

42. Robert Nozick, *Anarchy, State, and Utopia* (New York: Basic Books, 1974), pp. 30–3.

43. The reader will have noticed the use of the term "evil" in this paragraph. It is a hard and puzzling word not much used in formal tracts in theory, suggesting as it does a moral and even religious tone that is abrasive to the modern objective ear, though it has caught the recent attention of a number of theorists and philosophers. See the Review Essay by Kenneth Baynes, "Understanding Evil," *Constellations*, II, No. 3 (2004). Baynes examines books by Richard Bernstein, *Radical Evil: A Philosophical Investigation*, Susan Neiman, *Evil in Modern Thought: An Alternative Philosophy of History*, Maria Pía Lara, ed., *Rethinking Evil*, and Amelie Oksenberg Rorty, ed., *The Many Faces of Evil*. But however one treats the term, whether one reduces evil to psychological or sociological vocabularies, or locates it in a full and regrettable account of human nature, or adds to any of these reductions and assignments the thought that a full theory of justice is the device that helps us to demarcate evil, the appeal of talk is not likely to be a first-order choice in addressing this all-too-familiar phenomenon. Rawls (curiously enough) offers a definition of evil that suggests in dramatic terms the limits of reasoning and deliberation in politics. In distinguishing between the unjust, the bad, and the evil man, Rawls says that "the evil man aspires to unjust rule precisely because it violates what unjust persons would consent to in an original position of equality, and therefore its possession and display manifest his superiority and affront the self-respect of others. It is this display and affront which is sought after. What moves the evil man is the love of injustice; he delights in the impotence and humiliation of those subject to him and he relishes being recognized by them as the willful author of their degradation." See *A Theory of Justice* (Cambridge, MA: Harvard University Press,

1971 edition), p. 439. If we take evil as egregious and unacceptable actions on one's moral chart then discussion may not be an
option. But force is.

44. For a different and more critical (but complementary) set of arguments in favor of a public square "as being composed of a variety
of fluctuating subdialogues rather than a single dialogue among all
the members of society, and as focusing on the moral rights and
duties of the listener in a liberal society," see Douglas G. Smith,
"The Illiberalism of Liberalism: Religious Discourse in the Public
Square," *San Diego Law Review* (1997) 34, pp. 1571–1641
(quote on p. 1575).

45. P.S. Atiyah, *The Rise and Fall of Freedom of Contract* (Oxford:
Clarendon Press, 1979), especially the Introduction and chapter 3,
"The Intellectual Background in 1770." And (again for an histor-
ical account) Richard Tuck, *The Rights of War and Peace*
(Oxford: Oxford University Press, 1999).

46. See Geoffrey Garrett's recognition of the ways in which finance,
and international production and trade, are differentially regulated
in a global framework, in "The Causes of Globalization,"
Comparative Political Studies (2000) 33, No. 6/7, pp. 941–91. Or
Jeffrey A. Frieden's, arguments that sector influence on financial
capital, and investments in equities and sector-specific capital, are
quite different, in "Invested Interests: The Politics of National
Economic Policies in a World of Global Finance," *International
Organizations* (1991) 45, No. 4, pp. 425–51. Or, in a different
vein, see the classic work by Donald N. Levine, *Wax and Gold:
Tradition and Innovation in Ethiopian Culture* (Chicago:
University of Chicago Press, 1986), a study of the Ethiopian people that argues for a pragmatism that allows cultural context to
specify the pace of liberal programs of political development.

47. Here is one of the obligatory first texts in a sight reading of
Hobbes: In the state of nature "The laws of nature oblige in foro
interno—that is to say, they bind to a desire they should take
place—but in foro externo—that is, to the putting them in act—
not always." (p. 130 of the Liberal Arts edition of *Leviathan*). If
we take the laws of nature as rules of morality, then it is rational
to act morally only when security is guaranteed. Rational imperatives guide agents against following these laws when reciprocity
cannot be assured, this on the famous grounds of the need (natural law, right) to preserve the self. So it is rational to be moral
only in the conditions of state authority and rational, at least on

occasion, to be immoral in the absence of these conditions. It is precisely because rational agents would rather live in conditions where they can follow the dictates of natural law that occasions the "covenant, every one with every one" (p. 143, *Leviathan*) to establish that commonwealth, which guarantees reciprocity in human transactions.

Chapter 7

1. John Stuart Mill assigns conscience as the first entry in the appropriate region of human liberties justifiable on both deontic and utilitarian grounds: "It comprises, first, the inward domains of consciousness; demanding liberty of conscience in the most comprehensive sense;" in the Introductory, *On Liberty*, p. 13.

2. Tom Green, "A Linguistic History of Conscience" (manuscript copy), his book, *Voices: The Educational Formation of Conscience* (Indiana: Notre Dame Press), especially pp. 21–7, and a brief email (made available to me by Green) from JoAnne Sorabella on the Hebrew sources for conscience. The full quote from Green's book is: "There is self-appraisal even in such things as washing the car, planting the garden, getting dressed, or crafting a good sentence. Although these things are not normally viewed as matters of morality, they are without exception things that can be done well or badly in our own eyes. They are activities subject to the reflexive commentary of conscience. That it allows the extention of reflexive judgment on things that matter to activities of ordinary life is a considerable advantage of the term 'conscience,' " (p. 221).

3. Plato, *Euthyphro, Apology, Crito, Phaedo*, trans. Benjamin Jowett (Amherst, NY: Prometheus Books, 1988), p. 68.

4. A helpful collection of essays on conscience is Ian Shapiro and Robert Adam, eds., *Integrity and Conscience* (New York: NYU Press, 1998).

5. Here I am using the Penguin Classic edition of these early dialogues, *Plato: The Last Days of Socrates*, trans. Hugh Tredennick (Baltimore, MD: Penguin Books, 1964)

6. I am taking some of these observations from a presentation by Nicholas Smith, "Persuade or Obey," at a University of Miami campus philosophy colloquium on February 27, 2004. See also Thomas Brickman and Nicholas Smith, eds., *The Trial and Execution of Socrates: Sources and Controversy* (Oxford: Oxford

University Press, 2002), Brickman and Smith, *Socrates on Trial* (Princeton, NJ: Princeton University Press, 1990), for a comprehensive treatment of interpretations of the *Apology*, and Smith and Paul Woodruff, eds., *Reason and Religion in Socratic Philosophy* (Oxford: Oxford University Press, 2000).

7. Interview with Augusta Del Zotto on October 5, 2000.

8. I have come to see that this description of animal sacrifice is flawed in several respects, meaning that it is irregular when viewed from the frame of conventional Osha rituals. I am certain that Ms. Del Zotto has reported her experiences accurately, and so conclude that, perhaps because of his age, Nilo Tandrón was inadvertently mixing a number of rites from various traditions. Or (and this is one reason why I have included the account) the ritual may indicate random syncretism at local levels in one of the key rituals of the religion.

9. I have drawn the legal material on Lukumí from the District Court decision, the oral arguments before the U.S. Supreme Court, the U.S. Supreme Court decision, relevant articles in legal journals—especially one by the attorney who argued the case for the church in the appeal to the U.S. Supreme Court, Douglas Laycock's "Free Exercise and the Religious Restoration Act," *Fordham Law Review* (February 1994)—the two interviews with Pichardo, and interviews with some of the attorneys for the city of Hialeah and selected members of the Hialeah city council at the time of the legal dispute. These interviews (all conducted in Hialeah, Florida) include those with Dan DeLoach on May 5, 1994, and Herara Echeverria on May 21, 1994.

10. Smith, "Identities, Interests, and the Future of Political Science," *Perspectives on Politics* (2004).

11. Farrell, with Tony Bentley, *Holding On To The Air* (New York: Summit Books, 1990), p. 12.

12. For a concise and initial summary of these two models, Ralf Dahrendorf, *Class and Class Conflict in Industrial Society* (Stanford, CA: Stanford University Press, 1959).

Bibliography

Ackerman, B., Why Dialogue?, *Journal of Philosophy* 86(1) (1989), pp. 5–22.

Ackerman, B., *We the People: Transformations*, Cambridge, MA: Harvard University Press, 2000.

Ackroyd, P., *Thomas More*, New York: Anchor Books, 1999.

Aczel, A.D. *The Mystery of the Aleph: Mathematics, the Kabbalah, and the Search for Infinity*, New York: Four Walls Eight Windows, 2000.

Almond, G. and J. Coleman, (eds.), *The Politics of Developing Areas*, Princeton, NJ: Princeton University Press, 1960.

Alston, W., *A Realist Conception of Truth*, Ithaca, NY: Cornell University Press, 1996.

Amar, A.R., Intratextualism, *Harvard Law Review* 112, No. 4 (1999), pp. 747–819.

Arendt, H., *The Human Condition*, (2nd ed.), Chicago: University of Chicago Press, 1998.

Atiyah, P.S., *The Rise and Fall of Freedom of Contract*, Oxford: Clarendon Press, 1979.

Barash, D.P., Why Bad Things Have Happened to Good Creatures, *The Chronicle of Higher Education* XLVIII (49) (August 17, 2001), pp. B13.

Bastide, R., *The African Religions of Brazil*, Baltimore, MD: Johns Hopkins University Press, 1978.

Baynes, K., Understanding Evil, *Constellations* 11(3) (2004), pp. 434–44.

Bellotti v. Baird, 443 US 622 (1979).

Bird, C., Mutual Respect and Neutral Justification, *Ethics* 107(1) (1996), pp. 62–96.

Bissette, J., *The Mild Voice of Reason: Deliberative Democracy and American National Government*, Chicago: University of Chicago Press, 1994.

Bohman, J., *Public Deliberation*, Cambridge, MA: MIT Press, 1996, 2000.

Bohman, J. and W. Rehg, (eds.), *Deliberative Democracy*, Cambridge: MIT Press, 1998.

Bolling v. Sharpe, 347 US 497 (1954).

Botero, G., *The Reason of State*, (1598), (trans.) P.J. and D.P. Waley, (ed.) D.P. Waley, New Haven, CT, 1956.

Brickman, T. and N. Smith, (eds.), *Socrates on Trial*, Princeton, NJ: Princeton University Press, 1990.

Brickman, T. and N. Smith, (eds.), *The Trial and Execution of Socrates: Sources and Controversy*, Oxford: Oxford University Press, 2002.

Brandon, G., *Santeria from Africa to the New World*, Bloomington and Indianapolis: Indiana University Press, 1993.

Brown v. Board of Education, 347 US 483 (1954).

Brown, K.M., *Mama Lola: a Vodou Priestess in Brooklyn*, Berkeley, CA: University of California Press, 1991.

Burke, P., Tacitism, Scepticism, and Reason of State, in *The Cambridge History of Political Thought 1450–1700*, (ed.) J.H. Burns, Cambridge: Cambridge University Press, 1991.

Burnham, W.D., *Critical Elections and the Mainsprings of American Politics*, New York: Norton, 1971.

Burnham, W.D., Constitutional Moments and Punctuated Equilibria: A Political Scientist Confronts Bruce Ackerman's We the People, *Yale Law Journal* 108(8) (June 1999), pp. 2237–77.

Campos, P.F., Secular Fundamentalism, *Columbia Law Review* 94 (1994), pp. 1814–27.

Canizares, R., *Walking with the Night: The Afro-Cuban World of Santeria*, Rochester, VT: Destiny Books, 1993.

Canizares, R., *Cuban Santeria*, Rochester, VT: Inner Traditions Intl Ltd, 1999.

Carr, E.H., *The Twenty Years' Crisis: An Introduction to the Study of International Relations*, London: Macmillan, 1946.

Cespedes, R., The Mystical Powers of Elian, *The New York Times* (September 30, 2000).

Christian, W., *Meaning and Truth in Religion*, Princeton, NJ: Princeton University Press, 1964.

Christiano, T., The Significance of Public Deliberations, in *Democracy*, (ed.) D. Estlund, Massachussets: Blackwell, 2002.

Church, W.F., *Richelieu and Reason of State*, Princeton, NJ: Princeton University Press, 1972.

Clark, A., *Being There: Putting Brain, Body and World Together Again*, Cambridge, MA: MIT Press, 1998.

Clark, A. and D. Chalmers, *The Extended Mind*, St. Louis: Washington University Press, 1995.

Clark, M.A., Orisha Worship Communities: A Reconsideration of Organizational Structure, *Religion* 30(4) (October 2000), pp. 379–89.

Clark, M.A., ¡No Hay Ningún Santo Agui! (There Are No Saints Here!): Symbolic Language within Santeria, *Journal of the American Academy of Religion* 69(1) (March 2001), pp. 21–41.

Cohen, J., An Epistemic Conception of Democracy, *Ethics* 97 (1986), pp. 26–38.

Cohen, J., Deliberation and Democratic Legitimacy, in *The Good Polity: Normative Analysis of the State*, (eds.) A. Hamlin and P. Pettit, Oxford: Blackwell, 1989.

Cortez, J.G., *The Osha: Secrets of the Yoruba-Santeria-Lucumi Religion in the United States and the Americas*, Brooklyn, NY: Athelia Henrietta, 2000.

Dahrendorf, R., *Class and Class Conflict in Industrial Society*, Stanford, CA: Stanford University Press, 1959.

Damasio, A.R., *Descarte's Error*, New York: Putnam's, 1994.

Damasio, A.R., *Looking for Spinoza: Joy, Sorrow and the Feeling Mind*, New York: Harcourt, 2003.

Dante, A., *The Divine Comedy of Dante Alighieri; Hell, Purgatory, Paradise*, (trans.) H.F. Cary. New York: P.F. Collier, 1909.

Darwin, C., *On the Origin of Species by the Means of Natural Selection, or The Preservation of the Favoured Races in the Struggle for Life*, London: John Murray, 1859.

Davidson, D. and G. Hartman, (eds.), *The Logic of Grammar*, California: Dickenson, 1975.

Davenport, D., The New Diplomacy, *Policy Review* 116 (2002/2003), pp.17–30.

De Magalhÿes, J.C., *The Pure Concept of Diplomacy*, (trans.) B.F. Pereira. New York: Greenwood Press, 1988.

Devlin, P., *The Enforcement of Morals*, New York: Oxford, 1970.

Dewey, J., *How We Think*, Toronto, Canada: Dover Publications, 1997.

Dick, P.K., *Do Androids Dream of Electric Sheep?* London: Millennium, Orion Books Ltd., 1999.

Dick, P.K., *We Can Remember it for You Wholesale*, London: Millennium, Orion Books Ltd., 2000.

Dick, P.K., *Paycheck*, London: Gollancz, Orion Books Ltd., 2003.

Dick, P.K., *Minority Report*, London: Gollancz, Orion Books Ltd., 2005.

Doty, R.L., *Imperial Encounters: The Politics of Representation in North–South Relations*, Minneapolis, MN: University of Minnesota Press, 1996.

Doyle, M.W., *Ways of War and Peace: Realism, Liberalism, and Socialism*, New York: Norton, 1997.

Duffy, G., Frederking, B.K. and S. Tucker, Language Games: Dialogical Analysis of INF Negotiations, *International Studies* 42 (1998), pp. 271–94.

Dunn, D.H., (ed.), *Diplomacy at the Highest Level: The Evolution of International Summitry*, New York: St. Martin's Press, 1996.

Durkheim, E., *The Elementary Forms of the Religious Life*, (1965), (trans.) J.W. Swain. New York: The Free Press, 1912.

Dworkin, R., *A Matter of Principle*, Cambridge, MA: Harvard University Press, 1985.

Dworkin, R., *Taking Rights Seriously*, Cambridge, MA: Harvard University Press, 1978.

Dworkin, R., *Law's Empire*, Cambridge, MA: Harvard University Press, 1986.

Dworkin, R., The Original Position, in *Reading Rawls*, (ed.) Norman Daniels, Palo Alto, CA: Stanford University Press, 1989.

Dworkin, R., *Life's Dominion*, New York: Knopf, 1993.

Easton, D., *The Political System: An Inquiry into the State of Political Science*, New York: Knopf, 1953.

Eckstein, H., Authority Patterns: A Structural Basis for Political Inquiry, *American Political Science Review* 67(4) (1973), pp. 1142–61.

Eco, U. and S. Collini, (eds.), *Interpretation and Overinterpretation*, Cambridge: Cambridge University Press, 1992.

Edwards, T., Religion, Explanation, and the Askesis of Inquiry, in *The Insider/Outsider Problem in the Study of Religion*, (ed.) Russell T. McCutcheon, London & New York: Cassell, 1999.

El Obatala, *Creative Ritual*, York Beach, Maine: Samuel Weiser Inc., 1996.

Eliade, M., *The Sacred and the Profane: The Nature of Religion*, (trans.) W. Trask. New York: Harvest Books, Harcourt, Inc., 1968.

Elster, J., (ed.), *Deliberative Democracy*, New York: Cambridge University Press, 1998. *Employment Division v. Smith*, 494 US 872 (1990).

Engel v Vitale, 370 US 421 (1962).

Estlund, D., Who's Afraid of Deliberative Democracy? *Texas Law Review* 71 (1993), pp. 1437–77.

Estlund, D., The Insularity of the Reasonable: Why Political Liberalism Must Admit the Truth, *Ethics* 108(2) (1998), pp. 252–75.

Evans, B.N., *Interpreting the Free Exercise of Religion*, Chapel Hill, NC: University of North Carolina Press. 1997.

Everson v. Board of Education, 330 US 1 (1947).

Farrell, S. and T. Bentley, *Holding On To The Air: An Autobiography*, New York: Summit Books, 1990.

Fernández-Santamaria, J.A., Reason of State and Statecraft in Spain (1595–1640), *Journal of the History of Ideas* 41(3) (July/September, 1980), pp. 355–79.

Fierke, K., Links Across the Abyss: Language and Logic in International Relations, *International Studies* 46 (2000), pp. 331–54.

Fish, S., Normal Circumstances, Literal Language, Direct Speech Acts, the Ordinary, the Everyday, the Obvious, What Goes Without Saying, and Other Special Cases, *Critical Inquiry* 4(4) (Summer 1978), pp. 625–44.

Fish, S., Mission Impossible: Settling the Just Bounds Between Church and State, *Columbia Law Review* 97(8) (1997), pp. 2255–333.

Fish, S., Mutual Respect as a Device of Exclusion, in *Deliberative Politics: Essays on Democracy and Disagreement*, (ed.) S. Macedo, New York: Oxford University Press, 1999.

Fish, S., *The Trouble with Principles*, Cambridge: Harvard University Press, 2001.

Fishkin, J., *Democracy and Deliberation*, New Haven, CT: Yale University Press, 1991.

Fitzgerald, T., *The Ideology of Religious Studies*, New York: Oxford University Press, 2000.

Flathman, R., It all Depends. . . . On How One Understands Liberalism, *Political Theory* 26(1) (1998), pp. 81–84.

Foucault, M., *The Birth of the Clinic: An Archeology of Medical Perception*, (trans.) A.M. Sheridan Smith. New York: Vintage/Random House, 1975.

Frank, J., The 'Fight' Theory Versus the 'Truth' Theory, in *Courts on Trial: Myth and Reality in American Justice*, (ed.) J. Frank, Princeton, NJ: Princeton University Press, 1976.

Frankena, W., *Ethics*, Englewood Cliffs, NJ: Prentice-Hall, 1973.

Frankena, W., *Thinking About Morality*, Ann Arbor, MI: University of Michigan Press, 1980.

Freeman, S., Reason and Agreement in Social Contract Views, *Philosophy and Public Affairs* 19(2) (1990), pp.122–57.

Freeman, S., Deliberative Democracy: A Sympathetic Comment, *Philosophy and Public Affairs* 29 (2000), pp. 371–418.

Frieden, J.A., Invested Interests: The Politics of National Economic Policies in a World of Global Finance, *International Organization* 45(4) (1991), pp. 425–51.

Frohock, F., The Structure of Politics, *American Political Science Review* 72(3) (September 1978), pp. 859–70.

Frohock, F., *Rational Associations*, Syracuse, NY: Syracuse University Press, 1987.

Frohock, F., *Public Reason*, Ithaca, NY: Cornell University Press, 1999.

Frohock, F., "The Free Exercise of Religion: Lukumí and Animal Sacrifice," Institute for Cuban and Cuban-American Studies Occasional Paper Series, University of Miami (November 2001).

Frohock, F., Sacred Texts, *Religion* 33 (2003), pp.1–21.

Frohock, F., How I Learned to Stop Worrying and Love the Global System, *International Studies Review* (2006) 8, pp. 93–96.

Fuller, S., *Thomas Kuhn*, Chicago: University of Chicago Press, 2000.

Funk, R.W., *Language, Hermeneutic, and Word of God*, Harper and Row, 1966.

Gabel, P., Spirituality and Law, *Tikkun: A Bimonthly Jewish Critique of Politics, Culture, and Society* 18(3) (March/April, 2003), pp. 17–27.

Gauchet, M., *The Disenchantment of the World: A Political History of Religion*, Princeton, NJ: Princeton University Press, 1997.

Gaus, G., Reason, Justification, and Consensus: Why Democracy Can't Have It All, in *Democracy,* (ed.) D. Estlund, Massachussets: Blackwell, 2002.

Gauthier, D., Public Reason, *Social Philosophy and Policy* 12 (1995), pp. 19–42.

Geertz, C., Religion as a Cultural System, in *The Interpretation of Cultures*, New York: Basic Books, 1973.

Gellner, E., *Postmodernism, Reason and Religion*, New York: Routledge, 1992.

Geneva Conference on Laos, 1961–62 Washington, D.C., Library of Congress, Legislative Reference Service, 1968.

Gleick, J., *Isaac Newton*, New York: Vintage, 2004.

Goldstein, R., *Incompleteness: The Proof and Paradox of Kurt Godel*, New York: W.W. Norton and Co., 2005.

Goleman, D., *Emotional Intelligence*, New York: Bantam Books, 1995.

Gombrich, E.H., *Art and Illusion*, Princeton, NJ: Princeton University Press, 1969.

Gonzalez-Whippler, M., *Santeria*, New York: The Augustan Press, 1973.

Gonzalez-Whippler, M., *Santeria: La Religion*, St. Paul, Minnesota: Llewellyn Publishers, 1999.

Gottlieb, R., *Joining Hands: Politics and Religion Together for Social Change*, Cambridge, MA: Westview Press, 2002.

Gould, S.J., *The Structure of Evolutionary Theory*, Cambridge, MA: Belknap Press of Harvard University Press, 2002.

Grafton, A., "Humanism and Political Theory" in *The Cambridge History of Political Thought 1450–1700*, (eds.) J.H. Burns and M. Goldie, Cambridge: Cambridge University Press, 1991.

Graber, M., The Constitution as a Whole: A Partial Political Science Perspective, *University of Richmond Law Review* 33 (1999), pp. 343–76.

Grant, R., *Hypocrisy and Integrity: Machiavelli, Rousseau, and the Ethics of Politics*, Chicago: University of Chicago Press, 1997.

Gray, J., *Two Faces of Liberalism*, New York: The New Press, 2000.

Greeley, A., *The Catholic Imagination*, Berkeley, CA: University of California Press, 2000.

Green, T., *A Linguistic History of Conscience in Voices: The Educational Formation of Conscience*, Indiana: Notre Dame Press, 1999.

Grice, H.P., Logic and Conversation, in *Syntax and Semantics 3: Speech Acts*, (eds.) P. Cole and J. Morgan, New York: Academic Press, 1975.

Gutmann, A. and D. Thompson, Moral Conflict and Political Consensus, *Ethics* 101 (October 1990), pp. 64–88.

Gutmann, A. and D. Thompson, *Democracy and Disagreement*, Cambridge, MA: Belknap Press, 1998.

Gutmann, A. and D. Thompson, Reply to the Critics, in *Deliberative Politics: Essays on Democracy and Disagreement*, (ed.) S. Macedo, New York: Oxford University Press, 1999.

Guzzini, S., *Realism in International Relations and International Political Economy: The continuing Story of a Death Foretold*, New York: Routledge, 1998.

Haack, S., *Evidence and Inquiry*, Oxford: Blackwell Publishers, 1997.

Haack, S., *Manifesto of a Passionate Moderate*, Chicago: University of Chicago Press, 1998.

Hare, R.M., The Promising Game, in *The Is-Ought Question: A Collection of Papers on the Central Problems in Moral Philosophy*, (ed.) W.D. Hudson, New York: Macmillan, 1969.

Habermas, J., *Between Facts and Norms*, Cambridge, MA: MIT Press, 1998.

Hart, H.L.A., *The Concept of Law*, Oxford: Oxford University Press, 1961.

Hartman, F.H., *Germany Between East and West*, Englewood Cliffs, NJ: Prentice-Hall, 1965.

Hayek, F.A., *The Road to Serfdom*, Chicago: University of Chicago Press, 1994.

Hebrew Bible, New York: American Bible Society, 1991.

Hermann, M. and C. Hermann, Who Makes Foreign Policy Decisions and How: An Empirical Inquiry, *International Studies Quarterly* 33 (1989), pp. 361–87.

Hersh, S.M., Selective Intelligence, *The New Yorker* (May 12, 2003), pp. 44–51.

Hick, J., *An Interpretation of Religion*, New Haven, CT: Yale University Press, 1989.

Hobbes, *Leviathan*, (Penguin Classics). London: Penguin Books, 1982.

Holton, G., W. Heisenberg and A. Einstein, Paper presented at the Symposium: Creating Copenhagen, Graduate Center of the City University of New York, March 27, 2000.

Holy Bible, King James Version, Oxford: Oxford University Press, 1937.

Johnson, J., Is Talk Really Cheap? Prompting Conversation Between Critical Theory and Rational Choice, *American Political Science Review* 87(1), pp. 74–86.

Johnson, J., Arguing for Deliberation: Some Skeptical Considerations, in *Deliberative Democracy*, (ed.) J. Elster, Cambridge: Cambridge University Press, 1998.

Johnson, J. and J. Knight, What Sort of Political Equality Does Deliberative Democracy Require? in *Deliberative Democracy*, (eds.) James Bohman and William Rehg, Cambridge, MA: MIT Press, 1997.

Johnson, J. and J. Knight, Aggregation and Deliberation: On the Possibility of Democratic Legitimacy, *Political Theory* 22 (1994), pp. 277–96.

Juarrero, A., *Dynamics in Action: Intentional Behavior as a Complex System*, The MIT Press, 1999, 2002.

Kahn, V., Revising the History of Machiavellism: English Machiavellism and the Doctrine of Things Indifferent, *Renaissance Quarterly* 46(3) (Autumn 1993), pp. 526–61.

Karade, B.I., *The Handbook of Yoruba Religious Concepts*, York Beach, Maine: Samuel Weiser Inc., 1994.

Keohane, R.O., *Neorealism and its Critics: The Political Economy of International Change*, New York: Columbia University Press, 1986.

King, M.L., Letter from Birmingham Jail, in *Blessed Are the Peacemakers: Martin Luther King, Jr., Eight White Religious Leaders, and the 'Letter from the Birmingham Jail*, (ed.) J.S. Bass Baton Rouge, LA: Louisiana State University Press, 2001.

Kissinger, H., *Diplomacy*, New York: Simon & Schuster, 1994.

Koestler, A., *The Sleepwalkers: A History of Man's Changing Vision of the Universe*, Cambridge: Cambridge University Press, 1984.

Korematsu v. United States, 323 US 214 (1944).

Kornbluh, P., *The Pinochet Files*, New York: New Press, 2003.

Kratochwil, F., The Embarrassment of Changes: Neo-realism and the Science of Realpolitik Without Politics, *Review of International Studies* 19(1) (1993), pp. 63–80.

Kripke, S., *Naming and Necessity*, Cambridge, MA: Harvard University Press, 1980.

Kuhn, T., *The Structure of Scientific Revolutions*, Chicago: University of Chicago Press, 1962.

Lakatos, I., Falsification and the Methodology of Scientific Research Programmes, in *Criticism and the Growth of Knowledge*, (eds.) I. Lakatos and A. Musgrave, Cambridge: Cambridge University Press, 1970.

Lakoff, G., *Moral Politics*, Chicago: University of Chicago Press, 1996.

Langford, J.J., *Galileo, Science and the Church*, Ann Arbor, MI: University of Michigan Press, 1992.

Lara, M.P., (ed.), *Rethinking Evil Contemporary Perspectives*, Berkeley, CA: University of California Press, 2001.

Larmore, C., Pluralism and Reasonable Disagreement, *Social Philosophy and Policy* 11(1) (1994), pp. 61–79.

Larmore, C., *The Morals of Modernity*, New York: Cambridge University Press, 1996.

Laycock, D., Free Exercise and the Religious Restoration Act, *Fordham Law Review* 62 (February 1994), p. 883.

Lefever, H., When the Saints Go Riding In: Santeria in Cuba and the United States, *The Journal for the Scientific Study of Religion* 35 (September, 1996), pp. 3–27.

Lele, L., *The Secrets of Afro-Cuban Divination: How to Cast the Diloggun, the Oracle of the Orishas*, Rochester, VT: Destiny Books, 2000.

Lemon v. Kurtzman, 403 US 602 (1971).

Levine, D.N., *Wax and Gold: Tradition and Innovation in Ethiopian Culture*, Chicago: University of Chicago Press, 1986.

Lewis, M., *Liar's Poker: Rising Through the Wreckage on Wall Street*, New York: Penguin Books, 1990.

Lewis, M., *Moneyball: The Art of Winning an Unfair Game*, New York: W.W. Norton and Company, 2004.

Locke, J., *A Letter Concerning Toleration*, (1689). Indianapolis, IN: Bobbs-Merrill, 1950.

Lovejoy, B., World Religions: a Santeria Primer, *e.Peak* 1(100) (September 8, 1998). Available: [Online] http://www.peak.sfu.ca/the-peak/98-3/issue1/santeria. html

Luhmann, N., *Political Theory in the Welfare State*, New York: Walter de Gruyterm, 1990.

Luhmann, N., *Social Systems*, (trans.) J. Bednarz. Stanford, CA: Stanford University Press, 1995.

Luhmann, N., *Writing Science*, (trans.) W. Whobrey. Stanford, CA: Stanford University Press, 1998.

Lukumí v. Hialeah, 508 US 520 (1993).

Lyotard, J.F., *The Postmodern Condition: A Report on Knowledge*, (trans.) G. Bennington and B. Massumi. Minneapolis, MN: University of Minnesota Press, 1984.

Macedo, S., In Defense of Liberal Public Reason: Are Slavery and Abortion Hard Cases?, *The American Journal of Jurisprudence* 42 (1997), pp. 1–19.

Macedo, S., Transformative Constitutionalism and the Case of Religion: Defending the Moderate Hegemony of Liberalism, *Political Theory* 26(1) (1998a), pp. 56–80.

Macedo, S., Reply to Flathman, *Political Theory* 26(1) (1998b), pp. 85–89

Macedo, S., (ed.), *Deliberative Politics: Essays on Democracy and Disagreement*, New York: Oxford University Press, 1999.

Macedo, S., *Diversity and Distrust: Civic Education in a Multicultural Democracy*, Cambridge, MA: Harvard University Press, 2000.

MacIntyre, A., Is Understanding Religion Compatible with Believing?, in *Rationality. Key Concepts in the Social Sciences*, (ed.) Bryan R. Wilson, Oxford: Basil Blackwell, 1974, pp. 62–77.

Mackie, G., All Men Are Liars: Is Democracy Meaningless?, in *Deliberative Democracy*, (ed.) Jon Elster, Cambridge: Cambridge University press, 1998.

Mackie, J.L., *Ethics: Inventing Right and Wrong*, New York: Penguin Books, 1977.

Macpherson, C.B., *The Political Theory of Possessive Individualism: Hobbes to Locke*, Oxford: Clarendon Press, 1964.

Mark, L., Diplomacy by Other Means, *Foreign Policy* 132 (2002), pp. 48–56.

Mauge, C.E. and A. Fayomi, *Odu Ifa: Book One, Sacred Scripture of Ifa*, Mount Vernon, NY: House of Providence, 1994.

Mauge, C.E. and A. Fayomi, *Odu Ifa: Book Two, Sacred Scriptures of Ifa*, Mount Vernon, NY: House of Providence, 1994.

McAllister, J.W., *Beauty and Revolution in Science*. Ithaca, NY: Cornell University Press, 1996.

McKeon, Michael, Reciprocity, Morality, and Fraud: An Analysis of the Scope of Deliberation, Graduate seminar paper, Syracuse University, Spring 2003.

McGinn, C., An Ardent Fallibilist, *The New York Review of Books*, (June 27, 2002).

Mill, J.S., *On Liberty*, New York: Norton, 1975.

Miller v. California, 413 US 15 (1973).

Miller, D., Deliberative Democracy and Social Choice, in *Democracy*, (ed.) David Estlund, Oxford: Blackwell, 2002.

Mitchell, G.J., *Making Peace*, Berkeley, CA: University of California Press, 2001.

Moore, G.E., *Principia Ethica*, Cambridge: Cambridge University Press, 1903.

Morgenthau, H., *Politics Among Nations: The Struggle for Power and Peace*, New York: Knopf, 1948.

Murphy, J.M., *Santería*, New York: Beacon Press, 1988.

Musgrave, A. and I. Lakatos, (eds.), *Criticism and the Growth of Knowledge: Volume 4: Proceedings of the International Colloquium in the Philosophy of Science, London, 1965*, Cambridge: Cambridge University Press, 1970.

Nagel, T., *The View from Nowhere*, Oxford: Oxford University Press, 1986.

Nagel, T., Moral Conflict and Political Legitimacy, *Philosophy and Public Affairs* 16 (1987), pp. 215–40.

Nashi, Roald, Reasonableness in Rawls' Political Liberalism, Graduate seminar paper, Syracuse University, Spring 2003.

Neal, P., Vulgar Liberalism, *Political Theory* 21(4) (1993), pp. 623–42.

Neiman, S., *Evil in Modern Thought: An Alternative Philosophy of History*, Princeton, NJ: Princeton University Press, 2002.

Newton, I., *The Principia: Mathematical Principles of Natural Philosophy*, (trans.) I.B. Cohen and A. Whitman. Berkeley, CA: University of California Press, 1999.

Nicolson, H., *Diplomacy*, (Revision of 1939 edition). Oxford: Oxford University Press, 1951.

Nieguhr, G., Cuban Church: It's Weak But Unified, *The New York Times*, January 21, 1998.

Nietzsche, F., *The Genealogy of Morals*, (trans.) W. Kaufmann. New York: Vintage Books, 1989.

Nozick, R., *Anarchy, State, and Utopia*, New York: Basic Books, 1974.

Nozick, R., *Invariances: The Structure of the Objective World*, Cambridge, MA: Harvard University Press, 2002.

Nussbaum, M., *Love's Knowledge: Essays on Philosophy and Literature*, New York: Oxford University Press, 1990.

Nussbaum, M., Religion and Sex Equality, Occasional Paper Series: Women and Human Development: The Fifth Annual Hesburgh Lectures on Ethics and Public Policy, University of Note Dame, 1999.

Nussbaum, M., *Women and Human Development*, Cambridge: Cambridge University Press, 2000.

Nussbaum, M., *Upheavals in Thought: The Intelligence of Emotions*, Cambridge: Cambridge University Press, 2001.

Nussbaum, M., *Hiding From Humanity: Disgust, Shame, and the Law*, Princeton, NJ: Princeton University Press, 2004.

O'Hear, A., *Karl Popper*, New York: Routledge Kegan & Paul, 1992.

O'Neil, O., Political Liberalism and Public Reason: A Critical Notice of John Rawls' *Political Liberalism, The Philosophical Review* 106(3) (1997), pp. 411–28.

Ogden, S.M., *Is There Only One True Religion or Are There Many?*, Dallas: Southern Methodist University Press, 1992.

Okin, S., Political Liberalism and Gender, *Ethics* 105 (1994), pp. 23–43.

Onuf, N., *World of Our Making: Rules and Rule in Social Theory and International Relations*, Columbia, SC: University of South Carolina Press, 1989.

Ortiz, F., *Ètnia y sociedad: Selección, notas y prólogo de Isaac Barreal*, Habana: Editorial de Ciencas Sociales, 1993.

Otto, R., (1917), *The Idea of the Holy: An Inquiry into the Non-rational Factor in the Idea of the Divine and its Relation to the Rational*, (trans.) John W. Harvey. New York: Oxford University Press, 1950.

Owen, J.J., *Religion and the Demise of Liberal Rationalism*, Chicago: University of Chicago Press, 2000.

Pagels, E., *Beyond Belief: The Secret Gospel of Thomas*, New York: Random House, 2003.

Peirce, C., *The Essential Peirce: Selected Philosophical Writings 1893–1913*, Bloomington, IN: Indiana University Press, 1998.

Pellizzoni, L., The Myth of the Best Argument: Power, Deliberation and Reason, *British Journal of Sociology* 52(1) (2001), pp. 59–96.

Pichardo, E., Syncretism: An Opinion from Within, *The Church of Lukumí Babalu Aye Journal*, November 1999.

Pichardo, E., Rule or Diplomacy, The Church of Lukumí Babalu Aye Journal. Available: [Online] http://www.church-of-the-lukumi.org/ruleordiplomacy02.htm

Pichardo, E. and L.N. Pichardo, *Oduduwa: Obatalá*, Miami: St. Babalú Ayé, 1984.

Plantinga, A., *Warranted Christian Belief*, New York: Oxford University Press, 2000.

Plato, *The Republic*, New York: Penguin, 1955.

Plato, *Plato: The Last Days of Socrates*, (trans.) Hugh Tredennick. Baltimore, MD: Penguin Books, 1964.

Plato, *Euthyphro, Apology, Crito, Phaedo*, (trans.) Benjamin Jowett. Amherst, NY: Prometheus Books, 1988.

Planned Parenthood of Pennsylvania v. Casey, 505 US 833 (1992).

Popper, K., *The Logic of Scientific Discovery*, London: Hutchinson Publishing Group, 1968.

Popper, K., *The Open Society and Its Enemies*, Princeton, NJ: Princeton University Press, 1971.

Popper, K., *Conjectures and Refutations: The Growth of Scientific Knowledge*, New York: Routledge, 2002.

Posner, R., *The Economics of Justice*, Cambridge, MA: Harvard University Press, 1983.

Posner, R., *Economic Analysis of Law*. New York: Aspen Publishers, 1998.

Posner, R., *The Problematics of Moral and Legal Theory*, Cambridge, MA: Belknap Press/Harvard University, 1999.

Posner, R., *Law, Pragmatism, and Democracy*, Cambridge, MA: Harvard University Press, 2003.

Rappaport, R.A., *Ritual and Religion in the Making of Humanity*, Cambridge: Cambridge University Press, 1999.

Rawls, J., *A Theory of Justice*, Cambridge, MA: Harvard University Press, 1971, 1999.

Rawls, J., *Political Liberalism*, New York: Columbia University Press, 1993, 1996 (paper edition).

Rawls, J., Reconcilation through the Public Use of Reason, *Journal of Philosophy* 92(3) (1995), pp. 132–80.

Rawls, J., The Idea of Public Reason Revisited, *University of Chicago Law Review* 64(3) (1997), pp. 765–807.

Rawls, J., *Justice As Fairness: A Restatement*, (ed.) Erin Kelly, Cambridge, MA: Harvard University Press, 2001.

Reidy, D.A., Rawls's Wide View of Public Reason: Not Wide Enough, *Res Publica* 6 (2000), pp. 49–72.

Ricoeur, P., *Interpretation Theory: Discourse and the Surplus of Meaning*, Fort Worth, TX: Texas Christian University, 1976.

Ricoeur, P., The "Sacred Text" and the Community, in *Figuring the Sacred*, (trans.) David Pellauer, (ed.) Mark I. Wallace, Minneapolis, MN: Fortress Press, 1995, pp. 68–72.

Ridge, M., Hobbesian Public Reason, *Ethics* (April 1998), pp. 538–68.

Roe v. Wade, 410 US 113 (1973).

Rorty, A.O., (ed.), *The Many Faces of Evil*, New York: Routledge, 2001.

Rorty, R., The Pragmatist's Progress, in *Interpretation and Overinterpretation*, (eds.) U. Eco and S. Collini, Cambridge: Cambridge University Press, 1992.

Roth, P., *The Ghost Writer*, New York: Vintage, 1979.

Royal Institute of International Affairs Geneva 1954, *The Settlement of the Indochinese War*, Princeton, NJ: Princeton University Press, 1969.

Rubenstein, N., Italian Political Thought: 1450–1530, in *The Cambridge History of Political Thought 1450–1700*, (ed.) J.H. Burns, Cambridge: Cambridge University Press, 1991.

Rucker, R., *Infinity and the Mind*, Princeton, NJ: Princeton University Press, 1995.

Ryan, A., Liberalism, in *A Companion to Contemporary Political Philosophy*, (eds.) R. Goodin and P. Pettit, Oxford: Blackwell, 1993.

Sánchez S.M., Afro-Cuban Diaspora Religions: A Comparative Analysis of the Literature and Selected Annotated Bibliography, Institute for Cuban and Cuban-American Studies Occasional Paper Series, August 2000.

Sandel, M., *Democracy's Discontent: America in Search of a Public Philosophy*, Cambridge, MA: Belknap Press, Harvard University, 1996.

Sandoval, M.C., Afro-Cuban Religion in Perspective, in *Enigmatic Powers: Syncretism with African and Indigenous Peoples*, (eds.) Anthony M. Stevens-Arroyo and Andrés I. Pérez y Mena, New York: Bildner Center for Western Hemisphere Studies, 1995, pp. 81–89.

Sartori, A., The Might of the Pen: A Reputational Theory of Communication in International Disputes, *International Organization* 56(1) (2002), pp.121–49.

Schmitt, C., *The Concept of the Political*, Chicago: University of Chicago Press (reprint edition), 1996.

Schumpeter, R., *Capitalism, Socialism and Democracy*, New York: Allen & Unwin, 1950.

Searle, J., *Speech Acts: An Essay in the Philosophy of Language*, New York: Cambridge University Press, 1969.

Searle, J., *The Construction of Social Reality*, New York: Free Press, 1995.

Segal, R.A., In Defense of Reductionism, *Journal of the American Academy of Religion* 51 (1983), pp. 97–124.

Shapiro, I., Enough of Deliberation: Politics Is about Interests and Power, in *Deliberative Politics: Essays on Democracy and Disagreement*, (ed.) Steve Macedo, New York: Oxford University Press, 1999.

Shapiro, I., (ed.), *Abortion: The Supreme Court Decisions*, Indianapolis, IN: Hackett Publishing, 2001.

Shapiro, I. and R. Adam, (eds.), *Integrity and Conscience*, New York: New York University Press, 1998.

Sherbert v. Verner, 374 US 398 (1963).

Smart, N., *Worldviews*, Saddle River, NJ: Prentice-Hall, 2000.

Smith, D.G., The Illiberalism of Liberalism: Religious Discourse in the Public Square, *San Diego Law Review* 34 (1997), pp. 1571–641.

Smith, J.Z., (ed.), and W. Scott (assoc. ed.), *The HarperCollins Dictionary of Religion*, San Francisco, CA: HarperCollins, 1995.

Smith, J.Z., Religion, Religions, Religious, in *Critical Terms for Religious Studies*, (ed.) M.C. Taylor, Chicago: University of Chicago Press, 1998.

Smith, N., Persuade or Obey, University of Miami campus philosophy colloquium, February 27, 2004.

Smith, N. and P. Woodruff, (eds.), *Reason and Religion in Socratic Philosophy*, Oxford: Oxford University Press, 2000.

Smith, R., Identities, Interests, and the Future of Political Science, *Perspectives on Politics* (2004).

Sobel, D., *Galileo's Daughter*, New York: Walker and Company, 1999.

Soroush, A., *Reason, Freedom, and Democracy in Islam*, New York: Oxford University Press, 2000.

Sosa, J.J., *Sectas, Cultos y Sincretismos*, Miami: Ediciones Universal, 1999.

Stokes, S., Pathologies of Deliberation, in *Deliberative Democracy*, (ed.) Jon Elster, Cambridge: Cambridge University press, 1998.

Strauss, L., *Natural Right and History*, Chicago: University of Chicago Press, 1953.

Strauss, L., *Persecution and the Art of Writing*, Chicago: University of Chicago Press (reprint edition), 1988.

Sunstein, C., The First Amendment in Cyberspace, 104 *Yale Law Journal* 1757 (1995).

Sunstein, C., *Why Societies Need Dissent*, Cambridge, MA: Harvard University Press, 2003.

Swaine, L., How Ought Liberal Democracies to Treat Theocratic Communities, *Ethics* 111 (2001), pp. 302–43.

Swaine, L., Institutions of Conscience: Politics and Principle in a World of Religious Pluralism, *Ethical Theory and Moral Practice* 6 (2003), pp. 93–118.

Taylor, M.C., Introduction, *Critical Terms for Religious Studies*, Chicago: University of Chicago Press, 1998.

Tillich, P., *The Shaking of the Foundations*, New York: Charles Scribner's Sons, 1948.

Thiemann, R.F., *Religion in Public Life: A Dilemma for Democracy*, Washington, DC: Georgetown University Press, 1996.

Thompson, J.W. and S.K. Padover, *Secret Diplomacy: Espionage and Cryptography, 1500–1815*, New York: Frederick Ungar Publishing, 1963.

Thornburgh v. American College of Obstetricians and Gynecologists 476 US 747 (1986).

Thucydides, *History of the Peloponnesian War*, (trans.) Rex Warner. New York: Penguin, 1972.

Tuck, R., *The Rights of War and Peace. Political Thought and the International Order From Grotius to Kant*, Oxford: Oxford University Press, 1999.

Twain, M., *Following the Equator, Pudd'nhead Wilson's New Calendar*, Oxford: Oxford University Press, 1996.

Vega, M.M., *The Altar of My Soul: The Living Traditions of Santería*, New York: Ballantine Books, 2000.

Vernon, R., *Political Morality*, Cambridge: Cambridge University Press, 2000.

Viroli, M., *From Politics to Reason of State*, Cambridge: Cambridge University Press, 1992.

Wallace, D., *Everything and More: A Compact History of* ∞, New York: Norton, 2003.

Waltz, K.N., *Man, the State, and War: A Theoretical Analysis*, New York: Columbia University Press, 1959.

Waltz, K.N., *Theory of International Politics*, Reading, PA: Addison-Wesley, 1979.

Walzer, M., *Spheres of Justice: A Defense of Pluralism and Equality*, New York: Basic Books, 1983.

Weber, C., Good Girls, Little Girls, and Bad Girls: Male Paranoia in Robert Keohane's Critique of Feminist International Relations, *Millenium* 23(2) (1994), pp. 337–49.

Weber, M., *The Methodology of the Social Sciences*, (eds.) Edward Shils and Henry Finch, New York: Free Press, 1949.

Weber, M., *Political Writings*, Cambridge: Cambridge University Press, 1994.

Webster, A., Health and Body, www.salon.com, January 26, 2000.

Wendt, A., *Social Theory of International Politics*, Cambridge: Cambridge University Press, 1999.

Werner, L., Political Liberalism: An Internal Critique, *Ethics* 106(1) (1995), pp. 32–62.

Wertheimer, A., Internal Disagreements: Deliberation and Abortion, in *Deliberative Politics: Essays on Democracy and Disagreement*, (ed.) S. Macedo, New York: Oxford University Press, 1999.

White, M., *Isaac Newton: The Last Sorcerer*, Reading, MA: Perseus Books, 1997.

Wiebe, D., Does Understanding Religion Require Religious Understanding?, in *The Insider/Outsider Problem in the Study of Religion: A Reader*, (ed.) R.T. McCutcheon, London: Cassell, 1999.

Williams, A. The Alleged Incompleteness of Public Reason, *Res Publica* 6 (2000), pp. 199–211.

Wilson, D.S., *Darwin's Cathedral: Evolution, Religion and the Nature of Society*, Chicago: University of Chicago Press, 2002.

Winch, P., *The Idea of a Social Science and its Relation to Philosophy*, London: Routledge, 1958.

Wittgenstein, L., *Philosophical Investigations*, New York: Macmillan, 1963.

Wolfe, A., *The Transformation of American Religion: How We Actually Live Our Lives*, New York: Free Press, 2003.

Wolfe, A., A Fascist Philosopher Helps Us Understand Contemporary Politics, *The Chronicle of Higher Education* (April 2, 2004).

Index

Abolitionists, 62, 93, 126, 162, 195
abortion, 60–2, 78, 123, 125, 138, 139, 141
Africa, 1, 6–10, 50, 53
altruism, 48, 86
Amendment
    First, 14, 15, 43, 67, 80, 101, 106, 139, 182, 185, 187, 189, 190, 195
    Fourth, 43, 182
    Tenth, 59; *see also* free exercise clause, establishment clause
    Fourteenth, 63, 107
American Civil Liberties Union, 187
American dream, 3
Amicus Curiae brief, 13
analysis
    intent, 57
    intratextual, 60
    methods of, 70
    textual, 55–9, 61, 73, 103
anarchism, 34
anarchy, 35, 118, 150, 154–5, 164, 165, 170, 171
animal rights, 2, 12–13, 187–8
Aquinas, 9, 76, 80, 83, 101, 140, 141, 150, 152, 169, 193
Aristotle, 23, 26, 27, 44, 80, 101, 116, 141, 175, 193
ashé, 8, 52
axial religions, 25
    post-axial, 17, 25, 26, 27, 31, 76, 77
    pre-axial, 25, 31
babalawo, 7, 8, 49

background
    belief, 16, 42–8
    concept, 99, 148, 149, 152, 173, 193
    mechanism, 20, 126, 170;
        see also religious belief
Bellotti v. Baird, 61, 138
Benin, 6
Bill of Rights, 63
bioethics, 141
Bolling v. Sharpe, 60
bounded rationality, 37
braking systems, 117
Brazil, 9
break points, 23–5, 41, 80, 98
Brown v. Board of Education, 60, 63
Buddha, 26
Buddhism, 29, 100, 132

capabilities, 104–9
carcass, 2, 180, 185, 192
Castro, 11
Catholic, 2–14, 108
    see also under Christianity
Catholicism, 6–10, 73, 79
cheap talk, 165
Chile, 161
China, 25, 158
Christ, 26, 32, 76
Christianity, 6, 9, 10, 12, 20, 69, 101, 132, 193–4
    Baptist, 2
    Catholic, 2–14, 108
    evangelical, 2
    Jehovah's Witnesses, 2
    Protestant, 14, 108
    Puritan, 68

church-state, 15, 17, 29, 75, 76, 98, 106,
    110, 139, 181, 187; *see also*
    state-church
circles
    nested, 124
    concentric, 124
citizenship, 37, 66, 110, 152, 163
Civil Rights Movement, 6, 7, 95, 162, 195
cognitive science, 128–32, 142, 169
Cold War, 158
commensurable, 79
    compare incommensurable
commensurability, 79
    compare incommensurabilty
communion, 9, 12, 66
compelling
    government interest, 107
    interest, 189, 192
    state interest, 107, 189
comprehensive
    decisions, 139
    dissent, 93
    doctrines, 62, 87–9, 102, 121, 126–7,
        146, 162
    domains, 30
    framework, 102
    liberalism, 106
    resolutions, 140
    schemes, 102
    views, 66, 88, 127, 197
concept-formation, 18, 23, 28, 75, 76
Confucianism, 67
Confucius, 25
conscience, 19, 31, 77, 95, 98, 117, 124,
    131, 140, 152, 175–8, 189, 195–6
consciousness, 1, 26, 31–2, 52, 77, 131,
    179, 181
constitutional moments, 94
constructivism, 19, 48, 154, 163, 170
constructivist, 47, 76, 154, 170
context
    discursive, 87
    historical, 94
    language, 125
    legal, 187
    pragmatic, 84
    secular, 95
contract
    binding on benefits, 168
    business, 150, 168

marriage, 150
relying on correct beliefs, 169
romantic, 150, 159
social, 62, 150, 151, 163
theorist, 141
theory, 29, 32, 142, 149, 176
critical realignment, 94
crusades, 37
Cuba, 1, 4, 6–9, 11, 179, 190
Cuban-American, 4
cult, 14, 106, 188
culture, 6–10, 12, 27, 28, 35, 38, 57, 62,
    75, 77, 79, 95, 129, 133–5, 152,
    163, 177, 181
    African, 9
    of ambiguity, 7
    demarcation, 38
    dominant, 7
    Hispanic, 7
    indigenous, 27
    osha, 6
    political, 95
    popular, 12
    religious, 8
    slave, 6
    Stoic, 79
    Yoruba, 6, 9, 10

Dahomian, 9
Dante, 124
Darwin, Charles, 24, 41, 98, 127
    see also natural selection
decision
    rule, 101, 125, 126, 171
    theory, 125, 126
definition
    of politics, 25–32
    pre- and post-axial, 27
    of punctuated equilibrium, 94
    of religion, 32–6
    taxonomic, 75
deliberative democracy, 17, 87, 90–4,
    113, 114, 140, 141, 146, 152, 154,
    168, 172
democratic deliberation, 93, 124,
    159, 167
dialectics, 59, 65, 111, 115, 120, 127,
    131, 139, 143
difference principle, 39, 99
diplomacy, 153, 157, 158

diplomatic reasoning, 157
    see also reasoning
diplomatic talk, 157, 158
discourses
    collateral, 139
    critical, 83
    legal, 58
    moral, 59
    ordinary, 168
    political, 19, 46, 80, 97, 101, 104,
        114, 115, 166
    public, 83, 92, 102
    recursive, 197
    religious, 17, 37, 45, 47, 48, 65, 80,
        84, 98, 147, 148
    scientific, 65
    secondary, 84
    secular, 101, 131
disease, infectious, 185
disputation, 47
dispute
    adjudication of, 128, 154
    management of, 90, 91, 103, 111,
        113, 119, 138, 140, 145, 147,
        158, 159, 167, 168, 173
    religious, 84, 86, 100, 196
    resolution, 147
    synoptic, 95
divination, 8, 9, 49, 51
divine, 16, 20, 68, 71, 100, 116, 121,
    175, 178, 194, 195
divinity, 3, 17–21, 26, 55, 97–9, 114,
    117, 124, 132, 136, 175, 193, 194,
    195
Dominican Republic, 11
Dred Scott v. Sandford, 93
dualism
    practice, 90, 101, 130
    property, 31, 130, 142
    religious, 132
    substance, 31, 130
due process, 60
Dworkin, Ronald, 58, 59, 64, 149, 163

egoism, 48
Employment Division v. Smith, 16, 106,
    189
Engele v. Vitale, 139
Enlightenment, 109, 133, 194
epistemology, 37, 46

equal opportunity, 87, 99
equal protection, 60, 63
eschatology, 68,
Espiritismo, 2, 7
establishment clause, 101, 139
Eucharist, 12
Everson v. Board of Education, 139
exegesis, 100

facts
    objective, 103
    physical, 85
    religious, 85
    social, 85
    subjective, 103
fair terms of cooperation, 86, 89,
    110, 158
fairness, 83, 99, 109, 110, 111, 118,
    119, 152, 158, 159, 161, 168
falsification, 44, 45, 100, 122, 128
family resemblance, 80, 120, 154
Federal Humane Slaughter Act, 1958, 14
feminism, 105
    see also feminist theory
Florida, 1, 5, 11, 14, 15, 182–4, 187
Foucault, Michel, 76, 154
free exercise clause, 15, 80, 106, 107,
    182, 189, 190, 192
free speech, 66, 67, 95, 128, 143, 177
freestanding
    language, 80, 85, 114, 115, 140
    political conception, 88, 89
    political language, 18, 19, 150, 178
    political reasoning, 20; *see also*
        reasoning
fruit of the tainted tree, 43, 91
fundamentalism
    Enlightened Secular, 133
    Islamic, 133

Galileo, Galilei, 116, 121, 134
game theory, 96, 114, 126
    see also language games
general applicability, 15, 107, 190
genocide, 171, 177
geocentrism, 43
globalization, 141, 170
Gnostic tradition, 132
government, United States, 139
    see also U.S. government

Haiti, 9, 54
halting, 119
    devices, 117–19, 124
    points, 124
harm thesis, 24, 25, 41, 47, 103, 123
    see also John Stuart Mill
healing, 6, 50
Hebrew, 12, 26, 73, 175
Hebrew Bible, 157
heliocentrism, 43
Hialeah, 1, 2, 4, 13–15, 40, 181, 182,
    184–96
Hispanic, 7
Hobbes, Thomas, 117, 119, 120, 141,
    150, 165, 168, 172
holism, 136
holistic, 10, 30, 38, 50, 51, 60, 61, 79,
    134, 135, 177
Holy Bible, 12, 27, 199
human nature, 165, 172
hygiene, 14, 191

idealists, 170
identity, 9, 10, 38, 39, 66, 97, 101, 131,
    169, 175–8, 194–6
ideology, 100, 110
Ifá, 7, 8, 9, 11, 49, 51
illegal evidence, 43, 44, 91
immigrant, 11
incommensurable, 79, 80
    compare commensurable
incommensurability, 79
    compare commensurability
individualism, 32, 34, 77, 169
    methodological, 32, 61, 134, 136
    possessive, 149
infinite regresses, 113–43
    see also regresses
infinity, 116, 117, 124, 194
insensate realities, 17, 25, 29, 31, 41, 64,
    65–70, 72, 73, 178
intent
    analysis, 57
    of author, 56–8, 68
    original, 56–8
intentionalist fallacy, 57
international relations, 155, 159, 160,
    169, 170, 172
interpretation
    judicial, 59
    textual, 55, 62, 69, 77

intratextualism, 59–61, 73
Islam, 41, 84, 133

Jesuit, 83
judicial review, 139
justice
    distributive, 35
    political, 88, 90
    political conception of, 87, 88, 102,
        152
    principles of, 101, 118, 149
    theory of, 99, 138, 162

King, Martin Luther, 93, 95, 114, 176
Koran, 11
Korematsu v. U.S., 62
Kuhn, Thomas, 94, 122, 134

language
    game(s), 19, 48, 80, 125, 139, 140,
        147, 153, 154, 195
    ordinary, 33, 48, 71, 118, 125
    use, 57, 60, 87
languages
    of politics, 35, 79, 140
    political, 18, 19, 47, 75, 84, 114, 139,
        140, 143, 145, 153, 157, 172,
        173, 197
    recursive, 85
Lemon v. Kurtzman, 139
liberal
    democracy, 45, 65, 66, 67,
        101, 111
    democratic values, 84
    model of engagement, 93
    model of reason, 84, 91, 171
    political philosophy, 87
    political theory, 17, 19, 24, 84, 104,
        110, 150, 167, 168, 172
    principles, 92, 102, 140, 169
    state, 16, 20, 25, 77, 83, 87, 90,
        103–5, 109, 163, 165, 194
    theory, 84, 104, 106, 146, 148, 149,
        154, 160, 165, 167
    thought, 84, 141, 168
    values, 104, 106, 108, 109, 110, 111,
        145, 147, 161
liberalism
    political, *see under* political liberalism
    transformative, 19, 158, 166, 169,
        171, 172, 194

liberty, 24, 25, 35, 41, 46, 60, 87, 99,
    105, 141, 149, 151, 152, 164, 169,
    173
    see also religious liberty
liminal, 71
    post-liminal, 71
Locke, John, 17, 98, 99, 106, 166
logic
    pragmatic, 123
    predicate, 55
    recursive, 20, 116, 136, 146
    reflexive, 140
    secular, 76
Lukumí, 1, 2, 12, 13, 15, 16, 17, 52, 181,
    183, 184, 188, 189–93, 196
Lukumí Babalu Aye, 1, 183, 189
Lukumí v. Hialeah, 16
Luther, 101, 152, 193

Macedo, Stephen, 141, 152, 162, 166, 172
magic, 7, 49, 50, 54
    black, 54
Mao Zedong, 158
marriage, *see under* contract
Mariel boatlift, 11
Mass, 14
mathematics, 43, 116, 124, 143
McCulloch v. Maryland, 60
meaning, textual, 56, 57, 62
medicine, 50
Melian dialogue, 153, 166
Metaphysical, 1, 18, 35, 38, 194
Miami, 3–5, 187–8, 190
Mill, John Stuart, 24, 46, 128, 146
miracle, 7
modus vivendi, 79, 126 147, 159, 160,
    161, 167, 168, 171, 172, 173, 197
morality, 15, 29, 63, 91, 93, 95, 149,
    150, 163, 181
    Golden Rule, 29, 181
morals, 17, 25

narrative, 15, 16, 20, 31, 71, 73, 109, 135,
    141, 146, 182, 194, 195
natural law, 32, 176
natural selection, 41, 127
naturalism, 104, 119
neutrality, 15, 27, 87, 101, 165, 189,
    190, 192
    of content, 27
    test, 190

New Testament, 11
New York, 3, 11
Newton, Isaac, 68, 116, 134
Nicene Creed, 66
Nigeria, 5, 6
Northern Ireland, 138, 156
Nozick, Robert, 138, 167
number theory, 116
    see also under theory
Nussbaum, Martha, 104, 105, 107, 108

Obatalá, 178
objectivity, 26, 65, 77, 97, 102, 103,
    135, 163, 196
Olodumare, 8
olorisha, 2, 3, 13, 49–51, 179, 181
ontology, 17, 25, 32, 37, 38, 46, 50, 52,
    68, 84, 100, 135, 146
oracle, 46, 176
ordinances, 14, 15, 40, 181–6,
    189–90, 192
original position, 99, 118, 119, 124, 125,
    127, 149
orisha, 8, 9, 49, 50, 52–4, 178
Oshun, 8, 53
overlapping consensus, 86, 92, 102, 120,
    121, 150, 160, 161, 170, 171

parable
    religious, 72
    of the wedding feast, 71, 72
paradigm shifts, 94
Pichardo, Ernesto, 1–5, 14–16, 182–3,
    186–8, 190–3
Pinochet, Augusto, 161
*Planned Parenthood of Pennsylvania v.
    Casey*, 61, 138
Plato, 26, 32, 37, 52, 104, 115, 116,
    118, 120, 124, 131, 153, 166, 176,
    197
pluralism
    contemporary, 75
    deep, 140, 148
    democratic, 122
    divisive, 145
    moral, 24
    reasonable, 110
    religious, 41, 99
political liberalism, 19, 102, 105, 106,
    108, 111, 115, 145–8, 150, 152,
    156, 159, 161, 162, 163, 166

political talk, 114, 140, 164
political theory, *see under* theory
philosophy
  classical, 115, 116, 137
  moral, 48
  political, 19, 84, 117, 118, 120, 124,
    149, 169
Popper, Karl, 44, 63, 122, 128, 134, 146
positive law, 176
Posner, Richard, 74, 146
possession, 9, 53–4
post-liminal, *see under* liminal
postmodern relativism, *see under*
    relativism
postmodernism, 19, 27, 42, 76, 103,
    133, 134, 151, 194, 196
post-positivism, 154
post-realist, 154
post-Reformation, *see under*
    Reformation
prayer, 6, 49, 139
Preamble, 59, 63
predicate logic, *see under* logic
priest
  awolorishas, 8
  babalawos, 7, 8, 49
  babalorisha, 9
  Catholic, 9
  italeros, 5, 8, 51
  iyalorisha, 9
primary goods, 34, 35, 104
probabilities, 125, 126, 185
protective belt(s), 45, 46, 100, 107, 151,
    156
Protestant, 14, 108
  see also under Christianity
public health, 185
public reasoning, *see under* reasoning
publicity, 83, 86, 87, 157
Puerto Rico, 11
punctuated
  equilibrium, 94
  upheaval, 94
puzzle solving, 42, 44

racial desegregation, 93
racism, 92
raison d'état, 154
  see also reason-of-state

realism, 19, 31, 37, 48, 154, 155, 156,
    170, 172
  deep, 100
  in international relations, 153, 159
  legal, 58
  political, 173
  pragmatic, 140
  rational, 148
realists, 170
realpolitik, 20, 145, 148, 153, 154, 155,
    158, 170, 171
reason-of-state, 19, 89, 115, 148, 153,
    166, 171
  see also raison d'état
reasonableness, 89, 92, 102, 110, 111,
    122, 127, 148
reasoning
  collateral, 40, 138, 197
  deliberative, 17, 21, 83, 85, 114
  diplomatic, 157
  legal, 74
  models of, 19, 42, 97, 148, 155,
    159, 164
  moral, 104
  political, 19, 20, 45, 46, 86, 90, 91,
    94, 95, 103, 104, 115, 123–6,
    130, 140, 147, 148, 153, 158,
    159, 164, 169, 172
  private, 87
  public, 87–90, 94, 103, 126, 130, 138,
    140, 141, 146, 153, 158, 159,
    168, 173, 197
  scientific, 44, 97
reciprocity, 12, 86, 87, 89, 93, 95, 119,
    148, 158, 159, 165
recursion, 113, 123
recursive
  discourses, 197
  examinations, 116, 119, 124, 140
  functions, 137, 143, 145, 177
  inquires, 115, 127
  language, 85
  legal systems, 142
  logic, 20, 116, 136, 146
  mechanism, 124, 136
  organization, 140
  patterns, 196
  systems, 19, 20, 113, 115, 127, 140,
    142

reflective equilibrium, 118
reflexive
   judgment, 175, 176
   logic, 140
reflexivity, 176
   institutional, 177
Reformation, 14, 26, 47, 109, 137, 172, 193
   post-Reformation, 66, 76, 108, 152, 169
Regla de Osha, 6
regresses, 113–43
   see also infinite regresses
reincarnation, 52
relativism
   moral, 93
   postmodern, 42
relativity, 43
religious belief, 15, 16, 18, 25, 37, 66, 76–8, 83, 85, 99–102, 105–6, 109, 111, 128, 132, 134, 137, 146, 170, 175, 186, 189, 190, 194, 197
religious liberty, 99, 104
revelation, 38, 100, 133, 176
rights
   animal, 2, 12, 13, 187, 188
   human, 161, 171
   to life, 12, 141
   vocabularies, 12, 63
ritual slaughter, 12, 14, 182, 184, 189, 192
Roe v. Wade, 61, 79
rules
   of argument, 24, 41, 84, 90, 122, 153
   of evidence, 18, 41, 84, 111, 122, 153
   of inference, 18, 24, 41, 42, 84, 90, 122, 129, 153

sacrifice
   animal, 11–16, 40, 179, 181–97
   human, 9
Santería, 1, 2, 13, 40, 71, 178, 193
santero, 1
secularism, 41
semantics, 57, 156
sex equality, 108
sexism, 92
sexual equality, 109
Shangó, 3, 4, 8, 53, 179

Shari'a, 84, 121
slaughter, 12, 14, 182–4, 189, 192
slaughter laws, 182
slave, 6–11
slavery, 6, 93, 95, 167
social contract, see under contract
social theory, see under theory
soul, 16, 26, 31, 35, 38, 39, 41, 76, 79, 130, 176, 193, 197
sovereign, 36, 76, 117, 119, 120, 135, 141, 147, 153, 154, 155, 156, 159, 164, 165, 167, 168, 169, 172, 173, 176, 177
speech act, 57, 58, 61, 62, 86
speech act theory, see under theory
state
   libertarian, 35
   of nature, 117, 150, 165
   night watchman, 35
state-church, 114
stem cell research, 141
Strauss, Leo, 77, 96, 97
subjectivity, 102, 196
Sunstein, Cass, 130, 146
supernatural, 1, 7, 17, 19, 49, 51, 55, 71, 85, 98, 99
surveillance, 76, 77
syncretism, 6–11, 197
syntax, 57
systems
   braking, 117
   complex, 19, 95, 113, 123–5, 134–7, 140, 142, 143, 145, 169, 197
   recursive, 19, 20, 113, 115, 127, 140, 142
   theory, see under theory

taxonomy, 33, 34, 75, 80
text
   foundational, 67
   secular, 55, 74, 77, 103
textualism, 60
theism, 37
theocratic, 164
theology, 10, 11, 68, 73
theory
   collective choice, 40
   contract, 29, 32, 142, 149, 176
   decision, 125, 126

theory—*continued*
  feminist, 154
  of games, 96, 114, 126
  liberal, 84, 104, 106, 146, 148, 149,
    154, 160, 165, 167
  linguistic, 58, 155
  normative, 138
  number, 116
  political, 17, 19, 32, 33, 35, 37, 40,
    81, 99, 115, 118, 126, 128, 131,
    141, 149, 150, 153, 166, 197
  social, 23, 29, 77, 135, 149
  speech act, 58
  systems, 33, 34, 94, 124, 128, 133,
    135, 136, 142, 177
*Thornburgh v. Am. Coll. Of Obst. And
  Gyn*, 24
Thucydides, 166
tolerance, 47, 76, 83, 84, 106, 109, 110,
  111, 137, 140, 163, 164, 172, 173,
  192
transcendence, 26, 32, 80, 116, 117,
  132–4
tripping mechanisms, 40
truth
  epistemic, 31, 46, 62, 70, 74, 103,
    104, 123, 133
  realist, 29, 31, 45–7, 78, 79, 100, 103,
    133, 195
  revealed, 31, 64, 133

undue burden, 61, 138

United States
  Constitution, 43, 55, 56, 59, 62, 63,
    65, 66, 70, 93, 101
  Court of Appeal for the Eleventh
    Circuit, 188
  District Court, 15
  government, 139
  legal system, 99
  Religious Freedom Restoration Act,
    1993, 107
  Supreme Court, 3, 15, 16, 40,
    89, 90, 138, 139, 187,
    188, 195
use, as a source of meaning, 70
utilitarianism, 12, 29, 55, 74, 128

values
  deontic, 128
  nonpolitical, 88
  utilitarian, 128

Weber, Max, 33, 77
well-ordered
  deliberations, 95
  political system, 102, 126
  society, 95, 102, 126, 161
witchcraft, 7

Yoruba, 1, 3, 4, 6, 7, 9, 10, 13, 52, 53,
  179, 180

zoning, 183–4, 192